ROUTLEDGE LIBRARY EDITIONS:
ECONOMIC GEOGRAPHY

Volume 6

RETURN MIGRATION AND REGIONAL ECONOMIC PROBLEMS

RETURN MIGRATION AND REGIONAL ECONOMIC PROBLEMS

Edited by
RUSSELL KING

Routledge
Taylor & Francis Group

LONDON AND NEW YORK

First published in 1986

This edition first published in 2015
by Routledge
2 Park Square, Milton Park, Abingdon, Oxon, OX14 4RN

and by Routledge
711 Third Avenue, New York, NY 10017

Routledge is an imprint of the Taylor & Francis Group, an informa business

© 1986 Russell King

British Library Cataloguing in Publication Data
A catalogue record for this book is available from the British Library

ISBN: 978-1-138-85764-3 (Set)
eISBN: 978-1-315-71580-3 (Set)
ISBN: 978-1-138-85415-4 (Volume 6)
eISBN: 978-1-315-72230-6 (Volume 6)
Pb ISBN: 978-1-138-85436-9 (Volume 6)

Publisher's Note
The publisher has gone to great lengths to ensure the quality of this reprint but points out that some imperfections in the original copies may be apparent.

Disclaimer
The publisher has made every effort to trace copyright holders and would welcome correspondence from those they have been unable to trace.

RETURN MIGRATION AND REGIONAL ECONOMIC PROBLEMS

EDITED BY
RUSSELL KING

CROOM HELM
London • Sydney • Dover, New Hampshire

© 1986 Russell King
Croom Helm Ltd, Provident House, Burrell Row,
Beckenham, Kent BR3 1AT
Croom Helm Australia Pty Ltd, Suite 4, 6th Floor,
64-76 Kippax Street, Surry Hills, NSW 2010, Australia

British Library Cataloguing in Publication Data

Return migration and regional economic problems.
    1. Regional economics   2. Emigration and
    immigration
    I. King, Russell
    330.9   HT391

    ISBN 0-7099-1578-9

Croom Helm, 51 Washington Street, Dover,
New Hampshire 03820, USA

Library of Congress Cataloging in Publication Data
Main entry under title:

Return migration and regional economic development.

    The nucleus of this book is formed by six papers
presented at the IBG Population Geography Study Group
meeting on 'Return Migration' which formed part of
the Institute of British Geographers' Annual Conference
at Leeds in January 1985.
    Includes index.
    1. Return migration–Case studies–Congresses.
2. Alien labor–Case studies–Congresses. 3. Repatriation–
Case studies–Congresses. 4. Regional economics–Case
studies–Congresses. I. King, Russell.
JV6217.R48   1986   304.8   85-24288
ISBN 0-7099-1578-0

Printed and bound in Great Britain by Mackays of Chatham Ltd, Kent

CONTENTS

Preface

Contents

PREFACE

The nucleus of this book is formed by six papers
presented at the IBG Population Geography Study
Group meeting on 'Return Migration' which formed
part of the Institute of British Geographers' Annual
Conference at Leeds in January 1985. As convenor of
the return migration meeting I am pleased to acknowledge the support and encouragement of the Population Geography Study Group committee, and to thank
all participants at the meeting for ensuring a
lively and constructive debate.

The six papers presented and discussed at the
Leeds meeting now form Chapters 1, 2, 3, 5, 8 and 10
of the book. The other chapters are contributions
invited by the editor. I would like to thank all
authors for contributing their material more or less
on time -- a relatively rare experience, I imagine,
in edited volumes of this kind.

The chapters are mainly based on authors' field
surveys of returned emigrants in various parts of
the world -- Ireland, Italy, Portugal, Greece,
Algeria, Jordan, South Asia, Jamaica and Newfoundland. They provide a striking variety of geographical and migration settings and, I trust, a well-
chosen set of case-studies through which to examine
the actual and potential impact of return migration
on the regional economic structures of the areas of
origin. Although it is repeatedly acknowledged that
returning migrants can be a force for economic innovation and social change, the general conclusion
is that the extent to which this potential is realised is determined very strongly by the economic
environment of the area in which they resettle. Two
chapters fulfil rather different roles to the rest.
The first provides a general overview of the issues
and literature on return migration and regional
economic change, while the last provides a useful
review of these interrelationships within the
specific context of South Asia, an area where much
more research on return migration needs to be done.

Three final words of thanks and acknowledgement:
to Peter Sowden of Croom Helm for advice and encouragement; to Renie Groves for her expert typing of
the camera-ready manuscript under what turned out to
be unreasonable pressure; and to all the contributors
for so readily agreeing that we donate all royalties
from this book to African famine relief. The book
is dedicated to the thousands of returnees who, from
Newfoundland to Bangladesh, unwittingly provided the
raw material for the research on which this volume

Preface

is so solidly based. Like labour migrants everywhere, their lives provide a sharp counterpoint
between poverty and accumulation, sacrifice and
contentment, humility and pride. I only hope that
this book provides a fair elucidation of their
achievements and problems, and that it will appeal
to students and policy makers alike.

Russell King
Department of Geography
University of Leicester

Chapter One

RETURN MIGRATION AND REGIONAL ECONOMIC DEVELOPMENT:
AN OVERVIEW[1]

Russell King

INTRODUCTION: THE DEVELOPMENT OF RETURN MIGRATION LITERATURE

Before the 1960s the literature on migration made
little or no reference to the phenomenon of return
migration. If return migration was mentioned it was
only to lament that so little material existed on it.
It is true that Ravenstein, father-figure of migration studies, mentioned 'counterstreams' in both of
his seminar papers published one hundred years ago
(Ravenstein, 1885, p. 187; 1889, p. 387), but there
was some confusion over whether the counterflows
were mainly returnees or flows of migrants merely
moving in the opposite direction to the dominant
stream. Neither was this point clarified by Lee
(1966) in his reformulation of Ravenstein's 'laws'
80 years later. One indication of the lack of attention paid to return migration by the late 1960s is
the extensive migration bibliography compiled by
Mangalam (1968) which, in more than 2,000 entries,
lists only 10 references on return migration.
        The reasons for this lack of acknowledgement of
return migration are not hard to see. Return migration has always been one of the more shadowy features
of the migration process, principally because of the
difficulty of obtaining satisfactory data for this
phenomenon. The nets cast out in migration surveys
and national censuses usually allow return migration
to slip through. It was, therefore, not surprising,
though not entirely excusable, that so many studies
of migration proceeded as if no returns ever took
place.
        But return migration's statistical elusiveness
is not the whole story. In explaining the reluctance
to come to terms with return migration, there is a
lot to be found in the nature of traditional

1

frameworks for analysis used by migration researchers, and in particular in the strong and entrenched
'rural-urban' framework (Rhoades, 1979). So often,
migration is portrayed as a one-way process that
starts in the countryside and terminates in the city.
This, and the particular locational and disciplinary
perspective of the individual researcher, has influenced the types of migration analyses that have
been most common. Prior to the recent interest in
returns, three major foci could be identified for
migration research. Firstly there were studies of
the initial migration decision. These ranged from
sometimes highly abstract economic and mathematical
models to more individually-focussed behavioural
studies, and of course also included the familiar
'push-pull' rationales. Second, there have been
quite literally thousands of studies of migrant
adaptation, assimilation, acculturation, integration
(call it what you will) and of migrant-non migrant
interaction in the receiving society -- nearly always
an urban centre. Thirdly, some social scientists
have examined the consequences of emigration for the
sending communities and regions; these have tended
to look at the direct, immediate effects of out-
migration, not the impact of returns. These three
topics have nearly always been dealt with in isolation from each other. Rarely have they been examined in terms of any systematic whole to which they
are all related and in which return migration plays
a part.

Amongst the very few major studies of return
migration prior to 1965, pride of place must go to
Theodore Saloutos' pioneering study of Greeks returning from the United States -- a sensitive and sometimes humorous description of a group of migrants who
returned after more than half a lifetime across the
Atlantic (Saloutos, 1956). Another important, but
lesser-known, early study is the account by Useem and
Useem (1955) of the return of the 'Western-educated
man' to India.

The 'take-off' period for the return migration
literature was the 1960s when a number of studies
appeared under three general areas. The first of
these concerned further analyses in the context of
the United States' main suppliers of migrant labour
at that time: Italy (Cerase, 1967; Gilkey, 1967;
Lopreato, 1967), Puerto Rico (Hernández Alvarez,
1967; Myers and Masnick, 1968) and Mexico (Form and
Rivera, 1958; Hernández Alvarez, 1966). The second
were the studies of British return migration from
Australia (Appleyard, 1962; Richardson, 1968) and

Canada (Richmond, 1966 and 1968). The third were
the studies of return migration from Britain to the
West Indies (Davidson, 1969; Patterson, 1968;
Philpott, 1968). The major landmark study of this
period was the monograph by Hernández Alvarez (1967)
on return migration to Puerto Rico. Like Saloutos'
book it was a model of its type and was much referred
to in research published in the ensuing few years.
     The flow of return migration literature swelled
further in the early 1970s, and it is tempting to
suggest that this was due to the onset of world-wide
recession which, especially in the West European
arena, provoked sudden and marked turnabouts in migratory trends. The threshold of 1973/4 was when
countries like France and West Germany stopped ad-
mitting large numbers of migrants and pressures
mounted for repatriation and return (Kayser, 1977;
Lebon and Falchi, 1980; Lohrmann, 1976; Slater,
1979). The last ten years have therefore seen a
steady flow of return migration studies, many based
on empirical research. This introductory chapter is
not an appropriate place to make reference in any
complete sense to this work -- for a fuller biblio-
graphic listing the reader is referred to King and
Strachan (1983). Instead I shall concentrate on the
concepts and research findings that refer specifically to regional economic issues.

SOME DEFINITIONS

Whilst not wishing to get embroiled in a detailed
discussion of the definition and types of migration
-- a topic of potentially endless debate -- it is
clear that we must define exactly what is meant by
return migration. This is necessary because there is
much terminological sloppiness in the return migration literature. The simple schema on Figure 1.1
places return migration in the context of the migratory cycle, which consists of three static stages
linked by migration moves out and back. This introductory review is concerned primarily with the last
two elements of the schema, viz. the return move
itself, and the post-return situation. However,
inasmuch as return migration is often largely conditioned by earlier steps in the migration cycle,
these are occasionally referred to as well.
     Figure 1.1 is also an oversimplification in that
it does not admit a whole range of other possibilities that might stem from an original migration move.
Figure 1.2 looks at a range of possible migration

Figure 1.1: The Stages of the Migration Cycle

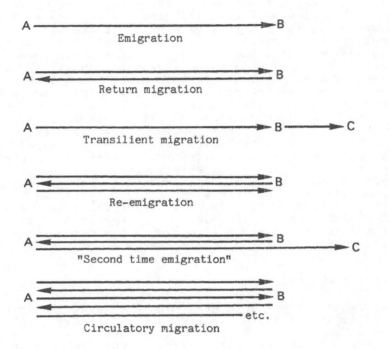

Figure 1.2: Migration: A Terminological Clarification (after Bovenkerk, 1974, p. 5).

paths that could result from an initial emigration. Note that Figure 1.2 portrays the case of international migration -- hence the use of the term emigration -- but it can easily be applied to internal migratory moves within a single country.

Following Figure 1.2 the following terms can be defined. Return migration is used when people return to their country or region of origin after a significant period abroad or in another region. When people move directly from the first destination B to a second destination C without returning to their home area A, as, for example, an Italian migrant

4

transferring from France to Germany (as many did in
the 1960s), then this is termed transilient migration.
When people emigrate once again to the same destination B after having returned for the first time, we
can call this re-emigration; but when people emigrate to a new destination C after having returned
from B, this is termed second-time emigration. When
the to-and-fro movements become repetitious, we term
this circular migration which may become seasonal
migration if the movements are regular, dictated
perhaps by climate or the seasonal availability of
certain types of work (harvesting, construction in
cold climates, holiday industry employment etc.).
The term repatriation is used when return is not the
initiative of the migrants themselves but is forced
on them by political events and authorities, or perhaps by some personal or natural disaster.

TYPES OF RETURN MIGRATION

Just as migration is a highly multifarious phenomenon, return migration too comprises a range of
different types. A preliminary typology can be
identified with regard to the differing levels of
development of the countries involved (King, 1978,
p. 175). Three cases may be envisaged. Firstly,
there are movements of people between countries of
roughly equal standards of living and levels of economic development, but with varying demands and opportunities for labour (e.g. British migration to
and from North America and Australia). A second type
involves movements of 'developed country' migrants
back from less developed, often colonial or former
colonial territories (e.g. French from Algeria,
Belgians from the Congo, British from Kenya, Portuguese from Angola, etc.). The third situation, and
numerically by far the most important, is the return
migration of workers and their families from the
more developed industrial countries to the labour-
supply countries (e.g. West Indians from Britain,
Puerto Ricans from the USA, Turks from West Germany,
etc).
    Aside from this 'developmental' typology, there
are many other types of return migration which need
to be mentioned. These 'marginal' types of return
movement include 'pilgrimage migration', circular
migration and what may be called 'ancestral return
migration'. Pilgrimage migration is most notable in
the case of the haj or pilgrimage to Mecca. Pil-
grims heading for Mecca from the countries of West

5

and Sahelian Africa take an average of eight years
to complete the journey: five out and three back
(Birks, 1975, p. 299). Returning West African pil-
grims are a prominent feature of the agricultural
labour force of the Sudan (Davies, 1964). Circular
migration is also predominantly African. Although
circular movement by definition embraces repeated
returns, these are often not identified as an object
of separate study: hence the marginality of circular migration to a study of return migration. The
circular migration of African wage labourers between
their villages of origin and their places of work in
the towns is normally a domestic movement which
takes place within a single culture area (Gmelch,
1980). Although there are obvious differences between life in the villages and urban society and
although circular migrants do have an impact on
their villages when they periodically return, the
migrants, their villages and the towns are really all
part of one continuous migratory system. Circular
migration can, however, take place across national
boundaries. Some African circular movement originated before present national boundaries became
established and still continues irrespective of these
boundaries. Seasonal labour migration in Europe is
also a form of circular migration; examples are
Spanish labourers working in French grape harvesting
and south Italian construction workers in Switzerland. Van Amersfoort (1978) draws attention to a
circular migration which is actually intercontinental: that of Moroccan workers in the Netherlands who
return each year to their villages in the Rif.

The third 'marginal' form of return migration
is what I have termed 'ancestral' return migration.
This involves the return of people to a homeland
that their ancestors came from but which they themselves were not born in. In fact many return movements include second generation children born in the
host country who return with their parents, but I
have in mind also the forced repatriation of long-
established colonial groups like the French pieds
noirs from Algeria, the Portuguese retornados from
Angola and the Dutch from Indonesia. Another interesting example of ancestral return is the 'return'
of diaspora Jews to their ancestral homeland in
Israel, a return separated by dozens of generations
and hundreds of years. In practice this can hardly
be regarded as true return migration. There is,
however, genuine return migration to Israel, mostly
of Israeli-born returning from spells of education
and work in Europe and the United States (Blejer and

Goldberg, 1980; Toren, 1976 and 1978). The Jewish
diaspora and return has, of course, an ironic counterpart in the desire for repatriation of Palestinians uprooted by the creation of Israel itself
(Barakat, 1973).
    A type of movement which is perhaps less equiv-
ocally return migration is 'brain return'. The
theme of brain drain and return is a major sub-field
within migration studies and has generated an extensive literature in its own right. The migration
of high-level manpower takes place in several developmental contexts. Richmond (1969 and 1981), Salt
(1981) and Wood (1976) have stressed the importance
of the movement of professional, scientific, technical and managerial personnel between highly industrialised or post-industrial countries and regions of north-west Europe and North America; indeed
for many of these 'hyper-mobile' groups migration is
almost the norm and is closely bound up with career
mobility. Little, however, has been written about
the return of these groups except for an analysis of
Canadian professionals returning from the United
States (Comay, 1971). Secondly, there is the migration of high-level personnel to less developed
countries where they often work as administrators,
advisers and supervisors on specific projects and
fixed contracts. Currently the oil-rich states of
the Middle East are a principal magnet for these
'elite migrants', but again little is known of these
groups when they return: their settling-in behaviour
or their propensity to emigrate again. Much more
thoroughly researched is the third situation, that of
brain drain from developing countries and the associated problems of non-return and of attracting back
the all too restricted intelligentsia to Third World
nations. Fortney (1970) estimates that the rate of
non-return of foreign students in the US is as high
as 50 per cent, higher for students from India,
Pakistan, Taiwan and Israel. In the key study of
'brain return' Glaser (1978) shows beyond doubt that
the commitment to return is very strong amongst high
level personnel working or studying abroad. Even
those who stay on beyond their initial planned term
still intend to return, although there are differences between countries and between professions and
subject specialisms. The return home is, however,
frequently accompanied by problems of loss of income,
difficulties of finding suitable employment and frustration with the local way of doing things, such as
the corruption of the bureaucracy.
    Some of the most thorough research on the return

7

migration of educated personnel has been done in the
Australian-Southeast Asian area (Hodgkin, 1972;
Keats, 1969). Hodgkin, in her study of 'innovators'
from Malaysia and Singapore educated in Australia,
describes the returnees as members of the 'Third
Culture'; they act as middlemen between the Western
culture of Australia and Malaysian culture. The
returnee who has both a commitment to progress and
an appreciation of indigenous values can play a
crucial role in the development of his home country.
Elsewhere, specific recommendations and policies for
encouraging brain return have been made: an OECD
project to bring back Greek scholars working abroad
(Haniotis, 1964); the Guyanese government-sponsored
scheme for filling gaps in the local labour market
by recruiting Guyanese migrants abroad (Strachan,
1980); and the Indian 'Scientists Pool' by which the
Indian government guarantees certain·highly educated
returnees a job in a government department for up to
two years (Abraham, 1968; Awasthi, 1966).

Very different from brain return as a species
of return migration is retirement migration. Of
course, by no means all retirement migration implies
a return to the point of origin; there are some
regions, such as the South of France, England's
South Coast, California and Florida where retirees
have no previous links, except perhaps holiday visits. In the case of international retirement migration, however, the return home at the end of the
migrant's working life is nearly always to the point
of departure where the desire is for a few quiet,
peaceful years in the 'native air'. The 'return of
retirement' is one of Cerase's (1974) four American-
Italian return migration types which I shall examine
in more detail shortly. International retirement
migration has also been studied elsewhere, in the
Philippines for example, where retired returnees
from Hawaii come back after maybe 40 years' absence.
These returned pensionados are usually very wealthy
by local standards and many build luxury homes and
take teenage wives (Griffiths, 1979; McArthur, 1979).
Retirees need not wait until they are 60 or 65
however; in Malta and Gozo retired returnees may be
as young as 35-40 years of age. For Maltese migrants
a concentrated period of 15-20 years of intense hard
work in North America may yield enough capital to
live off for the rest of the lives, for when they
return to Malta their living costs are very low (King
and Strachan, 1980).

Finally, the fundamental distinction between
internal and international return migration must be

8

stressed. Studies on international return migration, mainly from rich to poor countries, are by far the more numerous and these are the studies that other review papers (Bovenkerk, 1974; Gmelch, 1980; King, 1979) have concentrated on. Internal return migration has tended to be left aside as a topic for investigation. Nearly all internal return migration is urban to rural, although some inter-urban return takes place in highly urbanised countries such as the USA and Britain where the rural population has shrunk to a relatively small residuum. Among studies of internal return migration in industrialised countries may be mentioned Townsend (1980) on Northeast England, Bell and Kirwan (1979) and Beaumont (1976) on Scotland, Nicholson (1975) on Norway, Lee and Kim (1981) on Korea and the papers by Abe and Wiltshire on Japan (Abe and Wiltshire, 1980; Wiltshire, 1979; Wiltshire and Abe, 1978). Most of these are statistically-based 'desk studies' as is the plethora of studies on return migration within North America based on the analysis of official data sets (e.g. Eldridge, 1965; Lee, 1974; Long and Hansen, 1975; Vanderkamp, 1972). The effects of urban-rural return migration in Third World countries are reviewed by Dasgupta (1981), Lipton (1980) and Nelson (1976). Returnees coming back to villages act as vehicles for channelling the national urban culture to rural areas; this has been demonstrated in a variety of countries such as Nigeria (Adepoju, 1981), India (Crane, 1955), Greece (Friedl, 1959) and Spain (Brandes, 1975). In fact, because internal migration usually allows migrants to retain close links with their home villages, the effects of internal returnees on rural areas may be in the long term more profound, if less dramatic, than the impact of migrants returning from abroad.

FRAMEWORKS FOR ANALYSING RETURN MIGRATION

These range from the simple to the complex. Some are aimed at predicting the existence or scale of returns; others examine return's effect on local economic and cultural systems. Among the simpler frameworks for examining return are those based on distance, time and intention. For instance, one 'law' of migration that would seem to hold for return migration concerns the impact of distance; the shorter the distance of emigration, the higher the incidence of return. Another law concerns length of absence: the longer emigrants stay away the less the

9

likelihood of their return. Both these propositions
would seem generally to hold true in the experience
of southern European emigration. Emigrants from
Italy, for example, are much more likely to return
from European countries such as Switzerland and West
Germany than they are from long-stay visits to overseas countries like the USA and Australia.

A further temporal classification can be made
into occasional, periodic, seasonal, temporary and
permanent returns (King, 1978, p. 177). Occasional
returns are short term and include visits to see
relatives, for holidays and, perhaps, marriage or to
seek a marriage partner. Such brief visits do not
involve any real economic activity or employment:
usually the migrant returns for a period of relaxa-
tion and leisure. The same is true for periodic
returns, except that the return is regular, such as
every month or every weekend. A typical example is
the movement of certain types of 'frontier workers'
such as the north Italians who work in Switzerland
during the week and return home for weekends.
Seasonal returns are dictated by the nature of the
jobs followed: examples are crop harvesting, construction work and the hotel trade. Temporary returns take place when the migrant comes back, perhaps
at the end of a work contract or for personal reasons,
finds a job back home but intends to re-emigrate at
some future date. Permanent returns are those who
settle in their home areas without the intention of
emigrating again. Such differences in the length of
time spent back home will naturally condition the
kind of economic impact a return migrant can have on
his or her region of origin.

Of course, it should not escape notice that
these different types of return also reflect to a
considerable extent the types of migration that pre-
cede them. Douglass (1970) distinguishes permanent
emigrants, sojourners and 'birds of passage'.
Permanent emigrants by definition cannot return permanently, but they may still return for visits to
their communities of origin. Sojourners return for
longer periods from time to time; their roots are
often divided and they may feel ambivalent about
where they belong. Birds of passage have their roots
in their home villages; they work seasonally or for
shorter periods abroad and returns are dictated by
this short-term pattern.

Böhning (1974, pp. 61-67) deals comprehensively
with the role of returns in his well-known four-stage
model of the 'self-feeding process' of European
labour migration. In the first stage young single

male workers originating from towns form the bulk of
the migrants. As these 'pioneer' migrants come into
a country which has only just started to import labour, their duration of stay is likely to be very
short, partly because it is the intention of the
migrants and the immigration country that their return should come soon, and partly because they are
employed in marginal, insecure positions. Rates of
return are therefore high. In the second stage
married workers join the flow, although at this
stage they are not generally accompanied by their
families. Duration of stay increases slightly and
the rate of return slackens off a bit. Nevertheless
returns have a crucial effect in diffusing the message of migration possibilities and in enlarging the
areas of origin of the migrants from urban to rural
regions. The third stage sees the continued ageing
of the migration stream and a change in its sex composition as married workers send for their spouses.
Duration of stay increases further, especially for
families, and the rate of return decreases considerably. It is in the third stage that the migration
process becomes, to use Böhning's terminology, self-
feeding. The swelling number of migrants generates
its own consumer demands and begins to exhibit significant infrastructural requirements like schools,
health services and social care. Finally, in the
fourth stage of maturity the increasing length of
stay and the high degree of family reunion lead to
an enlargement of the migrant population with the
appearance of ethnic shops, employers, schools,
secular and religious leaders etc. Returns at this
stage are low, save for a steady trickle of migrants
going home to retire.

Another way of classifying return migration is
to look at migration and return migration intentions
and compare them with actual outcomes. Combining
the typologies of Bovenkerk (1974, pp. 10-19) and
Gmelch (1980, pp. 137-138), we arrive at the following four categories which are, however, only approximate since in practice many migrants do not have
definite plans but move on a trial basis leaving the
outcome open.

Firstly there are migrants who emigrated with
the intention of returning and who did in fact return. By returning, they are merely fulfilling
their original plans. Many temporary migrants can
be defined as 'target migrants' who migrate to work
abroad in high income countries in order to achieve
a certain amount of savings which they plan to invest in some project back home -- a new house, for

instance, or a shop or small business. As soon as
the target is achieved, and sometimes this takes
longer than anticipated because of the high cost of
living abroad and inflation at home, the migrant
returns to realise his dream. In other cases, the
'target' is not financial but has to do with the
acquisition of a certain kind of skill or training,
or even the experience of living abroad and seeing
a different way of life. Again, once the qualification is attained or the desire for a different experience is sated, the migrant returns, more or less
according to plan. Some labour migrants are on
fixed-term contracts and they know they will return
when the contract expires in, say, two or three
years' time. Often, in these circumstances, the
return is temporary, until the worker can find
another job, perhaps again on a fixed contract.
Otherwise, relatively few migrants have a precise
term of absence fixed in their minds at the moment
of departure. They may carry the intention of returning but be rather vague about when this might
take place. Often the return is postponed, either
because it proves to take longer than anticipated to
make worthwhile savings or because ambitions for
savings and possessions continually move upward
whilst the migrant is away. A migrant who leaves
with the vague intention of returning in one or two
years often stays for four or five, or longer.

If the intended return is postponed to such an
extent that it never happens, then we move to the
second type, intended temporary migration without
return. This phenomenon can often be observed
amongst students who go abroad to study and who stay
on after finishing their courses -- the classic brain
drain mechanism. Many labour migrants, whose intention is nearly always for a temporary migration, also
end up by settling for good. This occurs much more
readily when families can move en bloc or when wives
and children can join men who are already established. The existence of an already-established
ethnic community in the destination country, the
result of previous waves of migrants of the same
nationality, probably helps in this process of turning temporary migrants into permanent ones. So does
finding a secure and relatively well-paid job, and
becoming attuned to a higher standard of living and
housing than could ever be attained in the environment of origin. Nevertheless, the idea of return
always seems to live on. This 'ideology of return'
(Brettell, 1979; Rubenstein, 1979), also known as
the 'myth of return' (Anwar, 1979) or the 'return

illusion' (Hoffmann-Nowotny, 1978), is so common
that it must be considered as part and parcel of the
whole migration ethos. No matter how settled, migrants keep in their minds the possibility that one
day they will return. They take action towards this
end by keeping in close contact with home and by
sending remittances. At the same time, however, the
myth of return functions as a defence mechanism or
perhaps as a kind of moral justification for their
unwillingness or their inability to adapt more to
the culture of the host society. Amongst Asians in
Britain, for instance, 'the myth of return' is used
to legitimise continued adherence to the values of
the homeland and to condemn the assimilation of
English cultural values as irrelevant and destructive (Ballard and Ballard, 1977, pp. 40-41).

Intended permanent migration with return is the
third type. Again, the outcome is different from the
intention, but in the opposite way to the previous
type. Migratory movements from Europe to countries
like the USA and Australia have often been thought
of as flows of permanent settlers, and certainly
interpreted as such by immigration authorities in
the destination countries. The Australian government's use of the term 'settler' is an obvious expression of a stay that is anticipated as permanent.
Yet studies of return migration by Price (1963) and
Zubrzycki (1973) put the rate of 'settler loss' at
around one quarter or one third. Similarly Axelrod
(1972), in a review of nineteenth century migration
estimates for the United States, comes to the conclusion that the net migration gain has been consistently overestimated because of the failure to
appreciate the magnitude of return movements.

Such unintended returns take place for a number
of reasons. First, there are migrants who are forced
to return by some circumstance beyond their control
such as loss of job or a family crisis back home.
In a study of Italians returning home from Great
Britain King (1977) notes that many had to come back
to look after elderly or ill parents. Second are
those who do not adjust to the way of life of the
destination country and who therefore choose to return through nostalgia: Cerase (1974) calls this the
'return of failure'. Third are those who have
changed their minds not because of discomfort but
because of the improved economic conditions at home.
Although it can be statistically demonstrated that
return flows grow in proportion to the relative improvement of the home economy vis-à-vis the destination economy (cf. Lianos, 1975; Miller, 1973)

13

relatively few empirical studies have identified this as a primary motive for return. I shall return to this point later.

The fourth major category, <u>intended permanent emigration without return</u>, is obviously the least important of the four for the study of return migration, so it will not be discussed, except to note that there is some research on the homeward ties and feelings of permanently settled migrants.

A classification of returned migrants which has had a good deal of impact on recent return migration research is the typology developed by Cerase (1970; 1974) from his work on Italians returning from the United States. Cerase's main thesis is that the type of return and the post-return impact of migrants depend largely on the stage in the process of acculturation that the migrants had reached in America at the moment of return. The typology is shown schematically in Figure 1.3. Four types of return are recognised.

1) Return of Failure   0 - 5 years   ⎫ Orientation to
                                             ⎬ society of origin
2) Return of Conservatism   5 - 10 years   ⎭
- -
3) Return of Innovation   10 - 20 years   ⎫
                                             ⎪ Orientation to
4) Return of Retirement   > 20 years   ⎬ society of
                                             ⎪ destination
5) No Return   ⎭

Figure 1.3: A Typology of Return for Italians Returning from the United States (after Cerase, 1970)

Migrants for whom the move abroad is such a culture shock that they fail to cope return quickly, usually within a matter of months or a couple of years. As their process of integration into American society never really started, they are simply reabsorbed into Italian society as if they had never been away. This Cerase calls the <u>return of failure</u>, his first type.

For migrants who overcome the initial period of adjustment, finding satisfactory work and accommodation, perhaps within the ethnic community of a 'little Italy', the process of integration begins. They begin to identify with their work, their neighbourhood and perhaps with certain elements of the 'new society'. Their orientation remains, however,

to their home environment and towards a planned
return, usually desired sooner rather than later.
Linguistic acculturation may still be minimal, and
remittances are sent back regularly to kin in Italy.
Typically the return occurs when the migrant has
saved enough to achieve upward social mobility in
his own society through buying land, building a new
house or opening a small independent business. This
is the return of conservatism, so called because the
returnee behaves according to the values of his society of origin and thereby acts to reinforce that
social formation.

The migrant who stays on beyond the 'target
return' becomes increasingly part of the host society and sees himself increasingly with reference to
its system of social stratification. Sooner or
later, however, he comes to realise that because of
his ethnic origins, his accent, his religion and
other inherited cultural features, he can only advance so far. This is the third turning point.
Seeing his aspirations frustrated, he may turn his
thoughts again to his country of origin, but because
he has reached quite an advanced stage in the process of acculturation into the host society, he
takes new values back with him. This is the return
of innovation. Unfortunately, from the point of
view of change and development in the sending country, this type of return does not appear to be very
common. Even when it does take place problems
arise, for what can the returnee, full of new hopes
and ambitions, do in his village of origin? Potential for development in remote rural regions may be
limited in the extreme; initiative may be further
stifled by established political and social forces
which resent outside challenges to established patterns of authority.

Finally, for those who stay on in America, a
fourth turning point is reached on retirement.
Nostalgia reasserts itself with the desire to live
out a peaceful old age back home. The return of
retirement, then, brings back economically inactive
migrants who usually form a rather isolated social
group because of their prolonged absence from the
sending society. In spite of their 'Americanisation'
they have little political or economic influence.

The extent to which Cerase's model is valid for
other return migration contexts is unclear. Cerase
is also vague about exactly what acculturation involves -- this may vary with an individual's class,
position, location in a particular neighbourhood and
country of destination. There are many parallels in

15

Saloutos' (1956) work on the Greek-Americans and
some similarities to be noted in studies of other
long-distance returnees such as Spanish and Portuguese returning from Latin America (Brettell, 1979;
Kenny, 1976), Maltese returning from North America
and Australia (King, 1980) and returning Filipinos
(Griffiths, 1979; McArthur, 1979). The typology may
be less valid for shorter-distance and shorter-term
movements such as internal migration and intra-
European labour migration since the 1950s.

Finally, there are powerful arguments for analysing return migration within a systems framework
and therefore viewing it as an essentially linking
element in the whole migration syndrome. Mabogunje
(1970) sees return migration, along with letters
from migrants abroad or in the city and other forms
of contact from the emigrant community to the society of origin, as a form of feedback which cali-
brates the entire migratory system. If the feedback
is positive -- i.e. if the returnees come back with
glowing accounts of life and earnings in the city or
abroad -- then return acts as a boost to further
outmigration. If the feedback is negative, with
returnees telling of hard times and failures, further
outmigration will be depressed. Unfortunately, empirical studies of migration and return migration
through this kind of all-embracing framework are
difficult to carry out because of the impracticabil-
ity of conducting research at all stages and in all
locations of the migratory system. Recently, however, some anthropologists have succeeded in carry-
ing out field work at both ends of the migration
chain, and are able to claim a better understanding
of the processes of migration and return migration
than would have been possible by just looking at,
say, ethnicity or assimilation at the destination
end or the impact of emigration or of return migration at the sending end. Dahya (1973) in a detailed
and exemplary study of Pakistani migrants in Britain
and in Pakistan treats the migrant community abroad
and the society of origin as parts of a single system of socio-cultural and socio-economic relationships. Much the same approach is evident in Philpott's well-known work on Monserratian migrants, although he places less emphasis on return migration
(Philpott, 1973).

SUCCESSES AND FAILURES

A question which is often posed in studies of

returned migrants -- and one which has implications for returnees' potential contribution to the development of their home regions -- is whether the returnees are successes or failures. In other words, is return migration the consequence of a positive or a negative selection process? The numerous case studies available do not provide a uniformly clear answer to this question. Another problem is the criteria for definition of success or failure. The reception society tends to define as 'successful' a migrant who becomes thoroughly acculturated in terms of language, behaviour, etc. The society of origin, and perhaps the migrant himself, may define as successful a migrant who does not integrate but works and saves hard in order to return home. Further confusion arises from the fact that different studies compare return selectivity in different ways: some with the non-migrant population of the area of origin; others with the non-returnee migrant population of the destination country or city. Some of the more reliable (yet still conflicting) data can be summarised as follows.

Most studies of return migration to southern Europe, either from North America or from northern Europe, tend to find a negative selection on return. Both Gilkey (1967) and Cerase (1974) found that the most successful Italian migrants were the ones who did not return but stayed on to build America; and both Baučić (1973) for Yugoslavia and Bernard and Comitas (1978) for Greece found that returnees had lower educational standards than non-migrants and non-returnees. In a study of returns to north-west Ireland Foeken (1980) found that returnees were the ones who had made less occupational progress than non-returnees. Caldwell (1969), in a study of rural-urban migration in Nigeria, concluded that those who returned were the city's rejects: 'the old, the shabby and the sick'.

For certain longer distance migrations, however, it may be only the successful who can actually afford to return. This control is mentioned by Bovenkerk (1973) for Irish migrants in the USA, and by Davidson (1969) for Jamaicans in Britain. Latin American studies seem to be consistent in that here returnees are portrayed as being better educated and more skilled than non-returnees or non-migrants (Feindt and Browning, 1972; Hernández Alvarez, 1967; Sandis, 1970; Simmons and Cardona, 1974). It is also suggested that the failures do not go back, purely to avoid being branded as such by their communities of origin (Kenny, 1972). On the other hand, one also

reads that the <u>very</u> successful are not interested in
returning because this would involve giving up well-
paid jobs and good positions which would be unobtain-
able in the homeland (Gmelch, 1980, p. 142).
    Clearly, the evidence is contradictory. Gmelch
(1980, p. 141) concludes by suggesting that most
returnees are not clearly failures, but neither are
they the most successful. Bovenkerk (1974, p. 23)
thinks that it depends upon the type of migration
from which the return takes place: the returnees
from long distance, quasi-permanent emigration are
seldom failures; the returnees from temporary (e.g.
intra-European) migration are seldom successes.
Dasgupta (1981) divides internal returnees into two
main types: those who have been successful in the
towns; and those who are returning home because they
have failed. Each major type contains three sub-
types: successful returnees comprise retirees,
target migrants who achieved their target, and those
attracted back by village improvements; failures
comprise those who never succeeded in getting a job
in the city, those who did but then lost it, and
those who could not adapt to the social aspects of
urban life.

RETURN MIGRATION AND REGIONAL DEVELOPMENT

Moving now to the more strictly economic effects of
return migration, two main strands of debate can be
explored. One is the notion of returning migrants as
bearers of newly acquired skills and of innovative
and entrepreneurial attitudes. The second is the
use to which returnees put accumulated capital; this
includes both the savings they have put by and
brought back with them, and remittance income which
was sent back periodically during their absence.

Returnees as Innovators
Bovenkerk (1974, pp. 45-49) notes a number of factors
which may control the potential of return migration
to be an innovative force. The first is the <u>number</u>
<u>of returnees</u>. Large numbers of returnees to a com-
munity or region can provide the critical mass needed
to effect change, whereas small numbers are likely to
have little influence and be quietly absorbed. On
the other hand a massive repatriation or forced return might arouse hostility amongst the reception
community which might need to make sacrifices to
accommodate the incomers. On a similar note, the

<u>concentration of returnees in time</u> could also have
an effect. Migrants returning in dribs and drabs
would probably have less impact than the same number
coming in a single concentrated wave. Another
relevant variable is <u>duration of absence</u>. If this
is very short, say less than a year or two, the
migrant will have gained too little experience to be
of any use in promoting modernisation back home. If
the period of absence is very long, returnees may be
so alienated from their origin society, or they may
be so old, that again the influence exerted will be
small. Somewhere in between, an optimum length of
absence might be found whereby the absence is sufficiently long to have influenced the migrant and
allowed him to absorb certain experiences and values,
and yet sufficiently short that he still has time and
energy upon return to utilise his newly acquired
skills and attitudes. Next, returnees' <u>social class</u>
may have an effect in that returning professional
people or graduate students are more likely to have
an economic and cultural impact than uneducated
labourers. The <u>differences between the countries or
regions of immigration and emigration</u> also need to
be considered. A migrant returning from a metropolitan, industrial society to a traditional farming
area would have fewer relevant skills to offer than
if the return was to a town. Next there is the
<u>nature of the training</u> or skills acquired. Innova-
tion potential is probably greater for migrants
with general rather than highly specialised skills
which cannot be used in their home environment.
Finally, much may depend on <u>how the return is organ-
ised</u>. If it is spontaneous and unplanned, little
developmental impact may result; indeed, if the
movement is massive and uncoordinated, severe dis-
ruption could be caused. On the other hand, if the
movement is well organised and related to other
aspects of national and regional economic policy,
then potential benefits are increased.

The thesis of a gain in labour skills through
return migration rests on the belief that countries
and regions of emigration can acquire a skilled and
innovative labour force which will contribute use-
fully to the development of the home region. Generally, the countries of origin hope that their
returning workers will have learnt new industrial
skills which can be utilised for improving industrial
production back home. Certainly it has been shown
by Monson (1975) that Turkish workers receive a far
more efficient and economic training in industrial
skills in West Germany than they could get if they

stayed in Turkey. Sometimes, depending on the
nature of the local economy and the type of migration, it is anticipated that contributions may also
be made by returnees to agricultural improvement
and tourist development.

In practice, however, the 'improvement in human
capital' argument is repeatedly shown to be almost
entirely fallacious. A spell of foreign employment
does not effectively convert a mass of unskilled
rural labourers into an industrial workforce tailor-
made for the industrial development of the home
country. Several reasons account for this. Firstly,
a large proportion of migrant workers are employed
in unskilled jobs when away, consequently no skills
are imparted to them. A migrant who has 'learnt'
to sweep streets, collect refuse or mix cement is of
little use to a domestic labour market short of
skills. Paine (1974) estimates that less than a
tenth of Turks returning from West Germany have received any kind of useful training whilst abroad.
Secondly, the skills that are imparted to some migrants do not necessarily match those needed at
home. A migrant who has been trained to perform a
narrow range of tasks on a car production line is of
little use to his native labour market. It is true
that migrant workers may become more attuned to
factory work regimes, but this still does not satisfy the pressing demand in some migrant sending countries (in southern Europe, for example) for skilled,
intermediate and foreman-type personnel. Some
migrants actually experience downward occupational
mobility when they migrate, and forget the skills
(in craft activities, for example) that they had
before emigrating. Other problems are the already-
noted negative selection of migrants who return
(generally the more skilled migrants stay on) and the
unwillingness of industrial employers in the region
of origin to hire returnees because of their
'superior' attitudes, higher wage expectations and
trade union experiences.

The small proportion of migrants who take up
industrial jobs on return is revealed time and time
again in empirical surveys. A 1970 Greek study
showed that only one-tenth of returned migrants went
into industrial employment; the vast majority rejected factory work, preferring instead independent employment or even a return to farming (Kayser, 1972).
Abadan-Unat's surveys in Turkey reveal that most
Turkish returnees have pre-industrial attitudes, even
after their migratory experience in northern Europe.
After spending so many years of 'sacrifice' abroad it

20

is not the intention of the returnee to become a 'mere' manual worker in a factory when savings can buy him independence and prestige. Whilst the Turkish migrant finds it quite acceptable to do almost any kind of work whilst abroad, as soon as he returns he systematically rejects all dirty or strenuous work, thereby reflecting the scheme of traditional values. Especially for the Turks, going to Germany seems to convert peasants into petty traders, a process which robs the Turkish economy of the skilled and semi-skilled workers its long-term industrialisation requires. The scant willingness of returnees to engage in cooperative enterprises is also commented upon (Abadan-Unat, 1974 and 1976).

All this is not to suggest that no returnees participate in industrial or other forms of economic development. Digging around in the literature, it is possible to find some cases of returnee entrepreneurship which go beyond the 'small shopkeeper' model. Lopreato (1962) reported the case of an olive oil press cooperatively run by returnees in a south Italian village; Baučić (1972) mentioned a similar venture -- a cooperative textile factory organised by returnees in Dalmatia; Saloutos (1956) describes the introduction of industrialised milk production into Greece by returnees from the USA; and McArthur (1979) credits Filipino returnees with introducing many useful skills such as carpentry, welding and the use of heavy machinery. In parts of Yugoslavia, Italy and Greece returnees are quick to contribute to the development of the local tourist industries, as studies of Corfu, Rhodes, Calabria and Dalmatia show (Bennett, 1979; King, Mortimer and Strachan, 1984; Manganara, 1977). The Puerto Rico experience also supports the notion of the return of skills. Using data for the early 1960s Friedlander (1965) and Hernández Alvarez (1967) found that nearly half the returnees were white collar migrants who represented a 'middle sector' bordering on the nation's educational and occupational elite. The timing of the Puerto Rican surveys is, however, significant for they were carried out at a time of rapid expansion of the Puerto Rican economy which attracted home many professional and skilled migrants from the United States.

On the question of the impact of return migration on specifically rural or agricultural development, McArthur (1979) found that long-stay migrants returning from Hawaii to the Philippines were agriculturally innovative, buying rice land, planting new varieties and using fertiliser. Their example

was then followed by other villages. In India
Oberai and Singh (1982) found that many of the early
innovators in the Green Revolution areas of the
Punjab had had migrant experience and had therefore
accumulated the capital necessary to invest in tubewells and other elements of the Green Revolution
'package'. And in New Guinea returnees were amongst
the first to establish coffee plantations in highland areas (Mayano, 1973). Miracle and Berry (1970,
p. 96) point out the relevance of the physical environment in studies of return migration between
agricultural areas. A large proportion of technology
in farming is physical environment specific and if
the environments and systems of farming are different
there may be little that is transferable. Thus the
potential transfer of technology by Mexican migrants
from the arid north of Mexico working in nearby
Arizona or southern California is much greater than
it would have been if they had been working in the
apple orchards of Washington or the cranberry bogs
of Wisconsin (Wiest, 1978).

In general it does seem that in the rural societies of the more underdeveloped world, returned
migrants do play the role of catalysts in promoting
new farming practices, provided the opportunities are
available to profitably use their capital resources
(Adepoju, 1981). The situation is somewhat different, however, in what might be termed 'semi-devel-
oped' sending communities such as those in the
Mediterranean Basin and parts of the Caribbean. Here
the impact of return on farming is very slight. In
Spain, Yugoslavia and Turkey there has been some investment in farm machinery but much of this is ir-
rational: tractors are bought by returnees as
prestige symbols, agriculture becomes over-mechanised
so that more labour is driven off the land (Abadan-
Unat, 1976; Baučić, 1972; Rhoades, 1978). In many
Mediterranean countries returnees buy small plots of
land for building, speculation or hobby farming.
This returnee pressure on the land market drives up
the price of land making it impossible for farmers
to enlarge or rationalise their holdings. For southern Spain Rhoades (1978) shows that commercial farming and agricultural innovations are not a primary
concern of returning migrants. If anything their
actions combine to depress agriculture and further
fragment the landholding pattern. These conclusions
probably hold for other Mediterranean countries, and
maybe some other parts of the world too.

One further point needs to be made about the
role of returning migrants in introducing new work

skills. This is that the bulk of research has been done on return to rural areas. Here development possibilities are limited and to condemn returnees for their feeble economic impact is to run the risk of falling into the trap of tautological argument. Very few studies have been made of the migrant who returns to an urban area, where his influence could be quite different. Several chapters in this book[2] help to rectify this deficiency. Finally, the difficulty of disentangling returnee-induced effects from those caused by other agents of change (mass media, education, tourism, internal development policies etc.) should be noted. No rigorous research has yet been done on the diffusion of ideas and technology from returnees to the wider community (Gmelch, 1980).

Returnees' Capital and Investment

The second main strand of debate in the relationship between return migration and economic development is the use to which returning migrants' capital is put. Although an analytical distinction between remittances (sent back whilst the migrant is away) and savings (brought back when the migrant returns) should be made, in practice this distinction is often blurred, for remittances are in many cases used not only for the everyday support of family members remaining at home but are also channelled towards particular investments such as land, machinery or the acquisiton of a business. A comprehensive review of the use of remittances and savings by the sending society is contained in Connell et al (1976, pp. 90-120).

Migrants' savings are likely to be high, compared to what they could save at home, both because migrant incomes abroad or in the city are higher and because migrants make a greater effort to limit consumption. How much a migrant saves -- both in absolute terms and as a proportion of income -- depends on wage levels, the quantity of unavoidable expenses on accommodation, transport and subsistence, and the propensity to save. The amount of remittances or savings is likely to be less if the decision to migrate was taken independently by an individual, and greater if the migration decision was linked to the needs of the household, members of which are left behind. Remittances can also be seen as returns to the investment in the migrant's upbringing and education on the part of the household, and as an expression of the commitment to the home area and an

eventual desire to return. The amount of remittance
money sent usually increases with the distance and
cost of the migration, but the rate often declines
with the length of stay of the migrant in the urban
or foreign area (Dasgupta, 1981, p. 47).

Migrants returning after many years of hard
work and desperate saving may bring back very considerable sums. In addition to capital deposited in
savings accounts cash may also be obtained from the
sale of assets accumulated during the absence --
house, furniture, car etc. Rhoades (1978) has examined bank deposits of returning migrants to Spain
and there are other, more general, estimates of
remittance flows [e.g. Hume (1973) for intra-
European remittances]. Some studies make proportional estimates of remittance flows. For example,
Johnson and Whitelaw (1974) found that in their
study of 1,140 male migrants in Nairobi, 89 per cent
remitted regularly, the average proportion of income
sent back being 21 per cent. Hancock (1959) has
suggested that Mexican braceros are able to take
back or send home at least 55 per cent of their
incomes in the United States. Similar proportions
are reported for studies of South African migrant
groups (Houghton, 1960). In addition to the local-
scale function of supporting peasant communities,
remittances may also have an important part to play
in national balance of payments accounts, as Swanson
(1979) has shown for the Yemen.

Two things are clear. Many returnees are extremely well-off by local standards, rivalling in
many cases the wealth (but not necessarily the
status) of local elites. The second point is the
paradox that the greater the wealth and general well-
being on return, the greater are likely to have been
the sacrifice, self-denial and deprivation of the
migrants during the 'other existence' abroad.

The key question, however, is not how much
money migrants bring back but how they use it. Do
they invest in new enterprises such as industries,
new farming techniques or cooperatives which will
raise the productive capacity of their regions,
generating further employment and capital? Or is
their money spent largely on consumerism, to raise
the comfort and status of the returnee and his
family? Most of the empirical evidence suggests the
latter.

By far the most common target for returnee investment is housing. Baučić (1972) found that 69
per cent of returning Yugoslavs questioned said that
they intended to spend their earnings on a house,

and 51 per cent of returnee capital is actually spent on house construction. Most new migrant housing in Yugoslavia is excessively large, greater than family needs and therefore with many rooms unutilised, although in tourist and urban areas surplus rooms may be rented off. In Pakistan too migrant houses contain far more rooms than the family needs: 'the pakka structures, with their trellised balconies and loggias, multi-coloured glass windows, and surrounding fields, stand out for miles to vindicate to one and all the migrant's and his family's achieved status' (Dahya, 1973). One of the best descriptions of returnee housing comes from Rhoades' (1978) work in southern Spain where many villages have their centro alemán or 'German suburb'. Rhoades defines the behaviour of returnees in Andalusia as 'conspicuous consumption run amok'. The migrants returned from Germany are 'rabid Germanophiles' in their consumption tastes. 'This fervour for imitation includes plush sofas, chandeliers, and wall-long buffets that serve as display cases for German china and glass articles. The built-in bar is always well stocked with a multitude of liquors. Bathrooms and kitchen walls are tiled and hallways are decorated with plaques from German cities, Black Forest cuckoo clocks, and other tourist paraphernalia. Electronic gadgets abound...' (Rhoades, 1978, p.141).
    Many writers condemn such behaviour as anti-economic, pointing out that spending on housing could be more cost-effectively allocated elsewhere (Böhning, 1975), and that such consumer spending causes structural distortions in the economy since most consumer goods have to be imported (Cases Mendez and Cabezas Moro, 1976). This may be true, but is the returnees' behaviour so unnatural? Is not the house the near-universal prestige symbol? It can also be argued that such behaviour is not only for 'show' but has the effect of raising the status of the returnees, thereby giving them better access to other village resources, or perhaps increasing returned migrants' children's marriage prospects. Some employment is also created, and house construction also stimulates the development of local industries supplying bricks, tiles, cement, door frames, etc. Of course, it has to be borne in mind that the jobs created are of a temporary nature, their continuation being dependent on a regular flow of return migrants to maintain the housing boom.
    For most countries and regions affected by international return migration, investment in agriculture is imited. Many returning migrants are no

longer attracted to farming, either economically or
psychologically. Greek migrants are fairly typical
in this respect: while 30 per cent worked in agriculture before emigrating, only 8 per cent did after
return (Lianos, 1975). Returnees' lack of interest
in farming reinforces the land abandonment originally caused by rural outmigration. Investment in agriculture is also conditioned by the type of environment to which the migrant returns. The farm
structure itself may be a relevant variable. In
Spain, for instance, emigrants returning to a region
of smallholdings often invest their savings in a
small property, whereas those returning to an area
dominated by large estates turn to other activities
outside the agricultural sector (Livi Bacci, 1972,
p. 119). In a land-based peasant society the purchase of land by returnees is a bid for social position. But it has the effect of driving up land
prices and contributing to inflation. Under such
circumstances any consolidation of holdings or enlargement of farms is unlikely to occur. Nor are
the inflationary effects of returnee spending entirely local. Palmer (1975) writes that the entire
Jamaican economy faced inflation in the 1960s as a
result of an aggregate demand pushed continually
upward by the influx of emigrant remittances.
There are relatively few cases of a substantial
proportion of remittance capital being used for
productive investment in agricultural inputs, machinery or allied activities such as rice mills.
Where this does happen, as in the case of the Punjabi
migrants, the impact in the short run tends to replace hired labour by machines, but in the long run
investment in new forms of agriculture such as irrigation and multiple cropping may actually increase
-- as has happened in many areas where tractors and
tubewells have been introduced in conjunction with
the new high-yielding seed varieties (Dasgupta,
1981).
After housing and consumer needs, most indications are that the next category of return migrant
spending is on small businesses. Gmelch (1980, p.
150) found that in Ireland 30 per cent of returnee
households had established their own small businesses,
usually a shop or pub. Similar tendencies have been
noted for Spain (Rhoades, 1978), Portugal (Brettell,
1979), Italy (King, 1977), Yugoslavia (Baučić, 1972),
Greece (Unger, 1981), Turkey (Paine, 1974), Malta
(King, 1980), Jamaica (Taylor, 1976) and Monserrat
(Philpott, 1977). In nearly all cases these businesses imitate enterprises already established in the

locality and are concentrated in the service sector.
They do not introduce new forms of production. Any
profits tend to be ploughed back into family needs
or savings for old age rather than expanding the
enterprise.

In summary, it appears that there are relatively
few exceptions to the economically pessimistic view
of the use of remittances and savings. Large seg-
ments of migrant earnings are spent on supporting
families left behind and raising their standard of
living. Another significant portion goes on conspicuous consumption of large and elaborate housing.
Little of the money finds its way into productive
enterprises which yield a good return on investment
or create additional employment. Even where there
are institutional encouragements to channel migrants'
savings into industrial growth, as there have been
in Turkey, success may not be guaranteed (Abadan-
Unat, 1976; Penninx and van Renselaar, 1978).

A CONCLUDING CRITIQUE

The most strident critiques of the equilibrium model
of return migration aiding the development of the
region of origin come from Marxist writers. Amin
(1974) criticises sociologists for their lack of
systematic enquiry in this field and for their random and often conflicting observations. Amin main-
tains that return migration's variable contribution
to reinforcing traditional structures and to stimulating capitalist development are in fact part and
parcel of the same process of impoverishment and
underdevelopment, whereby real structural change
(i.e. lessening dependency) is prevented. Whether
the migrant returns as a petty trader or as an em-
bryonic capitalist 'planter' hiring paid labour, the
form of 'development' is that of 'a degenerated
agrarian capitalism, corrupted and poor' (Amin, 1974,
p. 104).

Castles and Kosack (1973, pp. 425-429) provide
a parallel set of arguments for the Mediterranean
countries locked into the European labour migration
system. The main economic benefit, according to
them, is experienced by the migrants themselves and
their families. A further, indirect, national benefit may derive from the inflow of remittances. Migration and return migration probably make the distribution of income in the sending society more
unequal, since the benefits of migration are confined
to a few (Lipton, 1980). On the other hand, there

seems little doubt that migration <u>could</u> be a real
aid to development. Migrants <u>could</u> be given relevant training by receiving countries. They <u>could</u> be
given incentives to invest their savings for the
general good of their societies. And industries
<u>could</u> be located in areas where they would use re-
turned migrants' skills. But these things can only
happen if there is a basic change in the relationship between the rich, migrant-receiving and the
poor, migrant-sending regions.

NOTES

1. This chapter is based on parts of two much
longer discussion papers (King, Strachan and Mortimer, 1983; King and Strachan, 1983) available from
the Geography Section, Oxford Polytechnic, Oxford,
England.
2. See especially Chapters 2, 5, 6, 8 and 10.

REFERENCES

Abadan-Unat, N. (1974) 'Turkish external migration
    and social mobility', in P. Benedict, E.
    Tümertekin and F. Mansur (eds.) <u>Turkey: Geo-
    graphic and Social Perspectives</u>, Brill, Leiden,
    pp. 362-402.
Abadan-Unat, N. (1976) 'Migration as an obstacle for
    re-integration in industry: the Turkish case',
    <u>Studi Emigrazione</u>, 43, pp. 319-334.
Abe, T. and Wiltshire, R. (1980) 'Reverse migration
    in Japan: a factor analysis of reverse migra-
    tion streams', <u>Science Reports of the Tohoku
    University, 7th Series (Geography)</u>, 30(2), pp.
    111-117.
Abraham, P.M. (1968) 'Regaining high-level Indian
    manpower from abroad, <u>Manpower Journal</u>, 3(4),
    pp. 83-117.
Adepoju, A. (1981) 'Migration and socio-economic
    change in tropical Africa: policy and research,
    in J. Balán (ed.) <u>Why People Move</u>, UNESCO,
    Paris, pp. 317-336.
Amin, S. (1974) 'Modern migrations in Western Africa',
    in S. Amin (ed.) <u>Modern Migrations in Western
    Africa</u>, Oxford University Press, London, pp.
    65-124.
Anwar, M. (1979) <u>The Myth of Return: Pakistanis in
    Britain</u>, Heinemann, London.

Appleyard, R.T. (1962) 'Determinants of return mi-
    gration: a socio-economic study of UK migrants
    who returned from Australia', The Economic
    Record, 83, pp. 352-368.
Awasthi, S.P. (1966) 'An experiment in voluntary
    repatriation of high level technical manpower',
    Development Digest, 4(1), pp. 28-35.
Axelrod, B. (1972) 'Historical studies of emigration
    from the United States', International Migra-
    tion Review, 6(1), pp. 32-49.
Ballard, R. and Ballard, C. (1977) 'The Sikhs: the
    development of South Asian settlements in
    Britain', in J.L. Watson (ed.) Between Two
    Cultures, Blackwell, Oxford, pp. 21-56.
Barakat, H.I. (1973) 'The Palestinian refugees: an
    uprooted community seeking repatriation',
    International Migration Review, 7(2), pp. 147-
    161.
Baučić, I. (1972) The Effects of Emigration from
    Yugoslavia and the Problems of Returning Emi-
    grant Workers, Nijhoff, The Hague.
Baučić, I. (1973) 'Yugoslavia as a country of emi-
    gration', Options Mediterranéennes, 22, pp. 56-
    66.
Beaumont, P.B. (1976) 'The problem of return migra-
    tion under a policy of assisted labour mobility:
    an examination of some British evidence',
    British Journal of Industrial Relations, 14(1),
    pp. 82-88.
Bell, D.N.F. and Kirwan, F.X. (1979) 'Return migra-
    tion in a Scottish context', Regional Studies,
    13(1), pp. 101-111.
Bennett, B.C. (1979) 'Migration and rural community
    viability in central Dalmatia (Croatia), Yugo-
    slavia', Papers in Anthropology, 20(1), pp. 75-
    83.
Bernard, H.R. and Comitas, L. (1978) 'Greek return
    migration', Current Anthropology, 19(3), pp.
    658-659.
Birks, J.S. (1975) 'Overland pilgrimage in the
    savanna lands of Africa', in L.A. Kosiński and
    R.M. Prothero (eds.) People on the Move,
    Methuen, London, pp. 297-307.
Blejer, M.L. and Goldberg, I. (1980) 'Return migra-
    tion - expectation versus reality: a case
    study of Western immigrants to Israel', in J.L.
    Simon and J. DaVanzo (eds.) Research in Popula-
    tion Economics, JAI Press, Greenwich, Conn.,
    vol. 2, pp. 433-449.

Böhning, W.R. (1974) 'The economic effects of the
    employment of foreign workers: with special
    reference to the labour markets of Western
    Europe's post-industrial countries', in W.R.
    Böhning and D. Maillat, The Effects of the
    Employment of Foreign Workers, OECD, Paris,
    pp. 41-123.
Böhning, W.R. (1975) ' Some thoughts on emigration
    from the Mediterranean Basin', International
    Labour Review, 111(3), pp. 251-277.
Bovenkerk, F. (1973) 'On the causes of Irish migra-
    tion', Sociologia Ruralis, 13(4-5), pp. 263-
    275.
Bovenkerk, F. (1974) The Sociology of Return Migra-
    tion: A Bibliographic Essay, Nijhoff, The
    Hague.
Brandes, S.H. (1975) Migration, Kinship and Commun-
    ity: Tradition and Transition in a Spanish
    Village, Academic Press, New York.
Brettell, C.B. (1979) 'Emigrar para voltar: a
    Portuguese ideology of return migration',
    Papers in Anthropology, 20(1), pp. 1-20.
Caldwell, J.C. (1969) African Rural-Urban Migration
    to Ghana's Towns, Columbia University Press,
    New York.
Cases Mendez, J.I. and Cabezas Moro, O. (1976) 'The
    relation between migration policy and economic
    development and the promotion of new employment
    possibilities for returnees (foreign investment
    and migrant remittances)', International
    Migration, 14(1-2), pp. 134-162.
Castles, S. and Kosack, G. (1973) Immigrant Workers
    and Class Structure in Western Europe, Oxford
    University Press, London.
Cerase, F.P. (1967) 'A study of Italian returning
    migrants from the United States, International
    Migration Review, 1(3), pp. 67-74.
Cerase, F.P. (1970) 'Nostalgia or disenchantment:
    considerations on return migration', in S.M.
    Tomasi and M.H. Engel (eds.) The Italian Ex-
    perience in the United States, Center for
    Migration Studies, New York, pp. 217-239.
Cerase, F.P. (1974) 'Migration and social change:
    expectations and reality. A study of return
    migration from the United States to Italy',
    International Migration Review, 8(2), pp. 245-
    262.
Comay, Y. (1971) 'Determinants of return migration:
    Canadian professionals in the United States',
    Southern Economic Journal, 37(3), pp. 318-322.

Connell, J., Dasgupta, B., Laishley, R. and Lipton,
    M. (1976) Migration from Rural Areas: the
    Evidence from Village Studies, Oxford University
    Press, New Delhi.
Crane, R.I. (1955) 'Urbanism in India', American
    Journal of Sociology, 60(5), pp. 463-470.
Dahya, B. (1973) 'Pakistanis in Britain: transients
    or settlers?', Race, 14(3), pp. 241-277.
Dasgupta, B. (1981) 'Rural-urban migration and rural
    development', in J. Balán (ed.) Why People
    Move, UNESCO, Paris, pp. 43-58.
Davies, H.R.J. (1964) 'The West African in the econ-
    omic geography of the Sudan', Geography, 49(3),
    pp. 222-235.
Davidson, B. (1969) 'No place back home: a study of
    Jamaicans returning to Kingston', Race, 9(4),
    pp. 499-509.
Douglass, W.A. (1970) 'Peasant emigrants: reactors
    or actors?', in R.E. Spencer (ed.) Migration
    and Anthropology, University of Washington
    Press, Seattle, pp. 21-35.
Eldridge, H.T. (1965) 'Primary, secondary and return
    migration in the United States', Demography,
    2(3), pp. 444-455.
Feindt, W. and Browning, H.L. (1972) 'Return migra-
    tion: its significance in an industrial metro-
    polis and an agricultural town in Mexico',
    International Migration Review, 6(2), pp. 158-
    166.
Foeken, D. (1980) 'Return migration to a marginal
    rural area in north-western Ireland', Tijd-
    schrift voor Economische en Sociale Geografie,
    71(2), pp. 114-120.
Form, W.H. and Rivera, J. (1958) 'The place of re-
    turning migrants in a stratification system',
    Rural Sociology, 23(2), pp. 286-297.
Fortney, J.A. (1970) 'The international migration of
    professionals', Population Studies, 12(2), pp.
    217-232.
Friedl, E. (1959) 'The role of kinship in the trans-
    mission of national culture to rural villages
    in mainland Greece', American Anthropologist,
    61(1), pp. 30-38.
Friedlander, S.L. (1965) Labour Migration and
    Economic Growth: A Case Study of Puerto Rico,
    MIT Press, Cambridge, Mass.
Gilkey, G.R. (1967) 'The United States and Italy:
    migration and repatriation', Journal of Devel-
    oping Areas, 2(1), pp. 23-35.
Glaser, W.A.(1978) The Brain Drain: Emigration and
    Return, Pergamon, Oxford

Gmelch, G. (1980) 'Return migration', Annual Review of Anthropology, 9, pp. 135-159.

Griffiths, S.L. (1979) 'Emigration and entrepreneurship in a Philippine peasant village', Papers in Anthropology, 20(1), pp. 127-144.

Hancock, R.H. (1959) The Role of the Bracero in the Economic and Cultural Dynamics of Mexico, Hispanic American Society, Stanford, Calif.

Haniotis, G.V. (1964) 'An exercise in voluntary repatriation in Greece', OECD Observer, 11, pp. 12-15.

Hernández Alvarez, J. (1966) 'A demographic profile of the Mexican immigraton to the United States, 1910-1950', Journal of Inter-American Studies, 8(3), pp. 471-496.

Hernández Alvarez, J. (1967) Return Migration to Puerto Rico, University of California Institute of International Studies, Berkeley.

Hodgkin, M.C. (1972) The Innovators: the Role of Foreign-Trained Persons in Southeast Asia, Sydney University Press, Sydney.

Hoffmann-Nowotny, H.J. (1968) 'European migration after World War Two', in W.H. McNeill and R.S. Adams (eds.) Human Migration, University of Indiana Press, Bloomington, pp. 85-105.

Houghton, D.H. (1960) 'Men of two worlds: some aspects of migratory labour in South Africa', South African Journal of Economics, 28(4), pp. 177-190.

Hume, I. (1973) 'Migrant workers in Europe', Finance and Development, 10(1), pp. 2-6.

Johnson, G.E. and Whitelaw, W.E. (1974) 'Urban-rural transfers in Kenya: an estimated remittance function', Economic Development and Cultural Change, 22(3), pp. 473-479.

Kayser, B. (1972) Cyclically-Determined Homeward Flows of Migrant Workers, OECD, Paris.

Kayser, B. (1977) 'European migrations: the new pattern', International Migration Review, 11(2), pp. 232-240.

Keats, D. (1969) Back in Asia, Australia National University, Canberra.

Kenny, M. (1972) 'The return of the Spanish emigrant', Nord Nytt, 2, pp. 119-129.

Kenny, M. (1976) 'Twentieth century Spanish ties with the homeland: remigration and its consequences', in J.B. Aceves and W.A. Douglass (eds.) The Changing Faces of Rural Spain, Schenkmann, New York, pp. 97-122.

King, R.L. (1977) 'Problems of return migration: a case study of Italians returning from Britain', Tijdschrift voor Economische en Sociale Geografie, 68(4), pp. 241-246.

King, R.L. (1978) 'Return migration: a neglected aspect of population geography', Area, 10(3), pp. 175-182.

King, R.L. (1979) 'Return migration: a review of some case studies from southern Europe', Mediterranean Studies, 1(2), pp. 3-30.

King, R.L. (1980) The Maltese Migration Cycle: Perspectives on Return, Oxford Polytechnic Discussion Papers in Geography 13, Oxford.

King, R.L., Mortimer, J. and Strachan, A.J. (1984) 'Return migration and tertiary development: a Calabrian case study', Anthropological Quarterly, 57(3), pp. 112-124.

King, R.L. and Strachan, A.J. (1980) 'The effects of return migration on a Gozitan village', Human Organization, 39(2), pp. 175-179.

King, R.L. and Strachan, A.J. (1983) Return Migration: A Sourcebook of Evaluative Abstracts, Oxford Polytechnic Discussion Papers in Geography 20, Oxford.

King, R.L., Strachan, A.J. and Mortimer, J. (1983) Return Migration: A Review of the Literature, Oxford Polytechnic Discussion Papers in Geography 19, Oxford.

Lebon, A. and Falchi, G. (1980) 'New developments in intra-European migration since 1974', International Migration Review, 14(4), pp. 539-579.

Lee, A.S. (1974) 'Return migration in the United States', International Migration Review, 8(2), pp. 283-300.

Lee, E.S. (1966) 'A theory of migration', Demography, 3(1), pp. 47-57.

Lee, O.J. and Kim, K.D. (1981) 'Adaption in the city and return home: a dynamic approach to urban-to-rural return migration in the Republic of Korea', in J. Balán (ed.) Why People Move, UNESCO, Paris, pp. 230-241.

Lianos, T.P. (1975) 'Flows of Greek outmigration and return migration', International Migration, 13(3), pp. 119-133.

Lipton, M. (1980) 'Migration from rural areas of poor countries: the impact on rural productivity and income distribution', World Development, 8(1), pp. 1-24.

Livi-Bacci, M. (1972) 'The countries of emigration',
    in M. Livi-Bacci (ed.) The Demographic and
    Social Pattern of Emigration from the Southern
    European Countries, Dipartimento Statistico-
    Matematico dell'Università di Firenze, Flor-
    ence, pp. 7-123.
Lohrmann, R. (1976) 'European migration: recent
    developments and future prospects', Interna-
    tional Migration, 14(3), pp. 229-240.
Long, L.H. and Hansen, K.A. (1975) 'Trends in return
    migration to the South', Demography, 12(4),
    pp. 601-614.
Lopreato, J. (1962) 'Economic development and cul-
    tural change: the role of emigration',
    Human Organization, 21(3), pp. 182-186.
Lopreato, J. (1967) Peasants No More, Chandler,
    San Francisco.
Mabogunje, A. (1970) 'Systems approach to a theory
    of rural-urban migration', Geographical
    Analysis, 2(1), pp. 1-18.
Mangalam, J.J. (1968) Human Migration: A Guide to
    the Literature in English, University of
    Kentucky Press, Lexington.
Manganara, J. (1977) 'Some social aspects of the
    return movement of Greek migrant workers from
    West Germany to rural Greece', Greek Review of
    Social Research, 29, pp. 65-75.
Mayano, D.M. (1973) 'Individual correlates of coffee
    production in the New Guinea Highlands',
    Human Organization, 32(3), pp. 305-314.
McArthur, H.J. (1979) 'The effects of overseas work
    on return migrants and their home communities:
    a Philippine case', Papers in Anthropology,
    20(1), pp. 85-104.
Miller, E. (1973) 'Return and non-return in-migra-
    tion', Growth and Change, 4(11), pp. 3-9.
Miracle, M.P. and Berry, S.S.(1970) 'Migrant labour
    and economic development', Oxford Economic
    Papers, 22(1), pp. 86-108.
Monson, T.D. (1975) 'Industrial learning experiences
    of Turkish migrants at home and abroad',
    Journal of Developing Areas, 9(2), pp. 221-236.
Myers, G.C. and Masnick, G. (1968) 'The migration
    experience of New York Puerto Ricans: a
    perspective on return', International Migration
    Review, 2(2), pp. 80-90.
Nelson, J.M. (1976) 'Sojourners versus new urbanites:
    causes and consequences of temporary versus per-
    manent cityward migration in developing coun-
    tries, Economic Development and Cultural Change,
    24(4), pp. 721-757.

Nicholson, B. (1975) 'Return migration to a marginal
    area: an example from north Norway', Sociolo-
    gia Ruralis, 15(4), pp. 227-245.
Oberai, A.S. and Singh, H.K.M. (1982) 'Migration,
    production and technology in agriculture: a
    case study in the Indian Punjab', International
    Labour Review, 121(3), pp. 327-343.
Paine, S. (1974) Exporting Workers: The Turkish
    Case, Cambridge University Press, Cambridge.
Palmer, R. (1975) 'A decade of West Indian migration
    to the United States 1962-1972: an economic
    analysis', Social and Economic Studies, 23(4),
    pp. 571-587.
Patterson, H.O. (1968) 'West Indian migrants return-
    ing home: some observations', Race, 10(1),
    pp. 69-77.
Penninx, R. and van Renselaar, H. (1978) A Fortune
    in Small Change, REMPLOD/NUFFIC, The Hague.
Philpott, S.B. (1968) 'Remittance obligations,
    social networks and choice among Monserratian
    migrants in Britain', Man 3(3), pp. 465-476.
Philpott, S.B. (1973) West Indian Migration: The
    Monserrat Case, Athlone, London.
Philpott, S.B. (1977) 'The Monserratians: migration
    dependency and the maintenance of island ties
    in England', in J.L. Watson (ed.) Between Two
    Cultures, Blackwell, Oxford, pp. 90-119.
Price, C.A. (1963) Southern Europeans in Australia,
    Chesshire, Melbourne.
Ravenstein, E.G. (1885) 'The laws of migration I',
    Journal of the Royal Statistical Society, 48(2),
    pp. 167-235.
Ravenstein, E.G. (1889) 'The laws of migration II',
    Journal of the Royal Statistical Society, 52(2),
    pp. 241-305.
Rhoades, R.E. (1978) 'Intra-European return migration
    and rural development: lessons from the
    Spanish case', Human Organization, 37(2), pp.
    136-147.
Rhoades, R.E. (1979) 'Toward an anthropology of
    return migration', Papers in Anthropology, 20
    (1), pp. i-iii.
Richardson, A. (1968) 'A shipboard study of some
    British-born immigrants returning home from
    Australia', International Migration, 6(4),
    pp. 221-238.
Richmond, A.H. (1966) 'Demographic and family char-
    acteristics of British immigrants returning
    from Canada', International Migration, 4(1),
    pp. 21-27.

Richmond, A.H. (1968) 'Return migration from Canada
    to Britain', Population Studies, 22(2), pp.
    263-271.
Richmond, A.H. (1969) 'Sociology of migration in
    industrial and post-industrial societies', in
    J.A. Jackson (ed.) Migration, Cambridge Uni-
    versity Press, Cambridge, pp. 238-281.
Richmond, A.H. (1981) 'Immigrant adaption in post-
    industrial societies', in M.M. Kritz, C.B.
    Keely and S.M. Tomasi (eds.) Global Trends in
    Migration, Center for Migration Studies, New
    York, pp. 298-319.
Rubenstein, H. (1979) 'The return ideology in West
    Indian migration', Papers in Anthropology,
    20(1), pp. 21-38.
Saloutos, T. (1956) They Remember America: the
    Story of the Repatriated Greek-Americans,
    University of California Press, Berkeley.
Salt, J. (1981) 'International labour migration in
    Western Europe: a geographical appraisal', in
    M.M. Kritz, C.B. Keely and S.M. Tomasi (eds.)
    Global Trends in Migration, Center for Migra-
    tion Studies, New York, pp. 133-157.
Sandis, E.E. (1970) 'Characteristics of Puerto Rican
    migrants to and from the United States',
    International Migration Review, 4(1), pp. 22-43.
Simmons, A.B. and Cardona, R.G. (1974) 'Rural-urban
    migration: who comes, who stays, who returns?',
    International Migration Review, 6(2), pp. 166-
    181.
Slater, M. (1979) 'Migrant employment, recessions,
    and return migration: some consequences for
    migration policy and development', Studies in
    Comparative International Development, 14(3-4),
    pp. 3-22.
Strachan, A. (1980) 'Government-sponsored return
    migration to Guyana', Area, 12(2), pp. 165-169.
Swanson, J. (1979) 'Some consequences of emigration
    for economic development in the Yemen Arab
    Republic', Middle East Journal, 33(1), pp. 34-
    43.
Taylor, E. (1976) 'The social adjustment of returned
    migrants to Jamaica', in F. Henry (ed.) Ethni-
    city in the Americas, Mouton, The Hague, pp.
    213-229.
Toren, N. (1976) 'Return to Zion: characteristics and
    motivations of returning migrants', Social
    Forces, 54(3), pp. 546-558.
Toren, N. (1978) 'Return migration to Israel',
    International Migration Review, 12(1), pp. 39-
    54.

Townsend, A. (1980) 'The role of returned migrants
     in England's poorest region', Geoforum, 11(4),
     pp. 353-369.
Unger, K. (1981) 'Greek emigration to and return
     from West Germany', Ekistics, 290, pp. 369-374.
Useem, J. and Useem, R.H. (1955) The Western Educa-
     ted Man in India, Dryden Press, New York.
Van Amersfoot, J.M.M. (1978) 'Migrant workers, cir-
     cular migration and development', Tijdschrift
     voor Economische en Sociale Geografie, 69(1-2),
     pp. 17-26.
Vanderkamp, J.(1972) 'Return migration: its signif-
     icance and behaviour', Western Economic
     Journal, 10(4), pp. 460-465.
Wiest, R.E. (1978) Rural Community Development in
     Mexico: The Impact of Mexican Recurrent Mi-
     gration to the United States, University of
     Manitoba Anthropological Papers 21, Winnipeg.
Wiltshire, R. (1979) 'Research on reverse migration
     in Japan (1): reverse migration and the con-
     cept of "U-turn"', Science Reports of the
     Tohoku University, 7th Series (Geography), 29
     (1), pp. 63-68.
Wiltshire, R. and Abe, T. (1978) 'Reverse migration
     in Japan: some evidence from the 1970 Census',
     Science Reports of the Tohoku University, 7th
     Series (Geography), 28(2), pp. 353-370.
Wood, P.A. (1976) 'Inter-regional migration in
     Western Europe: a reappraisal', in J. Salt and
     H. Clout (eds.) Migration in Post-War Europe,
     Oxford University Press, London, pp. 52-79.
Zubrzycki, J. (1973) Enquiry into the Departure of
     Settlers from Australia, Australian Government
     Publishing Service, Canberra.

Chapter Two

GASTARBEITER GO HOME: RETURN MIGRATION AND ECONOMIC
CHANGE IN THE ITALIAN MEZZOGIORNO

Russell King, Alan Strachan and Jill Mortimer

INTRODUCTION

Migration is one of the main features of the human
geography of southern Europe and indeed of much of
the Mediterranean Basin. The post-war period, in
particular the period between the late 1950s and the
early 1970s, has seen an emigration boom, sparked
off partly by the labour requirements of Western
Europe's industrial economies, and partly by the
continuing poverty of areas such as southern Italy,
northern Greece and rural Iberia. From the Italian
Mezzogiorno, as from Tras-os-Montes, Andalusia,
Macedonia and a dozen other Mediterranean regions,
farm labourers, peasants and other low status, low
income groups have flocked to the industrial regions
and conurbations of Western Europe where, until the
early 1970s, jobs -- of a certain range of types --
were available in abundance. By the watershed year
of 1973 this phenomenon of labour migration had
accumulated an estimated stock of nearly 10 million
migrants from the 'periphery' in the 'core' of
Western Europe.

     For the last ten years or more, however, this
trend has been reversed in the sense that counterstreams of returning migrants now outweigh the much
reduced outflows from southern Europe. At the outset, four main reasons may be intuitively advanced
for this migration reversal. First, it is often
attributed to the effects of the oil-induced recession which first struck in late 1973, creating
economic pressures for reducing employment in destination countries and for encouraging the repatriation of migrant workers and their families.
Secondly, these same pressures for return were
paralleled in the socio-political realm by what was
seen by some as a threatening build-up of ethnic

minorities and interracial tension. Thirdly, it could be hypothesised that return was encouraged by the development of the countries of origin where, in recent years, some new employment opportunities in industry and tourism have been opened. Finally, there is the essentially temporary nature of the labour migration cycle itself, with most migrants intending to return home at some stage, and being encouraged to do so by 'labour rotation' policy in most receiving countries. Their very labelling as Gastarbeiter ('guestsworkers') implies their short-term presence, in West Germany and Switzerland especially, and an anticipated return home.

The main purpose of this chapter is not to pronounce on the relative importance of these four suggested reasons for return. Its concern is with effects not causes of return. Nevertheless, it can be pointed out here that the real balance of factors giving rise to a return flow is highly complicated. Many studies based on interviewing returnees, including the present study and others in this book, have shown that most migrants return not because of redundancy in the host country but because of a much more complex mix of personal, family, emotional and economic reasons. The character of these reasons is relevant to the main theme of this chapter, however, in that it will tend to condition the kind of impact returnees have on their home regions.

The principal question to be examined, then, concerns the impact of return migration on southern Italy, a typical region of post-war emigration and, most recently, of return. Does return migration contribute to, or act as a force for, change, innovation and possible economic development in the region; or are the effects of return closely controlled or even stifled by the region's prevailing economic, social or political structures?

A brief look at the literature on this question reveals an interesting and rather sharp contradiction which was discussed in more detail in the previous chapter. Economists have pointed to return migration as a possible dynamic force for the development of migrants' countries and regions of origin. Returnees, it is postulated, bring in capital in the form of remittances and savings, as well as new ideas and experience of different types of work from their period abroad. And capital, training and innovation are all significant inputs into the development process.

However, the majority of empirical work carried out so far in southern Italy, and indeed in southern

39

European and Mediterranean countries as a whole, suggests that this developmental stimulus from return migration simply does not happen. Time and time again it is found that returnees come back with rather conservative ideas and limited ambitions. Their only desire seems to be to buy themselves a small plot of land and build themselves a new home. They do not engage in improving agriculture, nor do they set up appropriate rural industries (for example agricultural processing). Any entrepreneurial ambitions that returnees may have appear to be channelled into the creation of small-scale service-sector enterprises like shops and bars. From the economic point of view such concerns are marginal and precarious.

Part of this contradiction can probably be explained by the fact that previous empirical research on return migration in southern Italy (King, 1977; Lopreato, 1967; Merico, 1978; Reyneri, 1980) has been almost entirely in backward and remote rural regions (central Sicily, the Calabrian mountains, the Molisan hills) where economic opportunities are limited, as they always have been -- hence their high outmigration levels in the first place. Much the same situation is to be found with the research on other southern European countries: the best example is Rhoades's (1978; 1979) well-known work on villages in the Granada province of southern Spain. This focus on backward, poverty-stricken rural areas leads to a dangerously tautologous argument: return migration does not stimulate economic development largely because there are few development possibilities in these areas anyway.

The present study intends to break out of this circular argument by considering the impact of return migration on parts of southern Italy which can be statistically demonstrated to have made significant progress in recent years in economic and social development. The principal methodology is a questionnaire survey based on interviews with 705 returnees.

STRUCTURE OF THE RESEARCH AND ITS LOCATIONAL CONTEXT

The prime focus of the research[1] concerns the economic impact of returnees to southern Italy. Social dimensions of return and reintegration are considered only in passing. The main categories of questionnaire data analysed concern information on employment and on the use of savings and remittances.

Regarding the organisation and spatial location
of this research, we take as our point of departure
the criticism of previous questionnaire surveys of
returned migrants carried out in southern Europe,
which often select communities for interviewing on
what appears to be a strategy of convenience or at
best intuition. Obviously, where sample communities
are not selected rigorously, conclusions drawn for
such studies may not have much general significance.
The present study's sampling of south Italian settlements is based on two foundations: a profound knowledge of the geography of the Mezzogiorno, gathered
over many years' combined residence, travel and
fieldwork there; and statistical tabulations and
analyses of Italian census and other relevant data
at a variety of scales -- national, regional, provincial and commune.

Within the Mezzogiorno, which conventionally is
considered to embrace all of Italy south of Rome,
including the islands of Sicily and Sardinia, the
spatial frame of reference for this research is restricted to the three southernmost regions of the
mainland: Puglia, Basilicata and Calabria. This
spatial limit is partly dictated by the logistics of
the statistical analyses of official data, which
should not be too unwieldy, and partly by the desire
not to disperse field interviews across too wide an
area. The most important thing to note, however, is
that these three regions contain a good cross-section
of the economic geography of the Mezzogiorno, including areas of recent agricultural, industrial and
tourist development. The three regions comprise ten
provinces (Foggia, Bari, Brindisi, Taranto and Lecce
in Puglia; Matera and Potenza in Basilicata; and
Cosenza, Catanzaro and Reggio in Calabria), which
collectively contain 788 communes.

The statistical background to emigration and
return migration in southern Italy has been presented in detail in other papers by the authors and co-
workers on this research (King, Strachan and Di
Comite, 1982; Strachan and King, 1982). Very briefly
the three regions, which contain 11.6 per cent of
Italy's population, accounted for 31.2 per cent of
Italian emigration abroad during the period 1962-76.
Substantial numbers also migrated out of the regions
but within Italy; these internal migrants mainly
went to northern industrial regions around Milan and
Turin, and to the capital Rome. Whilst 934,763
emigrated abroad from the three regions during
1962-76, the return flow amounted to 653,587 over
the same period. These quantities represent

respectively 14.6 per cent and 10.2 per cent of the
1971 population of the three regions. Although
there may be some double-counting of emigrants (oc-
curing when individuals emigrate, return and then
re-emigrate), these figures are more likely to be
underestimates for it is widely acknowledged that
considerable numbers of people emigrate unrecorded
by the authorities. Since the mid-1970s, however,
the net balance of foreign migration has been inward
for most parts of the study area. In the late 1970s
these positive balances tended to diminish so that
the decade closed with most provinces experiencing
approximate parity between emigration and return.

Obviously it was not possible to interview in
all 788 communes in the study area. The choice of
sample communes was framed as rigorously as possible.
The first priority was to look for groupings of
communes exhibiting a fair degree of common ground.
This was achieved through an analysis of available
commune data relevant to the topic: migration data
(published annually in the ISTAT serial Popolazione
e Movimento Anagrafico dei Comuni); and the 1971
Census (Censimento Generale della Popolazione 24
Ottobre 1971), particularly those tabulations relating to population structure, employment, education and housing. The data set comprised 26 socio-
economic variables and 6 migration variables, for
each of the 788 communes. Two main techniques of
analysis were employed -- factor analysis, followed
by a grouping algorithm. A choropleth mapping procedure allowed direct computer mapping of the results
with a range of print symbols of varying density
filling in the patches of territory occupied by each
commune. The full set of factor and cluster maps is
published elsewhere (Strachan and King, 1982), but
Fig. 2.1 provides in a single map the most important
result of this analysis linking migration trends
with socio-economic health at the commune level.

Despite the absence of any contiguity constraint
in the clustering algorithm, certain clear patterns
can be seen on Fig. 2.1. Most prominent of all is
the spatial dominance of Cluster 1, and to a certain
extent of Cluster 2, over most of Puglia. In this
region the map stresses the strong relationship
between return migration and areas of economic
opportunity as reflected in good housing and employment opportunities, including a relatively well
developed specialised agriculture and recent
industrial development. These features cover most
of Puglia, except the north-western and south-
eastern extremities, and they extend over the border

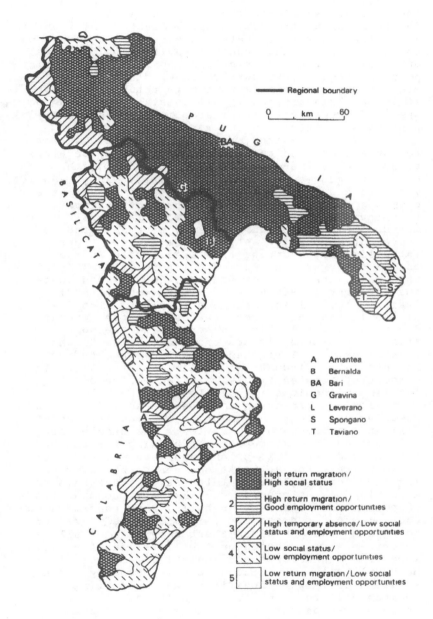

Fig. 2.1: Cluster Map of Migration and Socio-
Economic Data for the Study Area

43

into adjacent areas of Basilicata. In Calabria and
the rest of Basilicata the situation is the opposite,
for these areas are dominated by Clusters 3, 4 and 5.
Here, lower levels of return are seen as a response
to a poor social and economic environment. In most
of this predominantly highland zone, agriculture is
poor and industry virtually non-existent. The
limited areas of high status/high returns (Cluster
1) in Calabria are nearly all coastal, focussing on
areas of intensively cultivated lowland and on expanding administrative and resort towns.

As it was decided, for reasons stated earlier,
to concentrate the research in more highly developed
areas, Fig. 2.1 provided an ideal guide for the
choice of sample communes. Eventually, after a pilot
visit to check the situation 'on the ground', seven
communes were chosen, largely, but not entirely,
from the high-status Puglian belt. The sample
communes, indicated on Fig. 2.1, were selected to
represent a range of settlement sizes and types.
In Puglia they comprise the largest city in the
entire study region, Bari (1981 population 370,715),
the small rural town of Gravina (36,165) and three
smaller, rural settlements -- Leverano (12,603),
Taviano (10,893) and Spongano (3,672). Also included in the sample were the Basilicatan commune of
Bernalda (11,757) which is located in the more
prosperous part of Matera province, close to the
coastal belt of irrigated agriculture and to the
Basento Valley industrial estate, and the Calabrian
commune of Amantea (11,196), a centre for coastal
tourism and residential development.

Within these seven communes, a second level of
sampling was necessary in order to identify individuals and families for interview. The sample population was defined as persons of working age who had
been abroad for at least one year and who had been
back in Italy for at least one year, returning during the decade 1970-80. Interviewees were selected
according to two procedures. Firstly, commune lists
of returnees (held in town halls) were random sampled
for names and addresses. This procedure worked up
to a point but contained shortcomings: not all
returnees were recorded on the lists; and the lists
were often out of date and indistinct (especially if
hand-written). The second sampling strategy, run
simultaneously with the first, was a 'rolling
programme'. This involved identifying an initial
group of respondents via a range of intermediary
contacts such as local priests, school teachers and
shopkeepers, and then to ask each respondent, at the

44

end of the interview, to put the interviewer in
touch with another returnee of the respondent's
acquaintance. The interviewing, mostly carried out
by local graduates who had been specially trained in
the aims of the research, including interviewing
techniques, occupied the period between July 1982
and May 1983; 705 interviews were completed, 211 in
Bari and around 80-100 in each of the remaining
settlements.

The questionnaire took about 1-1½ hours to
administer. If spouses and working-age children of
the head of household were returnees, they were
interviewed also: the spouse perspective was felt
to be important since so many migration investiga-
tions are based on male heads of household, ignoring the possibly strong female influences on return
decisions and behaviour. Analysis of the questionnaire data was based on conventional statistical
techniques, using SPSS as the most suitable package
for handling large data sets. The data set was
subdivided along two distinct lines: by topic and
by community. The community split is being dealt
with in a series of separate papers on the various
sample settlements.[2] This chapter will focus,
therefore, on a topic-based analysis of the total
sample and will concentrate on those aspects of the
survey that are crucial to an understanding of the
migration process and the impact of return on such
variables as employment, investment, innovation and
attitudes to further migratory movement.

GENERAL CHARACTERISTICS OF THE SAMPLE

The 705 interviews comprised 486 households and
included 197 wives and 22 working-age children.
Returnees had worked in seven main countries of
destination: West Germany 40 per cent, Switzerland
23 per cent, Venezuela 8.9 per cent, France 7.8 per
cent, Belgium 4.5 per cent, USA 4.3 per cent and
Canada 3.4 per cent. There was some variation in
destination country by commune: Leverano, Gravina
and Bernalda were overwhelmingly orientated to West
Germany; Spongano consisted largely of seasonal
migrants to Switzerland; and Amantea had strong links
to the Americas, especially Venezuela. Bari was
more cosmopolitan in its migration destinations, with
some migrants from this city going to African and
Middle Eastern countries.

The typical migrant left between the ages of 17
and 29 years (63 per cent of respondents), visited

one (87 percent) or at most two (11 per cent)
countries and stayed an average of 9 years. Regarding the type of migration path, 76 per cent went for
a single period (though sometimes broken by brief
holidays back home), a further 15 per cent went for
two distinct periods broken by a period of at least
a year at home, and 6 per cent were seasonal migrants.
Over half (52 per cent) departed alone, including 16
per cent who were married at the time of departure;
19 per cent migrated to join a spouse already
abroad (these were mostly females joining up with
husbands). Most (58 per cent) were working at their
time of emigration; 14 per cent had worked but were
unemployed just before departure; 28 per cent were
young adults looking for their first jobs; and the
rest were schoolchildren or housewives when they
departed. The average age on return was 35 years,
and 84 per cent had returned by the age of 50.

Considerations of work dominate the sample's
motives for emigration, which is hardly surprising
considering the type of migration under study --
labour migration. Two-thirds of respondents
recorded wholly or mainly economic reasons for emigration; these were to do with lack of work, low
pay, poor prospects for job advancement, job
insecurity, etc. Most of the rest emigrated for
'family' reasons; these were primarily females
joining husbands who were already working abroad,
and children taken abroad with their parents.

The return motives, however, are much less
dominated by economic considerations. Here 'family'
and 'nostalgia' loom large, accounting for two-thirds
of return decisions. Family reasons include the
need to look after aged parents, the desire to have
children educated in Italian schools and, for single
migrants, the wish to find an Italian spouse. Some
returnees (7.1 per cent) also mentioned their own
poor health. Specifically economic reasons accounted
for only 13 per cent of returnee decisions: these
were divided roughly equally between economic
'pushes' from the destination country (unemployment
or threat of redundancy) and economic 'pulls' from
the origin region (improved job situation, desire
to start up a business, etc.). The low proportion
of respondents mentioning an economic attraction to
their home region (6.7 per cent of the total sample)
is significant in view of the research's focus on
return migration's hypothesised contribution to
economic change in southern Italy.

Table 2.1: Employment of a Sample of Returned Migrants
(n = 705)

	Before Migration		Abroad		Current Job		Desired Job	
	No.	%	No.	%	No.	%	No.	%
a) BY SECTOR								
Agriculture	130	31.6	2	0.3	122	23.7	46	8.7
Artisan								
(1-4 workers)	75	18.2	12	1.9	36	7.0	41	7.7
Small industry								
(5-49)	29	7.0	58	9.4	14	2.7	28	5.3
Large industry								
(50+)	19	4.6	280	45.2	28	5.4	84	15.9
Construction	77	18.7	119	19.2	84	16.3	68	12.9
Commerce	16	3.9	31	5.0	66	12.8	54	10.2
Private services								
(manual)	49	11.9	69	11.1	95	18.5	64	12.1
Public								
employment	11	2.7	25	4.0	53	10.3	63	11.9
Other	6	1.5	23	3.7	16	3.1	80	15.2
Economically								
inactive	293	41.6	86	12.2	191	27.1	177	25.1
b) BY POSITION								
Employee	299	72.6	566	91.4	285	55.4	286	54.2
Self-employed	61	14.8	25	4.0	113	22.0	111	21.0
Family								
enterprise	46	11.2	20	3.2	99	19.3	50	9.5
Other	6	1.5	8	1.3	17	3.3	81	15.3
Economically								
inactive	293	41.6	86	12.2	191	27.1	177	25.1

Note: Percentage figures refer to percentages of economically
active respondents, except for the bottom row in each section
(economically inactive as % of total sample).

Source: Authors' questionnaire survey.

EMPLOYMENT

A major part of the questionnaire data relates to
employment at various stages of the migration cycle,
and especially to jobs done since return and to post-
return attitudes towards and desires for different

types of work. Table 2.1 summarises the total
sample picture for employment before, during and
after migration, and also gives the jobs desired
upon return. The responses are categorised in two
ways: by sector (agriculture, commerce, etc.) and
by position (employee, self-employed, etc.). Note
that the percentage data refer to percentages of the
economically active respondents, not of the total
sample. The economically active total varies at
different stages of the migration cycle: before
emigration this figure was 412, abroad it was 619
and 'currently' it was 514. First we analyse the
sectoral data.

On going abroad a big shift in the pattern of
employment ensues. The marked drop in the proportion of economically inactive, from 41.6 per cent of
the total sample to 12.2 per cent, highlights the
importance of earnings to the migrant and the role
of female employment abroad. For most emigrants,
money is the raison d'être of the whole exercise:
to emigrate to save, to save to return. When abroad
nearly two-thirds of those who worked found their
principal employment in large industries (those employing at least 50 workers) or in the construction
sector. Employment in large factories was especially characteristic of respondents who had been in
Germany; construction was more prominent amongst
migrants in France and Switzerland. This pattern of
employment is tied closely to the pattern of foreign
residence -- overwhelmingly in large towns and
conurbations. Only two respondents worked in farming whilst abroad. Other types of employment abroad
include small industries (5-49 workers) -- common
amongst migrants to Switzerland and North America --
and the commerce/private services group, where
respondents in South America dominated. In the
'other' category, the largest single group comprised

migrants working as miners in Belgium.

     Summarising thus far, one may say that the
main occupational shifts which occur when south
Italians emigrate are wholesale movement out of
farming and artisan activities, and a major transfer
into the large industrial sector. In many cases
these are industries like steel, vehicle manufacture,
rubber, chemicals, etc., where the jobs the migrants
actually do are heavy, dangerous, boring and health-
sapping -- the very jobs which tend to be shunned by
the native workforces of the various host countries.

     Upon return a different pattern again emerges.
In general this shows greater similarity to the pre-
migration pattern than to the pattern whilst abroad.
Similar numbers are employed in agriculture (130
before migrating, 122 under the 'current employment'
column) although, because of the larger quantity of
economically active respondents upon return, the
percentage figures record a relative drop of interest
in farming from 31.6 per cent of economically active
individuals before emigration to 23.7 per cent after
return. There are, however, important differences
between the 'before' and 'current' columns, indicating new trends in employment after return. There
is, for example, a move away from artisan and small
industry: together these categories employed 25.2
per cent of the economically active prior to migration but only 9.7 per cent after return. Employment
in large scale industry (50+ employees) remains at a
low level (4.6 per cent before emigration, 5.4 per
cent currently) implying, on the face of it, a
minimal impact of the dominance of this branch when
abroad (45.2 per cent of the economically active)
upon the post-return pattern. The building sector
has held fairly constant (18.7 per cent before migration, 19.2 per cent abroad, 16.3 per cent current)
and this is the main sector where employment continuity right through the migration cycle is widespread. The final feature of interest in the
current employment pattern is the increased importance, relative to both of the previous columns
('before' and 'abroad'), of the service sector --
commerce, private manual services and public
employment. These three tertiary categories account
for 41.6 per cent of current employment compared to
only 20.1 per cent abroad and 18.5 per cent before
emigration.

     To a certain extent, these changes reflect
changing patterns of job availability and of job
prestige. Agriculture tends to be rejected and is
only taken as a last resort. The same holds for some

artisan activities. Many craft activities are
dying out anyway because of the penetration of mass-
produced goods into rural areas -- thus plastic
bowls replace locally-produced hand-woven baskets.
The building sector remains buoyant partly because
of the self-generated demand for new housing on the
part of returning migrants, a point to which we
shall return later. The increase in post-return
service sector employment reflects to some extent
the nature of jobs done abroad and includes both
private services and small-scale commerce (bars,
barbers, food shops, mechanical repair workshops,
etc.), and public employment. Most of the public
sector employment consists of unskilled or semi-
skilled jobs with local councils but in Bari some
returnees were to be found working in white collar
public employment.

Table 2.1's final column shows the distribution of returnees' desires for different sorts of
employment. In some cases these desires were
actually achieved, in others not. The figures show
an even spread across the various sectors, but two
features stand out: the low perceived desirability
of agriculture (only 8.7 per cent of respondents
wished to have a job in this sector); and the un-
satisfied desire for industrial employment, largely
conditioned, one can suggest, by the industrial employment experience accumulated abroad. The desire
for industrial employment was particularly strong
amongst younger returnees. There is, therefore, a
fair degree of mismatch between jobs desired and
those actually being performed, largely owing to the
lack of large industrial enterprises in and around
the sample communes, and also to the inability of
returnees to get jobs in those that do exist. It
should also be noted that the large number of
respondents falling in the 'other' category included
55 individuals who simply said 'anything' or 'any
job which pays' without specifying a job sector.
Overall, 59.8 per cent of those who specified a
desired job (i.e. 283 out of 473, excluding from this
the 55 who simply responded 'anything' etc.) managed
to find their desired employment; and of these 283,
83.4 per cent (236) were still doing that job at the
time of interview (of the remainder, 30 had moved to
another job, 6 were unemployed and 4 had retired).

The various columns in Table 2.1 were also
cross-tabulated in various pairings. Confining
ourselves here to those affecting the current and
desired employment, the following remarks can be
made. A large proportion of current agriculturalists

were agriculturalists before migration (57 out of
122); of the remaining shortfall (65), 42 came out
of the large rump of previously non-active individuals. Therefore virtually no-one moves into agriculture after return from another job sector before
migration. A similar pattern is evident, on a
smaller scale, for artisan activity: most post-
return artisans were artisans before emigration (24
out of 36), with 7 coming in from the non-active
pre-emigration sector. And much the same holds for
building: 46 out of the 84 current building employees were in construction before migrating, and 31
came in from the non-active pre-migration sector.
All these three sectors therefore have weak powers
of attracting return migrants from other pre-
emigration occupational backgrounds. Services and
commerce, however, not only retain high proportions
of individuals who were already in these sectors
prior to migration, but also attract in persons from
other sectors, especially from the agriculture and
artisan fields. It may be that the relative independence of working in these sectors is an attractive proposition. Some service sector jobs,
especially in the public sector, are secure and are
therefore greatly sought after. On the other hand
it must also be realised that small-scale commercial
and private sector service enterprises (mechanical
repair shops, bars, etc.) are relatively easy to
establish and are virtually the only employment
outlet for rural migrants who shun the insecurity,
low pay and low prestige of agriculture and
construction and have no opportunity to find
industrial jobs.
    Cross-relationships between current job and job
done abroad are fairly weak as would be expected
given the already-noted sharp shift in employment
patterns accompanying migrants moving between
southern Italy and industrial Europe. For example
returnees now working in agriculture (n = 122)
worked abroad in a wide range of sectors completely
unrelated to farming (45 per cent in industry, 16
per cent in building and 14 per cent in private
manual services). Some slight groupings are,
however, evident in other sectors. There is a
tendency for 'current' artisans to work abroad in
small rather than big industry; there is a trend for
construction workers to stick to this sector when
abroad; and similar tendencies hold for service and
commercial workers abroad to return to this sector.
It should, however, be stressed that these are
tendencies rather than strong trends or rules.

Jobs desired on return are also somewhat in-fluenced both by the pre-migration pattern and by experience of employment abroad. The relatively small number (46 or 8.7 per cent of the economically active sample) who desire farming jobs on return consist overwhelmingly of those with a pre-migration background in agriculture. Similarly those wanting jobs in artisan and building activity are dominated by those who have precisely these employment backgrounds. For industry, however, the pattern is different: 84 (16 per cent) of the economically active returnees were seeking jobs in big industry, yet hardly any of these had a pre-migration background in big industry, largely of course because such jobs hardly existed in southern Italy and those who had secured such jobs had no need of migration anyway. Instead those returnees who aspired to industrial jobs were those who had experienced industrial jobs abroad (59 out of 84 or 70 per cent).

Cross-tabulation of current job with job desired reveals the extent to which post-return employment aspirations are fulfilled and the extent to which people are forced into job sectors they do not really want to be in. Agriculture provides the best illustration of this point. Most of those wanting to find employment in farming have done so, but farming also contains a larger number who ideally would prefer other employment which they cannot secure. Building provides an analogous, though less extreme, case: 51 out of 84 (61 per cent) building workers actually desire to be in their job: 75 per cent of 'desired' builders have actually achieved their ambitions.

Some relationships by destination country are also evident, although the level of significance of these relationships is rarely very high. Those wanting to work, and currently working in, construction are proportionately dominated by returnees from France and West Germany; those working or wanting work in the commerce and private service sectors (shopkeepers, bar owners, small businessmen, etc.) are more likely to have returned from the UK, Argentina or Venezuela; agriculture and artisan activities are disproportionately attractive to returnees from Switzerland; whilst returnees from West Germany are also over-represented in big industry.

The employment survey can be completed by examining the position of individuals in terms of a classification into employees, self-employed, member of a family enterprise and 'other' (employer, member

of a cooperative enterprise, concessionary, etc.).
Before migration 72.6 per cent of economically
active respondents were employees, 14.8 per cent
were self-employed and 11.2 per cent were in family
concerns. Employees characterised especially agriculture and industry, the largest group being farm
labourers; self-employed dominated in the artisan,
commerce and private services categories; and family
concerns were mostly farms and workshops. Whilst
abroad the 'employee' category jumped to account for
more than 90 per cent of economically active respondents -- a clear indication of the dependent type of
employment status accorded nearly all migrant
workers. The post-return (current) situation showed
a return to the pre-migration pattern with roughly
equal numbers of employees (299 before migration,
285 currently), but with an approximate doubling of
numbers in the 'self-employed' and 'family' positions from 107 to 212. The desired pattern was not
dissimilar to the current pattern except for the
lower family enterprise figure and the large 'other'
category which again includes the 55 respondents who
had been unable to specify sector and position of
desired employment. It should also be borne in mind
that the near-identical figures for employees under
current and desired employment hide a marked
sectoral imbalance: many returnees desired to be
industrial employees whereas in actual fact they
were agricultural employees.
     To conclude this section, it appears that the
migration experience changes returnees' aspirations,
largely towards a preference for industrial jobs and
a rejection of farming. Their actual patterns of
employment, however, do not match up to these aspirations. There is some reduction in farming but not a
significant increase in industrial employment.
Instead there is an increase in tertiary employment
and in self-employment and small family businesses.
Partly these increases are desired, and partly they
are forced on returnees by the constraints of what
limited action an individual can achieve within a
segmented and overstretched local labour market.

EDUCATION, TRAINING AND INNOVATION

The educational background of most returned migrant
respondents is low. Indeed three-quarters have no
more than some elementary schooling, indicating that
a similar proportion are barely literate. Eighteen
per cent of the sample have achieved between one and

four years of the scuola media or middle school.
Only 7 per cent are in posession of a liceo (high
school) or university qualification, and of these
49, a disproportionate number (29 or 59 per cent)
are from Bari (which accounts for less than 30 per
cent of the total sample of respondents).

These low levels of educational attainment are
an important parameter defining the character of the
migrant workforce and they act as a major constraint
on the kinds of jobs migrants can get abroad. Such
educational deprivation also sets a powerful brake
on the ability of migrants to relate to and integrate with the society of the destination country.
To give a simple example, illiteracy or semi-
literacy in Italian is an obvious hindrance to the
ability to learn a foreign language except by
mimicry.

With this in mind, it is not surprising that
relatively few migrants seem to have been able to
use the period abroad to obtain formal qualifications. Only 109, 17.9 per cent of the economically
active migrants abroad, had followed some kind of
formal course or apprenticeship whilst abroad. The
training covered a wide range of skills but most
were fairly low grade technical or industrial qualifications including electrical and mechanical appren-
ticeships (18 respondents), clothing and textiles
(8), catering (5) and hairdressing (5). However, 27
of the 109 represented the educational achievements
of younger migrants who were taken abroad as children and who went to school there. In addition,
another 315 respondents (50.9 per cent of the
economically active sample abroad) claimed that they
had, through their work abroad, obtained some form
of useful experience or training, but without following a formal course or recognised apprenticeship.
These tended to comprise the same range of basic
skills and activities just mentioned: e.g. 71 in
the electrical/mechanical fields, 49 in clothing
and textiles, 20 in woodworking, 13 in chemicals/
pharmaceuticals/plastics, 12 in catering and 10 in
hairdressing. The relevance of this foreign work
experience to the process of getting a job back
home appears, in general, to be very slight. Only
19 respondents, 3.7 per cent of those economically
active after return, said that their foreign training had played a role in their securing employment
back in Italy.

With these figures in mind, one should not be
surprised at the limited evidence for returnees
bringing back 'innovations' from abroad. Only a

handful of respondents claimed to have been economically innovative when they returned, introducing
either technical innovations or new entrepreneurial
or organisational initiative based on their experience abroad. When these few cases are examined
more closely the nature of the 'innovation' tends to
appear less than earth-shattering: individuals who
have introduced new types of shops such as
'boutiques' into rural areas; or others who claim to
have campaigned for better working conditions for
farm workers, etc. The phrase 'technical innovation'
is also exposed as something of a sham: more typical
than real technical progress (e.g. in modernising
agriculture or in mechanising craft activities) is
the case of a hairdresser who claimed he had introduced new hairstyles in his salon!

These findings obviously go against the hypothesis of the returnee as an agent of innovation.
In general we may conclude that the post-war
European-oriented south Italian migrant does not
leave with grand plans in mind. He, or she, goes
for relatively short periods to do mostly low-grade
work from which few usable skills materialise. The
migrant is probably able to accumulate a certain
amount of capital which can be used for personal
and family needs (more on this shortly), but he or
she does not return charged with new ideas or
flushed with riches. His, or her, plans are at the
individual or family scales; they are not such as to
have a wide effect on employment or on the life of
the community to which the migrant returns. Indeed
in many cases returnees are forced into a somewhat
marginal socio-economic position when they return,
the very fact of migratory absence having removed
them from the nexus of the local community. Social
ties with the community are therefore inevitably
weaker than for the non-migrants, and the economic
links necessary for a viable enterprise are difficult
to establish.

REMITTANCES, SAVINGS AND INVESTMENTS

The financial question of remittances, savings and
investments was another area of the survey on which
detailed questionnaire data were obtained. More
than three-quarters of the sample said that they
were either 'better off' (24.7 per cent) or 'much
better off' (51.3 per cent) when they were living
abroad; only 2.7 per cent claimed that they were
worse off abroad than they had been before leaving

Italy. Against this background, it is not surprising that most respondents were able to remit and/or
save portions of their foreign income.

Nearly two-thirds of respondents (65.2 per cent)
had been regular remitters whilst abroad. Mostly
they sent money to parents (56 per cent) or spouses
(16 per cent), but occasionally they supported other
relatives or sent money directly to a home-based
financial insitution. Of those who were able to
make reasoned estimates (14 per cent of the'remitter'
sample could not), 46.3 per cent sent back, on
average, between 25 and 50 per cent of their foreign
incomes, 31 per cent sent back 50-75 per cent, 14.2
per cent sent back more than 75 per cent, and 8.5
per cent sent back less than 25 per cent.

A majority of respondents (59.5 per cent) were
able to save whilst abroad; and this includes some
who were also remitters. The proportion of earnings saved was generally lower than that remitted.
Leaving aside the 15.4 per cent of 'savers' who
could not estimate the proportion saved, 49.7 per
cent saved less than 25 per cent of their foreign
earnings, 42 per cent saved between 25 and 50 per
cent, 6.5 per cent saved 50-75 per cent and only
1.5 per cent over 75 per cent.

Remittances are related much more to short-
term and seasonal European migration, savings being
more the product of longer-term overseas movement.
By country, remittances are high for Switzerland
and Germany, low for the USA and Venezuela. Savings
on the other hand are high for North American,
Venezuelan and German returnees, lower for those
returning from France, Switzerland and Belgium.
This also impacts differentially on the various
sample communes. In Spongano, dominated by seasonal
migration to Switzerland, 80 per cent of respondents had been regular remitters but only 27 per cent
had made savings. In Amantea, where the modal group
had gone to Venezuela, only 49 per cent had remitted
whereas 63 per cent had accumulated savings.

Remittances and savings were also found to
be related to type of job done abroad and to length
of time abroad. The highest proportion of remitters
came from those who had worked in large industry or
in construction, whilst the proportion of savers and
the level of savings appeared to be unrelated to
employment abroad. The commitment to sending remittances remains constant with varying time abroad up
to about 15 years, after which it tails off. Level
of savings exhibits the opposite pattern, increasing
with time spent abroad, as one would expect. The

amount of savings and the proportion of respondents
who were able to save were also affected somewhat
by whether the spouse worked abroad: obviously two
incomes lead to greater savings potential within a
household than one. Pensions are another important
source of cash inflow into migrant communities, the
existence of a pension being obviously related to
time spent abroad and to the pensionable status of
the job performed. Of the total sample of 705, 55
(7.8 per cent) were already in receipt of a foreign
pension and a further 73 (10.4 per cent) expected to
receive a pension from abroad when they reached the
age of 60.

Although we have drawn an analytical distinction between remittances and savings, in practice
this distinction became blurred in many migrants'
minds and responses. How, for instance, does one
categorise money which is remitted regularly by a
migrant to his parents but is then banked by them
for some joint project like a new house or a farm?
It was, therefore, decided to concentrate on the use
and investment of accumulated migrant income, however
transferred back to Italy. Table 2.2 shows this
information.

Before examining the various categories of
spending and investment a few words are necessary
on the mechanics of how this spending takes place.
Firstly, some investments are made by individuals,
whilst others are made jointly by two or more members of the same family who have emigrated. Hence
the unit of investment can be either individual or
multiple. Secondly, some investments are only
partly made up of 'migration income'; they may also
involve post-return income or perhaps an inheritance.
Therefore the composition of the investment can be
either wholly or partly derived from foreign earnings. Thirdly there are variations to be noted in
the timing of the investment: it can either be made
before the migrant actually returns (often the case
with land purchase), or after he settles back, or a
combination of both. All these variations are recorded in Table 2.2.

The first priority of most returning migrants
seems to be spending on the perceived requirements
of an improved standard of living: a new home (52.9
per cent of the total sample), new furniture (48.7
per cent) and a car (36.5 per cent). The dominance
of housing over the pattern of returnee investment is
increased when one considers the additional numbers
who improved an existing dwelling (9.8 per cent),
those who also invested in second or even third and

57

Table 2.2: Investment of Migrant Savings by Returnee Sample

	Agric. Land	Bldg. Land	New House	Improve House	Extra House	Farming (not land)	Commerce Ent.	Service Ent.	Craft or Bldg. Ent.	Car	Dowry	Furniture	Repay Debt
All respondents:	74	135	373	69	60	26	65	39	47	257	73	343	43
Unit of invest:													
Individual	37	45	119	36	16	16	20	18	17	80	37	103	17
Couple/family	37	90	254	33	44	10	45	21	30	177	36	240	26
Make-up of inv:													
All foreign inc.	56	127	294	48	47	20	45	31	33	228	48	253	38
Part for. inc.	18	8	79	21	13	6	20	8	14	29	25	90	5
Timing of inv:													
Before return	22	79	162	21	15	5	--	2	6	106	12	60	11
After return	39	30	89	31	30	15	56	34	35	108	40	238	16
Combination	13	26	122	17	15	6	9	3	6	43	21	45	16

Source: Authors' questionnaire survey.

subsequent dwellings (8.5 per cent) -- usually for
renting out to tenants or in anticipation of their
children's future needs -- and those who purchased
building land (19.2 per cent).

Investment in agriculture, on the other hand, is
proportionately very modest. Only 10.5 per cent of
respondents bought farming land with migrant earnings. This does not, moreover, necessarily indicate
any great commitment to farming as a profession or
way of life, for many of these land purchases were
either for renting out so that some landlord status
could be enjoyed, or were tiny plots bought just to
potter about in. A more revealing figure is the 26
migrants (just 3.7 per cent of the sample) who made
non-land farming investments, i.e. in machinery,
irrigation equipment or other agricultural inputs.
The impact of returned migrants on improving and
modernising south Italian agriculture therefore
seems to be very slight. Indeed there was equal, or
greater, commitment to using migrant income for debt
repayment or for accumulating a dowry than for
farming.

The final category of migrant investment concerns business enterprise of various kinds. Collectively these were established by 151 respondents,
21.4 per cent of the total sample of returnees. As
can be seen from Table 2.2, these are mainly joint
or family enterprises, set up after the return has
taken place. Commercial concerns are the most
important branch of these enterprises. These comprise shops of various kinds ranging from a green-
grocer selling off a barrow to highly specialised
outlets dealing in products like furs or hi-fi equipment. Most, however, are small general food shops
-- a typical family-scale enterprise in southern
Italy. Service enterprises include bars, barbers
and hairdressers, taxis, garages and mechanical
repair workshops. Craft and building concerns comprise again mostly small-scale businesses; these
include not only straightforward building contractors
but also carpenters, plumbers, stonemasons, iron-
workers, tilers etc. Investment by returnees in
industry proper, or indeed in any kind of activity
which generates much employment or is a real
stimulus to the local or regional economy, is
lacking.

The pattern of investment and savings showed
some influence by type of job done abroad and, by
association, by country of destination. Building
workers, most common amongst returnees from France
and Switzerland, tended to invest more strongly in

property (both land and housing), whereas commercial
sector employees, characteristic especially of South
America, invested in commerce back home. Seasonal
migrants in Switzerland were the most avid purchasers
of farmland in Italy.

Spending of savings on big items such as a house
is obviously influenced by length of time abroad:
only the longer-stay migrants have accumulated
enough savings for a house (two-thirds of the
migrants abroad for more than 10 years had invested
in a house, compared to less than half of those away
for less than 7 years). Investment in a second
dwelling was almost entirely confined to those away
for at least 10 years, and commercial investments
seemed to be subject to a similar kind of threshold.
On the other hand, smaller-scale spending -- dowry,
furniture, car, etc. -- was unrelated to length of
absence. The fact of having a spouse working
abroad also boosted rates and amounts of saving,
allowing more rapid accumulation of capital for
bigger post-return investments.

DEVELOPMENTAL IMPACT OF RETURN MIGRATION

At this point it is useful to briefly recapitulate
the main findings of the questionnaire survey on the
economic impact of returnees, and to set these findings in the context of the original question, posed
at the beginning of this chapter, on the nature of
the developmental stimulus generated by returned
migrants.

The spatial mobility of migration brings economic mobility too. From a pre-migration background
in farming and other low-grade non-industrial occupations, respondents found employment overwhelmingly
in large factories and on building sites, mostly in
urban centres in West Germany, Switzerland and
France. These jobs reflect much more the need of
Western Europe's industrial and post-industrial
development to feed off flexible supplies of cheap
and easily-trained labour than the inherent desire
of the migrants to improve their work skills for the
future benefit of themselves and their home regions
when they return. Indeed to the extent that training courses taken abroad detract from the migrant's
earning power (through time off or reduced opportunities for overtime), they are perceived as generally
undesirable by many migrants intent on maximising
savings. Against this background it is small wonder
that the level of economically innovatory behaviour

amongst returnees was found to be so low in the
questionnaire survey. The experience of performing
urban-industrial jobs when abroad does, however,
alter migrants' job attitudes when they return.
Particularly amongst younger male returnees, there
is a desire to continue in secure, regularly-paid
factory employment back in Italy. This is combined
with a rejection of farming and other low status
rural occupations. Unfortunately jobs in industry
are scarce so that many returnees are forced back
into agriculture as a last resort, or they take
marginal and poorly paid tertiary sector employment.
There is a link between migration and industrial
development in southern Italy, but it seems to be
more in terms of industrialisation reducing levels
of out-migration than encouraging copious returns
(Rodgers, 1970). Where migrants have returned from
abroad with professional and industrial skills, the
lack of appropriate local institutional help prevents
the full capitalisation of these skills. We shall
return to this point on local institutions later.
     The pattern of investment of migrant capital
was broadly consistent with the relative lack of
managerial or technical training acquired by migrants
whilst abroad. There were virtually no instances of
investment in opening up or expanding new industrial
initiatives based on foreign-acquired skills or
experiences. The nearest the questionnaire survey
came to uncovering such a process was with certain
respondents with experience of a craft or service
enterprise from abroad who had put this to good use
on return by opening up concerns like carpenters,
hairdressers, bars, restaurants etc. In one of the
sample communities, Amantea, there was a strong
trend for returnees, especially those from Venezuela,
to set up small hotels and catering services for the
seasonal tourist trade which affects this part of
the Calabrian coast (King, Strachan and Mortimer,
1984). This was one instance of returned migrants
participating actively in pushing local development
initiatives.
     The principal outlet for migrant capital ex-
penditure is residential property. This is true not
only in southern Italy but also in many other return
migration contexts in southern Europe and beyond (cf.
King, 1979, pp. 21-22; King, Strachan and Mortimer,
1983, pp. 48-50). The building of the new home is
the key to social advancement in regions of out-
migration. Indeed it provides the modern continuation
of a trend established nearly a hundred years ago by
migrants returning to southern Europe from the

Americas. This lends support to the notion that
models or ideologies of returnee behaviour established as early as the late nineteenth century have
been handed down to the modern post-war period
(Brettell, 1979). Italian proverbial lore that 'he
who crosses the ocean buys a house' (Gilkey, 1967,
p. 23) is equally true for Italy's contemporary
intra-European labour migrants.

The building boom is undoubtedly the most
dynamic influence propagated by emigration and
return migration in rural areas of southern Italy.
This not only introduces a certain amount of employment in the construction industry and a demand for
building materials, some of which can be supplied
locally, it also acts to radically change the
physical appearance of settlements in the
Mezzogiorno. Spacious villas set in their own
gradens replace the insanitary peasant hovels of the
traditional, tightly-packed south Italian nucleated
settlement. Often returnees settle in their own
modern residential suburbs away from the old village
nucleus. Again there is a historical parallel in
the strings of new houses built by returnees from
the USA in southern Italian villages in earlier
decades (Gilkey, 1967, p. 30). The building boom is,
however, a 'cosmetic' form of development in that it
is not rooted in the natural economic resources of
the locality and fails to generate much long-term
prosperity and employment. It is a source of
modernisation which is externally funded and will
only continue if the flow of remittances and savings
from abroad continues unabated. Italian official
figures on incoming migrant remittances, although
they are incomplete estimates of the true size of
migrant financial transfers, have been falling in
real terms for the last ten years.

REGIONAL MEASURES

The foregoing discussion brings us to the question
of returning migrants as possible agents of regional
policy. From what has been said thus far returnees
obviously have significant impacts on the regions to
which they return. They contribute to changing demographic trends -- notably to the population revival
in rural areas of southern Italy -- as well as to
the regional economy, sending back and bringing in
considerable sums of capital. Their new and improved
houses play the leading role in the building boom in
rural areas over the past 15-20 years. They have

set new standards for rural housing and their construction activity has radically altered traditional
village settlement forms.

The question remains, however, as to whether
the most efficient use is made of returnees as potentially profitable inputs into the regional
economy. In particular, have they used their accumulated skills, new attitudes and investment
capital in ways that are most beneficial to themselves and to the regional economy? The independent,
uncoordinated and individualistic way in which
returnees have acted suggests that the answer to this
question is more negative than positive.

Some of the Italian regional authorities, aware
of the problems of economic and social reintegration
of returning migrants, have passed laws and established offices to help returnees (Ciaurro, 1980).
The north-eastern region of Friuli-Venezia Giulia,
for instance, passed a series of laws in the 1970s
to facilitate returnee resettlement, with grants
available for return travel and housing, and assistance in the fields of employment and education
(Saraceno, 1981, p. 93). Southern Italian regions
have been slower to develop initiatives, but some
progress has been made in Puglia which in November
1979 passed a 'regional law in favour of returning
migrants'. Briefly this regional law offers grants
and loans to returnees, either individually or in
cooperatives, who present 'rational plans' for
developing their agricultural holdings, or for expansion in the touristic, craft or industrial
sectors, including the construction industry. Loans
are also available for house construction, not only
in Puglia but also in Basilicata and Calabria. Such
measures are supposed to be publicised in communities' town halls, and it is through these commune
offices that applications are to be channelled.

The questionnaire included questions attempting
to gauge the effectiveness of these regionally-
operated incentives. The results were, in one sense,
highly revealing. Only 22 per cent (156) of respondents even knew of the regional measures; only 23
per cent (36) of these had actually applied for some
form of financial aid under the provisions of the
regional laws; and of these only 22 per cent (8) had
been successful (a further 3 were waiting to hear
the success of their applications). The 8 'successful' applicants were spread across a broad range of
sectors: agriculture, crafts and small industry,
building and the private service sector.

A policy which seems to have benefited only 1 per cent of returnees can hardly be deemed success- ful. There are obvious problems to be sorted out here with regard to publicity, communication and eligibility. Equally important is the apparent lack of desire on the part of returnees to actually apply. In attitude many returnees appear to be individual- istic and self-reliant, and therefore reluctant to enter into cooperation or partnership, either with each other or with local authorities and regional governments (Signorelli, 1980). Many returnees, in their answers to questions about the regional aids, exhibited mistrust of the bureaucracy and were cynical of their chances of success in any dealings with officialdom. Generally, migrants' experiences abroad have strengthened the traditional diffidence with which Italians view the institutions of their country. The regional measures, at least for the present, are therefore far from being effective -- but Italy is not unique in this respect (Rogers, 1981).

CONCLUSION

Although cast in a more developmental framework, particularly in terms of choice of sample communes, this study seems on balance to confirm the more pessimistic evaluations of other empirical work located in more backward and environmentally de- prived areas of southern Italy. Migration and return have not generally had positive long-term economic effects on southern Italy. At the individual scale of the returnees themselves, however, migration appears to be a successful and valued experience. This success is evaluated essentially in instru- mental -- i.e. financial -- rather than intrinsic terms. Emigration is not seen as a desirable end in itself but as the means to achieve certain goals, notably improved standards of living and material possessions and the enhanced social status and personal satisfaction that these bring. Emigration does not, however, generally lead to better job prospects upon return.

These statements on evaluation of migration are backed up by questionnaire information obtained at the conclusion of the interviews with returned migrants. Nearly 90 per cent of respondents judged their period abroad to have been useful and success- ful in various ways; only 5.8 per cent stated un- equivocally that it had not been useful. When asked

if they would advise another person to emigrate, 58
per cent of the respondents gave an unreserved 'yes'
and 24 per cent said 'yes, depending on the availability of work abroad'. Only 14 per cent replied
'no'; these included many who doubted whether the
sacrifices of emigration (separation from family and
friends, isolation in an alien culture, hard work,
etc.) were really worth the rewards.

This reaction of 'sacrifice' and 'duty to one's
family', a recurrent theme in the interviews, led
many to refuse to consider another spell abroad.
Only 6.7 per cent were planning to go abroad again;
64 per cent had no intention of re-emigrating, and
the rest were undecided as to their future moves.
A few people (3 per cent of the total sample) were
considering a move to another part of Italy where
they had relatives and where jobs were less difficult
to acquire. This general lack of anticipated future
mobility also partly reflects the achievement of the
original goals of migration.

Acquired skills and accumulated capital do flow
in with the returnees, but these inputs are not
utilised to their full potential. This is due
partly to the uncoordinated, individualistic and
familistic behaviour of returnees, and partly to the
lack of an effective institutional framework to
fully mobilise these inputs for the optimum benefit
of the local and regional economy. Continued return
migration brings instead a double pressure to bear
on the regional labour market: pressure from numbers returning, swelling the supply of labour and
increasing unemployment; and pressure from changed
job aspirations after a period of work abroad. The
'migration model' only works if there are continuous possibilities for employment abroad so that
generations of migrants from the Mezzogiorno can
find work and sustenance for their families. Since
the early 1970s this has not been the case, and it
may never be the case again.

NOTES

1. Supported by the Social Science Research
Council (now Economic and Social Research Council)
under grant GOO 23 0059, the research was based in
the Geography Department at Leicester University and
ran from 1980 to 1983. An enormous debt is owed to
many individuals and organisations in Italy for
their willing help and collaboration. In particular
we thank Prof. Luigi Di Comite, demographer at the

University of Bari, for hosting the 'Italian end' of the project in his department, the Institute of Economics and Finance of the Faculty of Jurisprudence. Dr. Clara Copeta, of the Department of Geography, University of Bari, and Prof. Luigi Za, Dr. Franco Merico and Dr. Anna Trono, all of the University of Lecce, also provided invaluable assistance.

2. See King, Strachan and Mortimer (1984) on Amantea; King, Strachan and Mortimer (1985) on Bari; King, Strachan, Mortimer and Trono (1985) on Leverano; and King, Strachan, Mortimer and Viganola (1985) on Bernalda.

3. Of course, Table 2.1 does not show the real continuity between migration phases for it could be that different individuals are involved at each stage along a sectoral row. To show real continuity each migration stage would need to be cross-tabulated with each of the others in turn. This has been done, but there is no space to present the full tabulated results in this chapter. Briefly, we can verify that there is, for certain types of employment, considerable sectoral stability in the migration cycle; for example 64 per cent of migrants who worked in construction before migration found the same job abroad.

REFERENCES

Brettell, C.V. (1979) '"Emigrar para voltar": a Portuguese ideology of return migration', Papers in Anthropology, 20(1), pp. 1-20.
Ciaurro, G. (1980) 'Il rientro degli emigrati', Affari Sociali Internazionali, 8(4), pp. 59-74.
Gilkey, G.R. (1967) 'The United States and Italy: migration and repatriation', Journal of Developing Areas, 2(1), pp. 23-35.
Griffin, K. (1976) 'On the emigration of the peasantry', World Development, 4(5), pp. 353-361.
Hume, I. (1973) 'Migrant workers in Europe', Finance and Development, 10(1), pp. 2-6.
King, R.L. (1977) 'Problems of return migration: a case study of Italians returning from Britain', Tijdschrift voor Economische en Sociale Geografie, 68(4), pp. 241-246.
King, R.L. (1979) 'Return migration: a review of some case studies from southern Europe', Mediterranean Studies, 1(2), pp. 3-30.

King, R.L., Strachan, A.J. and Di Comite, L. (1982) 'Return migration in southern Italy: a research framework', Economic Notes by Monte dei Paschi di Siena, 11(3), pp. 54-67.

King, R.L., Strachan, A.J. and Mortimer, J. (1983) Return Migration: a Review of the Literature, Oxford Polytechnic Discussion Papers in Geography 19, Oxford.

King, R.L., Strachan, A.J. and Mortimer, J. (1984) 'Return migration and tertiary development: a Calabrian case-study', Anthropological Quarterly, 57(3), pp. 112-124.

King, R.L., Strachan, A.J. and Mortimer J. (1985) 'The urban dimension of European return migration: the case of Bari, southern Italy', Urban Studies, 22(3), pp. 219-235.

King, R.L., Strachan, A.J., Mortimer, J. and Trono, A. (1985) 'Return migration and rural economic change: a south Italian case study', in R. Hudson and J. Lewis (eds.) Uneven Development in Southern Europe, Methuen, London, pp. 101-122.

King, R.L., Strachan, A.J., Mortimer, J. and Viganola, M.T. (1985) 'Back to Bernalda: the dynamics of return migration in a south Italian agrotown', in P. White and B. Van der Knaap (eds.) Migration: Contemporary Perspectives, Geo Books, Norwick, in press.

Lopreato, J. (1967) Peasants No More, Chandler, San Francisco.

Merico, F. (1978) 'Il difficile ritorno: indagine sul rientro degli emigrati in alcune comunità del Mezzogiorno', Studi Emigrazione, 50, pp. 179-212.

Reyneri, E. (1980) 'Emigration and sending area as a subsidised system in Sicily', Mediterranean Studies, 2(1), pp. 88-113.

Rhoades, R.E. (1978) 'Intra-European return migration and rural development: lessons from the Spanish case', Human Organization, 37(2), pp. 136-147.

Rhoades, R.E. (1979) 'From caves to Main Street: return migration and the transformation of a Spanish village', Papers in Anthropology, 20(1), pp. 57-74.

Rodgers, A. (1970) 'Migration and industrial development: the southern Italian experience', Economic Geography, 46(2), pp. 111-135.

Rogers, R. (1981) 'Incentives to return: patterns
    of policies and migrants' responses', in M.M.
    Kritz, C.B. Keely and S.M. Tomasi (eds.) Global
    Trends in Migration, Center for Migration
    Studies, New York, pp. 338-364.
Saraceno, E. (1981) Emigrazione e Rientri: il
    Friuli-Venezia Giulia nel Secondo Dopoguerra,
    Il Campo, Udine.
Signorelli, A. (1980) 'Regional policies in Italy
    for migrant workers returning home', in R.D.
    Grillo (ed.) 'Nation' and 'State' in Europe,
    Academic Press, London, pp. 89-103.
Strachan, A.J. and King, R.L. (1982) Emigration and
    Return Migration in Southern Italy: A Multi-
    variate, Cluster and Map Analysis, Leicester
    University Geography Department Occasional
    Paper 9, Leicester.

Chapter Three

THE OCCUPATIONAL RESETTLEMENT OF RETURNING MIGRANTS
AND REGIONAL DEVELOPMENT: THE CASE OF FRIULI-
VENEZIA GIULIA, ITALY

Elena Saraceno

The study of migration in Italy in recent years has
been approached from a number of perspectives. The
most common one looks at migration movements from a
quantitative point of view: how many leave; where
they go; how long they stay; what jobs they take;
who follows them; how many come back; whether they
have a family. This sort of accountant's study of
migration is interesting to policy makers and a few
academics, but leaves us without an explanation of
the significance of such movements in their specific time and place context.

A second and more sophisticated perspective
comes from the structural approach to migration
movements which tries to find out their function
within the labour market of sending and receiving
areas. Quantitative and qualitative imbalances between the demand and supply of labour become the
explanatory paradigm of such movements. This approach comes nearer to understanding migration within the specific socio-economic context which produces these movements.

However, this approach does not usually deal
with the historical or evolutionary aspects of migration. Migratory movements do not happen at any
time and place; there have been particular time
periods, for example during the change from a rural
to an industrial society, when migrations have become extremely widespread and massive. If read
within a wider process of modernisation, migration
movements become much more understandable: connected
to expectations of social mobility, savings and
local economic development.

The phenomenon of return migration has made the
need to combine the last two approaches even more
relevant. The issue of return migration should not
be studied purely quantitatively. It is certainly

necessary to know something about the numbers of
returnees involved and about the conditions of the
local labour market to which they return, but certain characteristics of returning workers cannot be
understood unless we bring in the migrant's projects
and expectations. Within this perspective the study
of migration movements becomes a privileged observ-
atory of local or regional socio-economic development.

From this theoretical perspective I will describe the professional resettlement of returning
migrants in the 1970s to Friuli-Venezia Giulia, the
region occupying the north-eastern corner of Italy,
and how this contributed to local development.
Since 1970 the Friulian regional authorities have
offered grants to returning migrants. To obtain a
grant applicants give information about occupation,
family, age and residence. Between 1970 and 1980
around 11,000 families took advantage of these return grants; this number represents about 80 per
cent of all those who came back during the decade.
The universe of grant recipients was used to frame
a sample survey of 1,500 families who were interviewed in 1982.[1] The sample was made statistically
representative of the different parts of Friuli-
Venezia Giulia region.

This chapter is in three parts. First, a brief
account of the circumstances surrounding return migration to Friuli-Venezia Giulia is given. Next,
an analysis of changes in the local industrial
labour demand will give the economic framework within which migration and return took place. The final
section is an analysis of the professional careers
of returned migrants and how this affected their
occupational resettlement.

CIRCUMSTANCES SURROUNDING THE RETURN

In 1968 returnees from abroad outnumbered outgoing
migrants for the first time in Friuli-Venezia
Giulia. In fact returns had been a constant feature
since the end of World War II when European countries replaced the Americas as the main destination
for Friulian migrants and migration became a temporary phenomenon. The earlier returns were predominantly of retired family-heads at the end of their
migration cycle who did not pose any problems of
work resettlement. The new fact in recent returns
-- since the 1960s -- was that the majority were
active, and therefore looking for jobs in the local

70

labour market. Only such active returnees will be
considered here.

The reason why at the end of the 1960s return
migration increased while at the same time outmigration practically stopped is that the migratory chain
which had been established between sending and receiving countries was gradually interrupted by the
changed conditions of the local labour market.
These changes in labour demand acted both as a pull
factor for migrants abroad and as an alternative
for those who were about to leave. To such pull
factors that were already operating at the end of
the 1960s, must be added push factors which started
to operate after the 1973 crisis. From the combined
action of these two forces, which both acted to
accelerate returns, we find that the returning migrants of this period represent a cross-section of
all the different generations present in the migratory chain: from the older migrants with long
periods abroad to younger ones recently emigrated.
It is because of the above-mentioned interruption
of the evolution of the migratory chain that active
returnees represented more than three-quarters of
total returns. This proportion gradually decreased
in favour of non-active returns in the late 1970s
due to the reduced number of outgoing migrants.

CHANGES IN THE LOCAL INDUSTRIAL LABOUR DEMAND

After the Second World War, Friuli-Venezia Giulia
represented a marginal area in the Italian economy.
A few industrial initiatives, mainly in the textile,
mechanical and food industries, were spatially concentrated around the capitals of the four provinces
(Trieste, Gorizia, Udine and Pordenone) that belong
to the region. The State started huge investment
projects near Trieste in shipbuilding. The industrial structure remained until the mid-1960s based
on big industries, mostly in the hands of outside
investors and located near the urban areas. Such
development was unable to provide jobs for most of
the rural population and during that period Friuli-
Venezia Giulia had one of the highest emigration
rates among Italian regions.

During the second half of the 1960s, a different industrial structure began to take hold. Small
and medium-sized enterprises, mostly based on traditional artisan crafts, started by local entrepreneurs
and located in a dispersed pattern over a wide rural
area, began to grow and consolidate themselves into

71

an extremely original and fast-growing process of
industrialisation. This did not happen only in the
Friuli-Venezia Giulia region but also in other
central and north-eastern regions of Italy during
the 1970s (Bagnasco, 1977; Fuà and Zacchia, 1983),
giving rise to what is now widely known as diffused
industrialisation. What is specific about the
Friulian case is that the areas in which this development took place were the same areas where migration was endemic, contradicting the normal view of
the unlikelihood of such an event. Diffused industrialisation has had the effect of changing the local
industrial labour demand. It reduced the necessity
to migrate and provided jobs for returning migrants
near their former places of residence. What is even
more surprising is that all this happened in a quite
spontaneous fashion, while official regional policy
was investing in big industrial sites, ignoring the
possibilities of this untidy 'bottom-up' industrial
development.

In our research the changes in the work activity
of migrants reflect this evolution of local industrial labour demand. The sectors in which migrants
worked were extremely varied: only 27 per cent of
returning migrants had worked all their lives in
only one sector (there could be changes in the level
of qualification, firm and of self-employment),
while the rest have different degrees of sectorial
variations which for a small minority (9 per cent)
reaches eight or more different sectors of activity.

The assumption made is that few or no changes
are indicative of a higher level of professional
qualification, while a higher number of variations
reflects a low qualification. The sample taken as a
whole indicates a rather high incidence of changes
in the sector of activity of returning migrants'
work histories and a relatively low professional
qualification. But if we look at the work histories
of different generations of returning migrants we
see that the higher number of variations coincides
with the older returning migrants (over fifty years
of age) while middle-aged migrants have two to three
activity changes and younger ones, one or two. This
implies migrant workers are not an undifferentiated
mass of people who adapt to whatever demand for
labour they find both in receiving and sending areas,
but that through time their qualification has become
higher and therefore their rigidity towards demand
has increased. It might be added also that most
variations have a definite and one-way pattern:
from building to the industrial or service sector.

Very often changes in the sector of activity coin-
cide with territorial mobility and have a different
meaning whether they have taken place before migration, abroad or after returning. We will only deal
here with changes at the time of re-entry.

Returning active migrants changed sector of
activity at the time of re-entry in 37 per cent of
the cases, and another 22 per cent changed after-
wards. This means that there has been significant
job stability at the time of re-entry and that the
structure of local labour demand did not differ
greatly, for migrant workers, from the immigrant
countries' demand. This is mainly due to the region's recent industrial development, especially in
the mechanical and building sectors. Of those who
changed sectors about a quarter moved towards the
tertiary sector, finding undemanding, very often
independent, pre-retirement jobs in commerce.

A second point is that the building sector does
not attract returning migrants. Although 53 per
cent of them worked in this sector in their last
year abroad and local demand was very high both before and after the 1976 earthquake[2] it is surprising
that 22 per cent chose to leave it at the time of
re-entry. This fact cannot be adequately explained
by the structure of local demand but rather by a
choice on the part of returning workers; probably it
is due to the relatively worse conditions (pay,
security, level of qualification) and fatigue connected with this type of work if compared with other
available jobs, for instance in the manufacturing
sector.

Apart from the minor changes and the relative
stability of different sectors of activity between
foreign and local labour demand, the extreme ease
with which a job was found by most returning migrants
should be stressed. About 35 per cent found a job
within a week of re-entry, another 31 per cent before
a month, 24 per cent before six months and only 9
per cent after six months. At the time of interviewing, only 0.5 per cent of returnees had never been
able to find a job since the time of return, and
only 1.6 per cent were unemployed. Although this
excellent work resettlement record is rather surprising when compared with return migration in other
Italian regions, the migrants themselves did not
perceive their work after re-entry in positive terms;
indeed they were highly critical of it. This could
be partly explained on the one hand by differences
in pay and job organisation -- by the fact that very
big industries were predominant abroad as workplaces,

while very small and medium industries were predominant in the local labour market. On the other hand, about 30 per cent of returning active male migrants have been self-employed at some time after re-entry. This shows a very high propensity towards independent work among returnees. The businesses started by returning migrants have almost always less than 20 employees. Small building companies are the most popular forms of enterprise started (accounting for 40 per cent of such businesses) and many were created after a first job as dependent workers in the building sector. In this case the impact of reconstruction after the earthquake has been very intense in stimulating the birth of enterprises which, even in the small time-span considered, have had a high mortality rate. The facility with which workers have been able to shift from a dependent to an independent status and vice-versa shows the great flexibility and number of opportunities present in the local labour market. We cannot call this form of independent work 'entrepreneurial' in the usual meaning given to this word, but it is an original form of cooperation between small groups of building workers, and it is extremely interesting and dynamic, putting together highly qualified workers who have acquired their experience in big companies abroad and who are able to adapt it to local market conditions.

A different picture comes from enterprises in the mechanical sector. Independent initiatives here are less frequent (15 per cent) but more stable through time. Few start mechanical businesses immediately after returning, but work for a while as dependent workers as if to prepare the new business. These cases are similar to the other small new initiatives of non-migrant entrepreneurs which have given rise to the recent diffused industrial development. In this sense it can be said that returning migrants share the same entrepreneurial spirit as non-migrants.

A third branch of independent activity, accounting for 36 per cent of enterprises, is in the tertiary sector. The particular meaning that this choice might have after re-entry has already been mentioned; it tends to take place and develop independent of what sector of activity was held abroad. It is much more common for tertiary businesses to be started immediately after re-entry, with savings acquired and probably the entire project thought out while abroad.

So, changes in local labour demand have been extremely helpful in providing work opportunities for returning migrants to Friuli-Venezia Giulia in the 1970s. The dispersed pattern of the new industrial locations has reduced the probability of having to move, post-return, from one place where jobs were not available to another one where they were. This has helped many migrants (82 per cent of the sample) to go back to their original home communes, where they have invested their savings in buying or reconstructing a house, often integrating the new jobs found in local enterprises with part-time farming activities on land inherited from their parents and relatives. The whole evolution that has taken place through migration seems to have worked extremely well, and rather spontaneously, without significant policy measures that would surely have been difficult to design and implement in any case.

THE OCCUPATIONAL RESETTLEMENT OF RETURNING MIGRANTS

The professional evolution of returning active migrants seems to have taken place in accordance with the different stages of the migration cycle (Table 3.1). Before emigration agriculture and construction professions are predominant; during the period abroad construction reaches its maximum weight while industry gains significance; after return construction loses its importance and is substituted by a predominance of industrial occupations. A slow and gradual process of tertiarisation that involves a relatively small portion of the migrating labour force can be seen throughout the cycle.

Parallel to this evolution from traditional to industrial professions, there is an increase in the level of skills acquired until the last position held abroad. After re-entry there is a partial setback, especially for specialised workers. The above-mentioned difference in the size of enterprises might explain this partial setback, since an informal organisation is still predominant in local enterprises, and the performance of a variety of tasks by an individual is rather common, resulting in a lower level of qualification and skill in local jobs.

The significance of the evolution of migrant occupations cannot be understood only by the characteristics of demand in the various places: the logic of the migrant worker seeking a

Table 3.1: Professional Evolution of Returning Active Males at Different Points of the Migration Cycle (Returns 1970-79; all data %)

Professional and Skill Sectors	Work Before Emigration	Last Job Abroad	First Job After Re-entry	Current Job (1980)
Agriculture	19.3	0.4	2.9	2.8
Construction	36.8	45.3	41.5	37.5
Mining	0.5	0.8	0.2	0.3
Mechanical	17.3	25.1	21.8	23.2
Woodworking	10.1	11.4	13.2	13.1
Other industrial	4.9	4.9	4.5	5.2
Total industrial	32.8	42.2	39.7	41.8
Commercial	3.6	4.4	6.9	6.0
Transport	2.0	2.8	4.0	4.5
Services	3.0	1.5	2.7	4.4
Technicians	1.8	3.4	2.3	3.0
Total tertiary	10.4	12.1	15.9	17.9
TOTAL	100.0[1]	100.0	100.0	100.0
Apprentices	16.3	-	-	-
Unskilled	35.4	14.0	23.8	25.0
Skilled	33.4	50.1	48.5	46.8
Specialised	13.1	32.5	25.4	25.2
Employees	1.8	3.4	2.3	3.0
TOTAL	100.0	100.0	100.0	100.0

Note: 1. Includes 0.7% with undefined professions.
Source: Author's survey.

professional change by moving from one place to the other must be brought out and underlined since it shows that through migration there has been a slow maturing of the labour force from rural and tradi-tional professions to modern industrial ones, and such an evolution provides a rationale for the whole migration project. Through this professional evolution the migrant worker acquires upward social

mobility, regardless of the industrial development
that might take place in the areas of origin.
However, this industrial change occurred in Friuli-
Venezia Giulia parallel to the migratory chain and
this allowed a continuity for returning migrants:
their expections of social mobility could go on even
after returning, due to the modernisation process
that had been taking place while they were abroad.

The building sector offered the highest professional mobility abroad; the typical sequence
was from handyman, to mason, to tiler, electrician,
plumber or master mason. Stability was more typical
in the manufacturing sector, especially if some
skill (mechanic or carpenter) was already possessed
at the time of departure. In this case it was not
only the original skill that reduced the possibilities of professional mobility abroad but also the
limited mobility allowed to foreign labour within
European manufacturing industry's organisation.

After re-entry in the region the opposite logic
seems to have worked with the building professions
providing very low upward mobility and therefore
being left, and manufacturing industries offering
the possibilities that were not permitted abroad.
The higher propensity for independent work shown
after re-entry seems to point to the fact that independent work could have been taken in order to
somehow compensate for the lower skill levels and
poorer organisation which characterise local
industry.

The professional resettlement after return is
therefore a rather complex process that cannot easily
be conceptualised in terms of the existing debate
about the advantages and disadvantages of the work
experience during migration. The slow process of
maturation of the labour force through several migration cycles of succeeding generations cannot be
considered as endlessly reproducing itself: as
migrants who leave from agriculture diminish, the
scale of outmigration decreases. The more 'mature'
the migration labour force the less mobility they
are likely to experience; and therefore the expectations of change as a result of migration are greatly reduced. And this happens regardless of the
development that might take place in the places of
origin, as in the case of Friuli-Venezia Giulia.
Here the decision to return was more a choice than
an imposition, and has proved beneficial both to
returning migrants and local labour demand.

NOTES

1. This survey is a continuation of a series of research enquiries into return migration in the Friuli-Venezia Giulia region. For earlier phases of this work see Saraceno (1980; 1981).
2. The Friuli earthquake of 6 May 1976 caused widespread destruction across an area covering 100 communes and a population of half a million. Nearly 1,000 people perished, 2,400 were injured and 32,000 had their homes totally destroyed. For an excellent account of the earthquake and its aftermath see Geipel (1982).

REFERENCES

Bagnasco, A. (1977) Tre Italie: La Problematica Territoriale dello Sviluppo Italiano, Il Mulino, Bologna.

Fuà, G. and Zacchia, C. (1983) Industrializzazione senza Fratture, Il Mulino, Bologna.

Geipel, R. (1982) Disaster and Reconstruction: The Friuli (Italy) Earthquakes of 1976, Allen & Unwin, London.

Saraceno, E. (1980) 'Indagine sui rimpatri nel Friuli-Venezia Giulia', Studi Emigrazione, 58, pp. 174-202.

Saraceno, E. (1981) Emigrazione e Rientri: Il Friuli-Venezia Giulia nel Secondo Dopoguerra, Il Campo, Udine.

Chapter Four

LAND TENURE, RETURN MIGRATION AND RURAL CHANGE IN
THE ITALIAN PROVINCE OF CHIETI

Laurence Took

Within the general context of rural socio-economic
change, land tenure and migration have separately
been the object of many enquiries. Little work has,
however, been carried out on the interactions between these two phenomena. This chapter attempts to
explore the tenure-migration interface by means of a
questionnaire administered to a sample of 82 returned migrants interviewed in three villages in the
Lower Sangro Valley in the Italian province of Chieti
located in central-southern Italy, facing the
Adriatic Sea.[1] Because of its location, physique
(predominantly hilly), demography (traditional heavy
losses due to outmigration, followed by recent gains
due to returning migrants) and agrarian structure
(similar to the national pattern), Chieti can justi-
fiably be considered as broadly representative of
rural conditions in most of peninsular Italy.

LAND TENURE

Land tenure is best understood within the broad context of social relationships, for the various ways
in which land is farmed, owned, rented or otherwise
used by a rural community are fundamental to that
community's social organisation. The study of land
tenure is, therefore, as Davis (1973) has pointed
out, the study of relationships between people.
Land tenure is historically the foundation of the
'traditional' class structure of rural Italy south
of the Po Plain, for it dictated the fundamental distinction that existed between, on the one hand, the
great land owners (baroni), and on the other hand,
the landless peasants and labourers (braccianti),
sharecroppers (mezzadri) and other tenant farmers
operating at a subsistence level (Rossi-Doria, 1958).

In central and southern Italy today, land tenure is
still of critical importance to any analysis of
social change since most people, even if they are no
longer principally employed in the agricultural
sector, still maintain some contact with the land in
one way or another, perhaps as part-time or 'hobby'
farmers or as owners of varying amounts of ancestral
land. Land ownership is still a symbol of prestige
and an individual's relationship to the land -- his
'tenure position' -- is still important as a determinant of social status.

The Italian Central Statistical Institute
(ISTAT) recognises four main categories of land tenure. These correspond to distinctive agrarian systems and agricultural modes of production. Firstly,
there are family farms: small units operated directly by the person who owns or rents the land
without recourse to outside labour beyond the help
of family members. In the past family farms were
heavily subsistence oriented but recently, since the
war, increasing amounts of produce are offered for
sale commercially. Secondly there is the commercial
estate or 'capitalistic' sector made up of large
farms operated by hired labour. Such labour may
enjoy relatively secure contracts of a year or more,
or it may be hired by the day or week for casual
harvest work. The insecure labourer class are the
notorious braccianti whose poverty and exploitation
constitute one of the saddest chapters of Italian
rural social history. The third category is the
mezzadria, prevalent in central Italy. This too is
based on large estates, but the estates are frac-
tioned into small or medium sized farms which are
tenanted by sharecroppers on stable, secure leases
which may even be passed on through inheritance.
Under the traditional mezzadria contract the mezzadro (share-tenant) divided his produce equally with
his landlord. Recently the balance has shifted more
in favour of the mezzadro, even to the extent of
converting them into owner-farmers. The fourth category, quantitatively unimportant and decreasing, consists of miscellaneous local forms of land tenure,
mostly anachronistic and insecure sharecropping
arrangements.

Whilst a detailed analysis of the changing
weighting of these tenure types is out of place here,
it is important to note that the last two categories
are rapidly disappearing from the Italian rural
scene, at a national scale and in Chieti province,
whilst the relative importance of the 'family farm'
sector is increasing and the commercial estate

category remains stable (for a closer analysis see King and Took, 1983).

More useful for the ensuing analysis of this chapter is a division between individuals who have stable, direct links to the land, and those who do not, for this will be shown to have a bearing on migratory behaviour. Those who have stable links to the land tenure structure comprise landowners who live from farming (primarily individuals in the 'family farmer' class) and farmers such as mezzadri who rent or sharecrop land on a secure contractual basis. These cases are defined by their relationship to the land. Individuals who do not have direct links to the land tenure structure comprise both those who earn a living from farming but who do not actually own or lease a holding (e.g. braccianti and youngsters who help out on their parents' or relatives' farms), and those whose full-time occupation is non-agricultural (e.g. construction workers or artisans).

MIGRATION IN CHIETI PROVINCE

Chieti province has demographic and migratory characteristics that are typical of the highland districts of central and southern Italy. Its demographic history between 1861 and 1981 -- the respective dates of the first and the most recent Italian censuses -- falls into three distinct periods. The first 90 years was a period of gradual population increase (274,484 in 1861 to 400,210 in 1951) which early waves of emigration to the Americas did little to check, partly because of the continuing high birth rate. The picture then alters abruptly in 1951 with an ensuing 20-year period of decline, by 12.2 per cent, to 351,567. In mountainous districts of the province rates of population decline reached 40 per cent over the 1951-71 period. The third and final period under consideration -- 1971-81 -- re-established the trend toward population growth in most parts of the province. The province as a whole gained 4.9 per cent during this most recent intercensal decade, the increases being most marked along the coast and around the main towns of Chieti and Lanciano.

Emigration and, more recently, return migration, have played the key role in this demographic evolution. Early moves were to the USA, Argentina and Venezuela. This transatlantic link continued into the early post-war period but after the 1950s European destinations became progressively more important, first to France and Belgium and then, in the mid-1960s and early 1970s, to Switzerland and West Germany. The post-war wave of emigration abroad was also accompanied by large numbers of domestic migrants mainly to Lazio and Lombardy, and especially to these regions' respective capitals, Rome and Milan. Since 1971 annual population register data for the province record a steady net inflow of about 1,500-1,800 returnees annually.[2] Although returns have taken place to all parts of the province, including the mountainous interior, they have been most intense to the coastal strip and to industrial nodes being developed at Vasto and in the Lower Sangro Valley near Lanciano (Took, 1984, pp. 85-93). There would seem, therefore, to be a degree of correlation between areas of high return migration and the availability of industrial employment, but this relationship was not the main theme of the investigation.

SOME HYPOTHESISED RELATIONSHIPS BETWEEN MIGRATION AND LAND TENURE

Having outlined the land tenure and migratory background of the study area, it is now appropriate to suggest some possible ways in which these two key phenomena might be related. Some of the hypotheses will look at ways in which land tenure can exert an influence on migration behaviour; others will examine how migration in turn affects land ownership and tenure, and the wider rural economy.

First, let us consider how land tenure might affect the pattern of emigration. Does an individual's tenure status (estate owner, small owner-farmer, sharecropper, part-time farmer, bracciante etc.) influence the pattern of his or her migratory activity? It would be reasonable to infer that individuals with weak or precarious links to the land (labourers, insecure tenants or short-contract sharecroppers) would have a higher propensity to migrate than individuals with a solid hold on landed resources, such as estate owners or other categories of owner-farmers. An examination of ISTAT small area statistical evidence (for communes and agrarian zones) available for the province of Chieti shows that outmigration has been highest from the hilly areas (dominated by mezzadria tenure) and from mountainous districts (dominated by family farms) where the nature of the terrain limits agricultural

potential. This would seem to contradict the hypothesis stated above but, of course, the small area
data tell us nothing about individual behaviour; the
migrants could be precisely those excluded from the
secure benefits of the dominant family or <u>mezzadria</u>
farming. To resolve this conundrum, a questionnaire
survey is essential.

Secondly, we may hypothesise about the effects
of migration on land tenure and land use. These
effects may in turn be considered at two different
stages of the migration cycle: the impact at the
time of departure and possibly also whilst abroad;
and the impact at, and after, the time of return.
At the time of departure, the crucial question arises
as to what happens to land owned or rented by departing migrants. Is this land sold (and if so, to whom)
or rented out; is it retained and worked (perhaps
less intensively) by remaining family members who do
not migrate; or is it simply abandoned with no change
of ownership or tenure? Then there is the impact of
returning migrants on the land market. Do returnees
buy land? And for what purposes? Are they interested in working the land or just owning it, either for
speculative purposes or for renting out to others?
Are different forms of returnee land behaviour related to different types of migrant (e.g. seasonal
versus long-term)? Or, stated differently, what
kind of migrant leaves with investment in land in
mind as a personal goal?

FIELDWORK METHODOLOGY

Fieldwork in the province of Chieti was carried out
between April and October 1981. Three main strategies were employed. The first was the questionnaire
survey mentioned in the introduction. Lists held by
commune offices of migrants returned from abroad
were random sampled and interviews carried out with
82 returnees in three communes: Paglieta, Mozzagrogna and Santa Maria Imbaro. These villages were
carefully checked to screen out any atypicalities.
The questionnaire, which took about an hour to administer, was designed to appropriate respondents'
thoughts or actions on the use of land. It served
to highlight specific effects of migration on land
tenure and local agriculture. It included questions
concerning the respondents' general characteristics
(age, sex, pre-migration employment and education,
etc.), their migration history, their history of
land ownership and renting, and various aspects of

post-return economic behaviour. From the quantifiable responses to some of the questions, data could
be generated to test some of the hypotheses mentioned above. Difficulties over the legendary suspicion
of outsiders by southern Italian rural people were
overcome partly by a process of 'courtship' whereby
most respondents were visited several times on an
informal basis before the questionnaire was administered, and partly by the fact that my mother's
family had originated in the area; this reinforced
to a certain extent my 'credibility' since I had
visited the area frequently since childhood and was
reasonably familiar with the local dialect and cus-
tom. There was, therefore, a certain amount of
participant observation in the fieldwork, and this
was the second strategy. Thirdly, fieldwork also
involved structured and unstructured interviews with
key local informants such as agricultural trade
unionists, priests, teachers, lawyers and politicians. The results of these 'key interviews' were
recorded on tape and then critically analysed in the
light of all the other information arising from the
field survey.
     The three villages are situated in the centre
of Chieti province, at an intermediate location between the narrow coastal plain and the interior
mountains. Each village is perched on a hill over-
looking the Sangro Valley. Paglieta has a population of 4,405 (1981), the other villages are somewhat smaller -- Mozzagrogna has 1,884, Santa Maria
Imbaro 1,122. All villages, like the province as a
whole, lost population due to the excess of net
outmigration over natural increase during 1951-71,
then gained population due to return migration
during 1971-81. Local records indicate France,
Switzerland and West Germany to be the main migrant
destinations. All villages are primarily agricultural in character, the proportion of the employed
population working in farming being as high as 90
per cent in 1951, falling to 45-50 per cent in 1971.
Land tenure data from the 1961 and 1970 Agricultural
Censuses show a decline in mezzadria holdings and an
increase in family farms and commercial estates;
again these are trends characteristic of the province
as a whole. Table 4.1 presents a selection of ISTAT
census data for the post-war period on the three
villages.

Table 4.1: Population, Employment and Tenure Characteristics
of the Sample Villages

		Paglieta	Mozza-grogna	Santa Maria Imbaro
Population:	1951	5,090	2,502	1,041
	1971	4,176	1,833	1,012
	1981	4,405	1,884	1,122
Active population (%):	1951	51.7	52.8	61.4
	1971	36.5	39.9	39.4
% employed in agriculture:	1951	80.8	84.5	91.2
	1971	46.7	50.1	48.4
% employed in industry:	1951	7.6	6.2	2.7
	1971	21.5	21.3	18.8
% employed in tertiary:	1951	11.6	9.3	6.0
	1971	31.8	28.6	32.8
No. of family farms:	1961	515	297	175
	1970	579	300	201
No. of commercial estates:	1961	19	7	0
	1970	35	35	6
No. of mezzadria holdings:	1961	151	100	58
	1970	103	58	14

Source: Censimento Generale della Popolazione 1951, 1971, and
1981, ISTAT, Rome; Censimento dell'Agricoltura 1961, 1970,
ISTAT, Rome.

RESULTS OF THE QUESTIONNAIRE SURVEY

General Characteristics of the Sample
Only three of the 82 respondents were female. Women
were difficult to approach independently, either because they were unwilling to admit a male into their
homes or because they abdicated responding to the
questionnaire in favour of their husbands. Three-
quarters of the respondents had been born in the
village in which they were interviewed. Eighty of
the 82 respondents were married; only 7 had no children. Forty per cent of respondents were aged 35-45
years; this was very much the modal age group.
     At the time the interviews were carried out 18
respondents (22 per cent) were working in agriculture, 19 (23 per cent) in construction, 23 (31 per
cent) in miscellaneous small businesses, 9 (11 per
cent) were retired, and the remaining 11 respondents

were unemployed. A far higher proportion -- 76 per
cent -- had been engaged in some agricultural occupation prior to emigrating. These 62 individuals
comprised 19 'family farmers' who had owned only
modest amounts of land (mostly between 3 and 5
hectares), 22 mezzadri who were secure share-tenants
on somewhat larger holdings (but who had to cede half
their yield to the landlord), 18 braccianti and 3
individuals who had been youngsters working on
family land for pocket-money. The remaining 20 respondents had pre-emigration occupations that were
non-agricultural: 12 had been employed in industry
(including craft trades), 4 in construction, 3 had
been self-employed and one unemployed. Of these 20,
only 3 owned any land prior to departure, the amounts
being very small.
     The majority of the sample had been to Switz-
erland (34 respondents), West Germany (29) and
France (10). Only small numbers had been to other
European countries or to overseas countries. Whilst
abroad exactly a half were employed in the construction industry, and about a quarter had worked in
manufacturing industries.

Migratory Types
The respondents' migratory profiles were generalised
to four types. The first were seasonal migrants,
defined as those making regular seasonal migrations
lasting a few months on an annual basis. Migrants
of this type form a distinctive group who came mostly
(23 out of the 27 'seasonals') from an agricultural
background (Table 4.2). The occupation of farming
itself has a seasonal character which often permits
the farmer, mezzadro or agricultural labourer to
leave when the growing and harvesting seasons are
over and seek work abroad. The second category consists of short or medium term multiple movers --
those who have made two or more migrations separated
by one or more distinct periods back home during
which they worked or sought work. Sixteen of the
sample population had this profile, the overwhelming majority of these once again being former agricultural workers, half of whom were mezzadri (Table
4.2). The third category, containing 26 respondents,
comprised those who migrated only once, usually for
several years. Any visits home were brief, for
holidays or festivals. Interestingly, it is those
individuals who had less definite links with the
land tenure structure (braccianti, youths, industrial
employees) who figure most prominently in this
86

Land Tenure and Return Migration in Chieti

Table 4.2: Migration Type by Occupation Prior to Emigration

Pre-migration Occupation	Seasonal	Multiple Movers	Single Term	Mixed	Total
Family farmers	8	4	5	2	19
Mezzadri	8	7	3	4	22
Braccianti/youths	7	2	9	3	21
Artisan, industrial and construction workers	3	2	8	3	16
Other	1	1	1	1	4
Total	27	16	26	13	82

Source: Author's survey.

Table 4.3: Migration Type by Tenure Status

Tenure Status	Seasonal	Multiple Movers	Single Term	Total
Formal	16	11	8	35
Weak	10	4	17	31
Total	26	15	25	66

Chi-square 9.64; d.f.2; p.<0.01

Source: Table 4.2

'single-shot migration' group, a pattern which contrasts strongly with that observed for seasonal migrants where tenure-defined groups like owner-farmers and mezzadri were most numerous. The remaining 13 respondents fall into a fourth category, comprising those whose migratory histories combine elements of both a seasonal and multiple nature. Most migrants in this category started off as seasonal movers and then turned to longer-term migrations. These individuals are more or less evenly distributed across all pre-migration occupational categories.
From the above, there would seem to be a direct relationship between tenurial background and migration behaviour. This relationship is put to the

Table 4.4: Occupational Status Before Migration and After Return

Occupation Before Migration	Occupation After Return					
	Agriculture	Craft and Manufacturing	Construction	Self-employed	Retired or pension	Total
Family farmers	9	3	2	4	1	19
Mezzadri	5	2	5	5	5	22
Braccianti	3	3	7	2	3	18
Craft or manufacturing	0	1	1	10	0	12
Construction	1	0	3	0	0	4
Self-employed and others	0	1	1	5	0	7
Total	18	10	19	26	9	82

Source: Author's survey.

test in Table 4.3 which is essentially a condensed version of Table 4.2. It combines family farmers and mezzadri into one category defined by formal tenure status, and merges braccianti and industrial employees into a non-tenure group. The 'mixed' migratory category is omitted, as is the 'other' occupational category. The relationship is highly significant: it would seem, therefore, that formal tenure status predisposes an individual to take up a seasonal or multiple pattern of migration, whereas those with weak links to land holding are more likely to be found making single, long-term migrations.

Shifts in Occupation and Tenure Status over the Migration Period

Table 4.4 compares the occupations held by migrants prior to migration with those taken up on return. The first point to be noted is that of the 59 respondents actively employed in agriculture prior to migrating, only 18 returned to agriculture after their period abroad. Seventeen of these comprised family farmers, mezzadri and braccianti, all of whom subsequent to migration set themselves up as administrators of a family farm. Only one respondent previously employed in a non-agricultural occupation (a construction worker) returned to take up farming. Fourteen of the 18 returnees to agriculture had formal tenure status prior to migration.

A complementary exodus of no less significance seems to have taken place from craft and manufacturing industry. Twelve respondents were employed in this sector prior to migration. Of these only one returned to this occupation. One other went to work in the construction industry but more significantly 10 returned to invest in small businesses and became self-employed. The vacuum they left in manufacturing industry was filled by 8 returnees previously employed in agriculture. The 10 who left industrial employment represented some of the more educated respondents. Thus while the number of respondents in industry fell from 12 to 10 over the period of migration experience, the numbers of self-employed swelled dramatically from 7 to 26, a development largely due to those migrants who had left local industry and therefore those who had no land tenure status (in fact 17 of the 26 respondents in this group fell into that category).

Only 4 of the 82 migrants, prior to migration, were employed in the construction industry. This compares with 19 after return. Three reasons may

be advanced for this startling increase. The first
is that, as mentioned above, the majority of the
respondents worked on building sites whilst abroad
and might therefore, having experience of such work,
want to return to take up employment of this kind.
Secondly, 7 of those who returned to work in the
construction industry were ex-agricultural day
labourers, used to working short contracts of the
type issued by construction companies. Thirdly,
returning migrants had themselves stimulated work of
this type by commissioning new homes. This construction boom was also reinforced by industrial firms
building new plants in the Sangro Valley in the
1970s.

Overall, then, there was a complete move away
from sharecropping and 'day-contract' agricultural
work, and a more general exodus from agriculture as
a whole. Many of those moving out of agriculture
went into manufacturing industry, from which many
left to become self-employed. Some ex-agricultural
day labourers and mezzadri went into the construction industry which, as a whole, figured quite
prominently in the post-return occupational structure of the 82 respondents. Those respondents,
therefore, with formal tenure status, as defined
earlier in this chapter, fell in number from 41 to
18, or from one half to little more than one fifth
of the sample population -- an important change.

Tenure Status, Migration and Land Investment
The majority of respondents (56 out of 82, or 68 per
cent) had not owned any land prior to migrating.
This was reflected in all four migration categories.
For instance, 17 of the 27 seasonal migrants, 10 out
of the 16 multiple migrants, and 20 out of the 26
single-term migrants, did not own land. At the time
the interviews were carried out, i.e. post-return,
49 per cent of the sample (40 cases) had come into
the possession of land. Table 4.5 indicates the
connection between their tenure status prior to migrating and their present position with regard to
land ownership. A clear relationship is shown to
exist between current land ownership and pre-migration land tenure status: those who already possessed
or sharecropped some land prior to emigration are
more likely to be land owners after return.

In answer to the question 'With savings made
abroad did you invest in any land?' 40 respondents,
almost half the sample, said that they had. For 26
(65 per cent) of those who had invested in land, the

Table 4.5:   Land Ownership after Migration by Tenure Status

Tenure Status	Land Owned	Land not Owned	Total
Formal	27	14	41
Weak	13	28	41
Total	40	42	82

Chi-square 9.62; d.f.1; p<0.01

Source: Author's survey.

purchase represented an entirely new investment; for
the remaining 14 the investment was additional land
to that which they had owned prior to migrating.
Twelve respondents who had owned land before working
abroad bought no more land and 30 respondents (37
per cent of the total sample) remained without land.
The proportion of respondents investing in land
declines as one passes from seasonal to multiple to
single-term migrants. Most seasonal migrants (16
out of 27) invested in land and for the majority (11
cases) this represented an entirely new investment.
Exactly half the 16 multiple movers invested in land
and once again for half of these (4 cases) it was a
new investment. Less than half the single-term
migrants (11 out of 26) invested in land, and fewer
still in the mixed category.
    The respondents who had invested in land were
then asked whether their action represented the ful-
filment of an intention to invest in land that they
had entertained since before migrating. This question was partly designed to isolate those individuals
who may have migrated with land acquisition specifically in mind. Bearing in mind the methodological
problems of a question such as this, which asks
respondents to impute motives to actions retrospec-
tively, the results are suggestive and worthy of
comment. The majority (representing 57.5 per cent
of those who did invest in land) maintained that it
had been their intention since before migrating to
invest savings made abroad in land. It would not
necessarily be logical to infer from this that the
same number were spurred on to migrate precisely by
the thought of owning land, but it does give an indication of those who migrate with some form of
organised or semi-organised investment programme
with regard to land in mind. Cross-tabulation reveals

that 'planned' land investment is particularly characteristic of multiple and single-term migrants, less so of seasonal and other migrants (Took, 1984, p. 146).

One quarter of the 40 returnees who invested in land did so because they felt it was something that would earn value. In an area where land prices are rapidly inflating such an idea was not without foundation. Other reasons included the desire to purchase something that could be handed on to children, and the contribution it could make to the family budget in its capacity to provide home-grown produce. Four respondents specifically stated that they wanted land to build a house on. Only 7 respondents thought that it had been a bad investment.

In 15 cases out of 40 the land which the returnee bought was purchased from large local landowners and in 11 cases the land had been, prior to purchase, demanio, or land of the state. This indicates on the one hand the break-up of large estates in the area and on the other the inaccessible nature of a local land market where land mostly changes hands through laws of inheritance and not through commercial transactions, a situation forcing prospective investors to buy up unclaimed common land. Less than a quarter of the 40 who had bought land had in fact done so from local farmers, relations or friends. Only 3 individuals had bought land being sold off by departing migrants, a fact which indicates the apparent lack of a land market operating specifically amongst migrants themselves. Indeed of the 82 respondents in the sample as a whole only one had sold his land when he migrated and similarly only one had hired it out. The overwhelming majority had thus left their land in the care of relatives, which in many cases meant the wife of the respondent who had remained behind whilst her husband went abroad.

Returnee Investment Priorities

In an attempt to assess the importance attached to land investment relative to other possible items in an investment strategy, the respondents were asked to rank in order of preference a number of possible choices -- a car, land, a new house or improvements to an existing structure, a small business like a shop, and, if relevant, something else not specified in this list. Respondents were also asked to explain the reason for their choice, particularly with regard to land. The items chosen for this exercise

Table 4.6: Return Migrant Investment Priorities

| | Priority | | | | |
Investment	1st	2nd	3rd	4th	Total
House	47	28	2	1	78
Land	16	16	22	26	80
Business	15	12	15	34	76
Car	2	23	38	14	77
Other	2	3	5	7	17
Total	82	82	82	82	

Source: Author's survey.

in hypothetical investment were those which previous studies[3] and my own personal experience of the area led me to believe were the most common. The sample as a whole responded in the pattern indicated in Table 4.6.

The results show that a majority of respondents (57 per cent) thought a house to be first priority. Land took second place as first priority (19.5 per cent) and a business third place (18 per cent). Furthermore, investment in a house was nearly always either a first or second priority. Investment in land was more evenly spread although it figured more prominently as a low priority. A car was seen by most as a third priority and a business as a fourth. It is worth noting, however, that land was nominated by more people than any other category of investment.

When these investment responses are broken down by tenure status prior to migration further relationships emerge. The 47 respondents who listed a house as their first priority were equally divided amongst formal and weak tenure status. This applied also to those who declared a house to be their second investment priority. The 16 respondents who nominated the land to be their first priority were also equally divided, but the 16 who listed land as their second choice were drawn overwhelmingly from those with formal tenure status (12), whereas of the 26 who listed land as their fourth priority 18 had weak tenure status. Land, then, was given greater priority by those who, prior to migration, had formal tenure status. Conversely, of the 12 who listed a small business as their second choice 10 had weak tenure status, whereas of the 34 who listed such an

93

item as their fourth choice only 12 had such status.
    The picture which emerges from these patterns
of response is as follows. A house is clearly given
the greatest priority and a car emerged as essentially a third choice, these being the cases regardless of tenure status. The decisions concerning
second and fourth priority, however, did seem to be
linked to tenure status, the two items in competition for these places being investment in land or in
a small business. Often, however, building a house
requires the purchase of some land and this point
should not be overlooked, for in this sense the
house construction market could have an effect on
certain sectors of the land market too. It is also
worth noting that of those 18 respondents who, after
migration, returned to work in agriculture and maintained, therefore, their formal tenure status, 7 set
a house as their first priority and 6 the land.

CONCLUDING DISCUSSION

I conclude this chapter by re-examining the hypotheses and questions set out earlier on, both in the
light of the questionnaire results just described,
and with reference to perspectives shed on these
issues by the key interviews and by participant observation. This concluding discussion will look at
the effects of both emigration and return migration
on the socio-economic environment of Chieti province,
with particular reference to agriculture and the
rural economy.
    The notion that emigration removes surplus pop-
ulation so that a more balanced equation between
population and land resources is achieved -- the
equilibrium argument -- seems not to work in practice. The equilibrium model has been forcibly
stated by a number of economists looking for beneficial economic effects of emigration (e.g. Dasgupta,
1981; Griffin, 1976; Lipton, 1980; Miracle and Berry,
1970). Little evidence to support this model is
forthcoming from Chieti province or southern Italy,
although there are cases of more beneficial effects
in certain Third World countries in Africa and South
Asia (see the discussion in Chapter 1). As far as
my own observations in the province of Chieti are
concerned, emigration appears to have generated a
momentum of its own so that it has snowballed far
beyond the margins of any notional equilibrium state.
This is especially the case in highland areas of the
province where the rural economy seems pitched into

a trajectory of headlong decline. Here a workforce
depleted by emigration struggles unsuccessfully to
maintain previous levels of agricultural output.
The rural scene is dominated by abandoned land, although down on the coast and on the lower, gentler
hillsides just inland agriculture continues to
flourish under a virtual monoculture of vines.

The problem of the retreat from the agricultural margin is not a new phenomenon in Italian
agriculture, having been present in the Alps and
certain upland districts of the peninsula for at
least a hundred years. Contemporary accounts of the
earlier wave of emigration (e.g. Foerster, 1919)
provide vivid descriptions of land falling into dis-
use and villages crumbling into ruins in the early
years of the present century. However, in the post-
war period, due to the growing numbers who have
migrated or turned to employment in other sectors of
the economy, the phenomenon has gathered fresh momentum. Part of the cause of this is that many of
the women left behind by the menfolk -- the
vedove bianche or 'white widows' -- find it difficult or impossible to manage fields that are situated some way from the village. As a result they
continue to farm only the plots nearby, abandoning
the distant plots. This damages the fertility both
of the neglected distant fields, abandoned to scrub
or grazing, and of the remaining plots which are
often not properly rotated or fertilised.

Abandonment of cultivation of land, however,
does not necessarily mean abandonment of land ownership. Questionnaire results show that none of the
26 respondents who possessed some land prior to
emigrating disposed of this land by selling it when
they migrated. And only 3 of the 40 returned migrants who bought land since their return (or during
their absence) purchased the land from departing
migrants. The notion that emigration leads to a
rationalisation of farm holdings by the spontaneous
amalgamation of abandoned plots -- another branch of
the equilibrium model of migration -- cannot in this
instance be supported. Emigration does not lead to
consolidation and enlargement of farms; if anything
it actively prevents such a process taking place by
removing buyers and sellers from the actual market
for land.

The effects of return migration have been interpreted in widely differing ways. Those who stress
beneficial effects -- usually economists and government agencies -- focus on the return of human capital
with new skills and an innovatory outlook and on the

95

return of financial capital in the form of remit-
ances and savings. Lopreato (1967), for instance,
has claimed that returning migrants are the key
element in modifying the social structure of rural
Calabria; they bring in new ideas and values and
constitute a new social stratum of semi-retired
nouveau riche. Some of my key interviewees also
suggested that changes in local class relations
could be attributed to the impact of pluralistic
social values and militant 'shop-floor' ideology
introduced into the area by returning migrants from
industrial societies to the north. Local research
conducted by Bolino (1973) also stresses return migration's role as a powerful agent of cultural
change, introducing critical perspectives on the
status of religion and questioning the hitherto
hierarchical rigidity of society and its closed
system of values.

My own observations in Chieti province suggest
that these are not the dominant processes, however.
Far from being agents of radical change, I see
returnees more often than not as apostles of a deep
conservatism. Their behaviour does not really alter
rural class relations but rather serves to relocate
them within the existing social structures. To this
end they construct large houses or palazzi which in
some respects are reminiscent, in a modern form, of
the great houses where the old landowning barons
used to live. In other cases the style of the
palazzo reflects the migrant's particular experience: thus French-style villas or Swiss chalets
have appeared as incongruous inserts into the local
architectural scene. Inside, the returnee houses
are filled with beautiful furniture and a menagerie
of electrical gadgets. Returnee values are petit
bourgeois, consumerist and essentially conservative.

Furthermore it is difficult to see how return
migrants have generated real economic or political
changes in their villages of origin. Remittances
are certainly sent home by most Italian migrants
working abroad. Indeed ten years ago, at the height
of the migratory boom, over £1 million was deposited
in the local post office at Paglieta by residents of
the commune who were temporarily working abroad.
However, the effects of this considerable inflow of
exogenous capital do not necessarily procure economic development: it depends what the money is used
for. Table 4.6 showed only a low percentage of
respondents putting a high priority on the establishment of a business enterprise. Most migrant
capital goes on the famed new house, on furniture

and consumer durables to fill it and on a car. Investment in land is common but this is rarely related to increased agricultural productivity. Returnees buy land for investment, speculation,
prestige and possibly for future building sites.
Their holding of land for prestige purposes is highly reminiscent of the landowning practices of the
rural aristocracy. The changes that this import of
capital bring are therefore purely cosmetic (cf.
Rhoades, 1978). Voltage requirements for new
electrical appliances are too low and water pressure
unsuited to the blocks of apartments built by some
returnees. Therefore remittances do not generally
act to transform the system but only act within it;
they tend to preserve intact the archaic structural
features of the Italian rural economy, forestalling
the time when they must be rationalised and re-
organised (King, 1976).

Neither do returnees return as leaders of local
opinion or as active local politicians. Few returnees were found to be politically active either within local political parties or in local union or
cooperative organisations. These organisations
thrive on continuity and therefore are largely in
the hands of non-migrants.

Cerase (1974) has pointed out that a returned
migrant can be an agent or catalyst of socio-
economic change only when he has achieved a significant degree of integration with the life and culture
of the nation to which he migrates. Without this
experience his effect is, if anything, to counteract
on his return the indigenous development which has
taken place in his absence and to recall his local
society to the values and standards which he left
behind. The latter serves to promote the creation
of a facsimile of so-called 'modern' social values
whilst the former paradoxically generates a more
critical response, open to a re-interpretation of
the status quo, including a re-evaluation of the
position of agriculture. Unfortunately, it is my
belief, based on fieldwork in the Sangro Valley,
that the conservative returnee greatly outnumbers
his innovative counterpart.

NOTES

1. The research was supported by a Social
Science Research Council Linked Studentship in Land
Tenure Studies, held by the author during 1980-82
and supervised by Dr. Russell King in the Geography
Department, Leicester University. The full results

of this research are contained in my M.Phil. thesis (Took, 1984).

2. These annual population data are, however, far from accurate. Generally they underestimate the migratory flows since many migrants, especially those temporarily or seasonally abroad, do not bother to record their departure or re-entry. Nor are all local authorities assiduous in keeping records up to date.

3. Other studies which have provided data on migrants' post-return investment patterns include Baučić (1972) for Yugoslavia, King (1980) for Malta, Merico (1978) for southern Italy, and Rhoades (1978) for southern Spain.

REFERENCES

Baučić, I. (1972) The Effects of Emigration from Yugoslavia and the Problems of Returning Migrant Workers, Nijhoff, The Hague.

Bolino, G. (1973) Lo Spopolamento dell'Abruzzo: Aspetti Sociologici dell'Emigrazione Regionale, Editrice Itinerari, Lanciano.

Cerase, F.P. (1974) 'Migration and social change: expectation and reality. A case study of return migration from the United States to Italy', International Migration Review, 8(2), pp. 245-262.

Dasgupta, B. (1981) 'Rural-urban migration and rural development', in J. Balán (ed.) Why People Move, UNESCO Press, Paris, pp. 43-58.

Davis, J. (1973) Land and Family in Pisticci, Athlone Press, London.

Foerster, R. (1919) The Italian Emigration of our Times, Harvard University Press, Cambridge, Mass.

Griffin, K. (1976) 'On the emigration of the peasantry', World Development, 4(5), pp. 353-361.

King, R.L. (1976) 'Long-range migratory patterns within the EEC: an Italian case study', in R. Lee and P.E. Ogden (eds.) Economy and Society in the EEC, Saxon House, Farnborough, pp. 108-126.

King, R.L. (1980) The Maltese Migration Cycle: Perspectives on Return, Oxford Polytechnic Discussion Papers in Geography 13, Oxford.

King, R.L. and Took, L.J. (1983) 'Land tenure and rural social change: the Italian case', Erdkunde, 37(3), pp. 186-198.

Lipton, M. (1980) 'Migration from rural areas of
    poor countries: the impact on rural product-
    ivity and income distribution', World Develop-
    ment, 8(1), pp. 1-24.
Lopreato, J. (1967) Peasants No More, Chandler, San
    Francisco.
Merico, F. (1978) 'Il difficile ritorno: indagine
    sul rientro degli emigrati in alcune comunità
    del Mezzogiorno', Studi Emigrazione, 50, pp.
    179-212.
Miracle, M. and Berry, S. (1970) 'Migrant labour
    and economic development', Oxford Economic
    Papers, 22(1), pp. 86-108.
Rhoades, R.E. (1978) 'Intra-European return migra-
    tion and rural development: lessons from the
    Spanish case', Human Organization, 37(2), pp.
    136-147.
Rossi-Doria, M. (1958) 'The land tenure system and
    class in southern Italy', American Historical
    Review, 64(1), pp. 46-53.
Took. L.J. (1984) Land Tenure, Migration and Social
    Change in an Italian Province, M.Phil. thesis,
    University of Leicester, Leicester.

Chapter Five

THE ECONOMIC IMPACT OF RETURN MIGRATION IN CENTRAL
PORTUGAL

Jim Lewis and Allan Williams

INTRODUCTION

The links between international migration and economic development in labour exporting countries have
often been reviewed but no agreement on their relationship has yet been reached. In large part this is
because the actual impact of emigration, as well as
the effects of subsequent return flows of migrants
and money, are dependent on so many contingencies,
such as the characteristics of the emigrants, the
duration and nature of their experiences abroad, the
basic economic, social and political features of
both their home area and the area to which they return and the time period considered. Thus no simple
positive or negative relationship between emigration
and development is likely to be identified at the
national level. Even in one country, or group of
similar countries, the effects of emigration are
likely to vary both spatially and temporally.
     Within the general debate on international mi-
gration, there has been in recent years a marked
increase of interest in questions about the impact
of remittances and return migration, both of which
are closely tied to the temporary nature of most
labour migration. Welcome as this emphasis on remittances and returnees may be to many political act-
ors in labour exporting countries, it has suffered
from the tendency to study relationships at the
national level alone. The neglect of regional variations in possible impacts within a country should
be a matter of concern not only for those directly
concerned with the processes of spatially uneven
development but also for all those who are conscious
of the problems of overgeneralisation in evaluating
the consequences of emigration.
     Two types of overgeneralisation result from a

lack of attention to the regional dimension in
studies of remittances and returned emigrants.
First, survey results from one area are treated as
being applicable to others with different characteristics. An obvious example of this is to be seen in
the treatment of Gilani, Khan and Iqbal's (1981)
results on remittances to Pakistan as if they held
for other countries involved in the Gulf migration
system. Similar analytical flaws can also happen at
the subnational scale. Anyone who quotes Unger's
(1983) evidence that 36 per cent of returned Greek
emigrants work in industry to disprove the over-
generalised claims that returnees shun 'productive'
activities, without stressing that this refers to
urban returnees alone, would be guilty of overgeneralisation themselves. Therefore, research intended
to produce meaningful generalisations should use
ever finer regional distinctions. The second problem of analyses conducted solely at the national
level is that the economic behaviour of returned
emigrants is almost always isolated from that of the
rest of the population. This leads to blanket
statements about migrants' consumption levels or
aversion to industrial investments when, in fact,
the behaviour of rich returnees has more in common
with rich non-migrants than it does with poor returned emigrants.

It is with these dangers of overgeneralisation
in mind that this chapter sets out an analysis of
the economic behaviour of returned emigrants, refugees and non-migrants in contrasting regions of
Central Portugal.

Portugal provides excellent opportunities to
examine the relationships between international migration flows and regional economic development
because of the overall importance of migration nationally and the variety of economic conditions within the country. The fact that the principal emigrant
destinations have changed over recent years from the
Americas and the African colonies to Northern Europe
makes possible a comparison between two types of
returning migrants: regressados, workers coming
back from Northern Europe; and retornados, refugees
from the ex-colonies. Furthermore, the regionally
uneven character of Portuguese economic development
means that there are marked variations in the economic environments from which emigrants depart and to
which they return. It is thus possible both to
establish the extent to which the behaviour of emigrants varies between types of region and to evaluate the contribution of returnees to the differential

development of regions in Portugal.

The chapter first summarises the principal features of Portuguese emigration and then describes the evolving pattern of regional development in the country. The bulk of the chapter consists of a case study of the economic impact of returned emigrants and their remittances in three contrasting locations within the country's central region, paying special attention to returnees' investments, consumption patterns and occupational changes as the major means by which regional development processes are affected. Finally, the scope for generalisation from this study is considered in the conclusion.

PORTUGUESE EMIGRATION

Emigration has been a feature of Portuguese society for centuries, but there have been particularly significant changes in its scale, character and geographical patterns over the past 30 years.

First, the numbers of emigrants increased dramatically from levels of around 30,000 per annum in the 1950s to a peak of 173,267 in 1970. Hence during the decade of the 1960s an estimated one million legal and illegal emigrants (from a population of less than 9 million) left Portugal. This increase was partly the result of the economic under-development of the country (particularly its rural interior) as well as domestic political conditions -- especially the desire of young men to avoid conscription for the colonial wars in Africa (which meant that in 1970 at least 62 per cent of the emigrants left illegally). More important, however, was the growth of labour demand in the rapidly expanding economies of Western Europe, especially France but also West Germany, Luxemburg and Switzerland.

The fact that this demand was for temporary workers, often employed on an annual contract, made the new type of emigration different from the previously dominant intercontinental permanent or semi-permanent emigration flows. Labour circulation within Europe differed from overseas emigration for settlement in more than just its duration as it tended to involve more movement by single people (predominantly male) than by families -- at least initially. Additionally, the nature of the work available, combined with relative proximity to Portugal, provided more scope for the unskilled and poor to participate in the migratory system. Precisely because this kind of emigration is understood as temporary and involves the stretching of poor household economies across national boundaries, it usually gives rise to substantial flows of money in some form of remittances, and Portugal was no exception to this. To put the current levels of remittances in context, they normally represent over half the value of Portugal's merchandise exports and around 10 per cent of the Gross Domestic Product. In 1982 they were worth around £200 per capita, more that 30 per cent higher than Yugoslavia, which was the next most important Southern European country, and dwarfing by twelve times the per capita remittance figure for Italy.

The third significant change in emigration was in the pattern of destinations. International emigration in the first half of the twentieth century had been directed primarily to the Americas. Even as late as 1960 39 per cent of migrants went to Brazil and 33 per cent to the USA or Canada, compared with only 11 per cent to France and West Germany. However, by 1970 this pattern was reversed with 63 per cent of legal emigrants going to France or West Germany but only 3 per cent to Brazil and 24 per cent to North America. Migration to the African colonies -- principally Angola and Mozambique -- followed a very different pattern over this period. For a start, it was treated as internal migration and, rather surprisingly, has been poorly documented and little analysed except by Ferreira (1976). Comparison of the 1950 and 1960 censuses reveals a doubling in the number of Portuguese resident in both Angola and Mozambique. In the 1960s the metropolitan government encouraged further emigration to the colonies as part of a consolidation strategy in the face of escalating guerilla warfare. However, by the early 1970s the deteriorating military position of the Portuguese army meant that emigration rates were starting to fall and levels of return were on the increase. In all probability there were approaching a million Portuguese settlers (including second and third generation offspring) resident in Angola and Mozambique by 1974.

Although the foreign destinations of emigrants changed, there was relative stability in the regional distribution of their origins within Portugal. The south of the country consistently had very low emigration rates; instead, the southern interior region, the Alentejo, has been a major source of internal migrants to the Lisbon area. The Lisbon metropolitan region, although important in absolute terms, had relatively low rates of emigration, and

it was the northern and central regions which had
the highest relative rates. Over the period 1960-75,
the distritos of Viana do Castelo, Leiria, Aveiro,
Bragança and Guarda all had annual legal emigration
rates in excess of 7 per 1,000 inhabitants.
      Since 1974 there have been important changes in
the nature of emigration from Portugal, as from
other Southern European countries. First, in view
of the recession in the world economy, there has
been a substantial decline in the number of emigrants. From a peak of 173,267 legal and illegal
emigrants in 1970, numbers fell sharply to 44,918 in
1975, then more gradually to 21,862 in 1982, then
tumbling to a mere 6,905 in 1983. Secondly, the
destinations of the emigrants have also changed in
response to the lower levels of labour demand in
Northern Europe and the imposition of stricter legal
controls on immigrants by France and West Germany in
particular (Castles, Booth and Wallace, 1984). Consequently, the Americas have re-emerged as a principal destination, with Venezuela and the USA taking
28 per cent and 18 per cent respectively of Portuguese emigrants in 1982, compared with only 6 per
cent to France and West Germany. In addition, new
destinations are emerging, amongst which Australia,
Spain and the Middle East are prominent. A third,
and particularly dramatic, feature was the arrival
in Portugal of the retornados, Portuguese settlers
who had become refugees from Angola and Mozambique.
Most arrived around the time of decolonisation in
1975. Estimates of the numbers involved vary considerably and the 450,000 suggested by a special
census of retornados was widely regarded as an underestimate with the true figure lying between 800,000
and 1 million. However, the rapid and continuing
re-emigration of retornados to new destinations means
that their true figure will never be known.
      Taken together, these changes have transformed
the balance between emigration and return migration.
Although no official statistics on 'normal' return
are available, conservative estimates of about
30,000 per annum since 1976 suggest that rates of
return are up to 50 per cent higher than those of
emigration. Combined with the large number of
retornados -- almost 1 in 10 of the population -- it
is clear that few communities have been left untouched by return migration over the past few years.
      Until recently there were no official statistics
to permit an accurate assessment of the regional
pattern of return. However, the 1981 population
census provides some indication of this since it

records, by distrito, those who were resident elsewhere in Europe and in the African possessions in
1973. The regressados (roughly 140,000 people)
only constitute 1.5 per cent of the total population
but make up more than 3 per cent of current residents in the northern and interior distritos of
Bragança, Guarda, Castelo Branco and Viana do
Castelo. Only Leiria amongst the littoral distritos
had a similar proportion. Given the low levels of
initial emigration it is not surprising that below
average figures for regressados are found in the
rural south. Despite high absolute numbers, regressados form only 0.9 per cent and 0.8 per cent of the
populations of Oporto and Lisbon respectively. In
contrast, the distribution of retornados shows an
above average proportion in Lisbon (8.1 per cent of
the city's population), reflecting the fact that one
third of all retornados are now resident in the
capital. The other part of the Lisbon conurbation
in Setúbal distrito contains a similarly high proportion. Faro on the south coast, which contains
the Algarve tourist area, stands out as the other
economically developed area in which retornados are
an important element of the population. Their
greatest relative weight, however, is in the northern interior where the distritos of Bragança, Guarda
and Vila Real all had over 5 per cent in 1981; this
is a reflection of their roles as centres of initial
emigration in the 1950s and 1960s. Elsewhere, we
have argued that retornados initially tended to
settle in those areas where they had family connec-
tions (primarily the northern interior) or where
they were housed temporarily (in the vacant hotels
of Lisbon or the Algarve). However, by 1981 it seems
that a limited shift has occurred to the littoral
region -- especially to Lisbon, Oporto and Setúbal
-- representing rural-urban migration after initial
settlement (Lewis and Williams, 1985).

REGIONAL UNEVEN DEVELOPMENT IN PORTUGAL

After decades of relative stagnation, there was
rapid economic growth of the Portuguese economy from
the late 1950s onwards. This was partly a consequence of the ending of a period of autarchic policies under the Salazar regime, and partly a result
of investments in traditional manufacturing industries and physical infrastructure. The main foci of
growth were multinational companies, state investments in basic industries and a small number of

indigenous finance capital groups (Baklanoff, 1979;
Porto, 1984). During the 1960s, high economic
growth rates were maintained (an average of 6 per
cent per annum), although these were sectorally uneven, being greatest in manufacturing while agriculture continued to stagnate due to a lack of investment and the government's inability to use land
reform to tackle the problems of either small-scale
producers in the North or inefficient large estates
in the South. In the mid-1970s growth faltered due
to the world economic crisis, compounded by the
political uncertainty which followed the 1974 military coup. Subsequently, in the face of depressed
demand for both its traditional exports (e.g. textiles) and those added during the 1960s (e.g. ships),
as well as new conditions of production in the
newly-restored democratic era, economic growth has
been modest and uncertain (Macedo and Serfaty, 1981).

In common with other Southern European countries,
the nature of economic development in Portugal has
been dependent on its specific role in the evolving
international division of labour (Hudson and Lewis,
1985; Williams, 1984). The consequent characteristics of its economy have been a lack of control
over its own resources, a growing reliance on foreign investors, an increasing dependence on tourist
earnings for foreign exchange and the country's involvement in international migration systems as a
source of cheap labour for the more advanced economies of Western Europe.

Development in Portugal has been spatially as
well as sectorally uneven, for particular regions
have been differentially affected by an evolving
national spatial division of labour and, more
generally, greater integration into the international division of labour has tended to exacerbate
existing regional inequalities (Lewis and Williams,
1981). Although it is not possible here to present
a detailed account of patterns and processes involved, it is important to outline the main features
of uneven regional development in Portugal, especially the fundamental (if over-simplified) differen-
tiation between the interior and littoral regions
(Ferrão and Jensen-Butler, 1984).

Agricultural activities continue to dominate
the interior and far north of the country and accounted for between 50 and 70 per cent of employment in all interior distritos in 1970. Even in
1981, when the national figure was just under 20 per
cent, agricultural employment shares of 53 per cent,
51 per cent and 50 per cent were recorded in Vila

106

Real, Bragança and Viseu respectively. Manufacturing has traditionally had little importance here
except for some isolated pockets, such as the wool-
len textiles industry in Covilhã and Gouveia, while
the tertiary sector is also weakly developed, due in
no small part to the massive spatial centralisation
of public sector administration during the Salazar-
Caetano era. This pattern was somewhat modified in
the 1970s with a marked increase in employment and
in industrialisation evident in the sedes (administrative centres) of the interior distritos. Towns
such as Guarda and Portalegre have received investments by multinationals such as Renault and ICI, and
have also gained from the limited decentralisation
of public sector jobs in post-1974 Portugal. Hence
increasing care must be exercised in distinguishing
between the dynamics of different economic environments within the interior of the country. Nevertheless, in the marked absence of any sustained, extensive economic development, the principal economic
role of the interior regions in recent years has
continued to be the supply of labour to more economically advanced areas, both within and outside
Portugal.

In contrast, there has been sustained growth in
the littoral region, especially that part which
stretches from Setúbal in the south to Braga in the
north. This coastal region had 77.5 per cent of
national GDP in 1970, has GDP per capita levels well
above the mean and is the most industrialised and
urbanised part of Portugal. There are two main
nuclei within this zone, the metropolitan areas of
Lisbon and Oporto, each with its own distinctive
features. Industrial activity is larger in scale
and more capital intensive in the southern metro-
polis, where growth is spatially polarised around
the margins of the Tagus. Lisbon, as the capital of
both country and, until 1975, empire, also dominates
the tertiary sector. Oporto, however, is the centre
of a more decentralised, and sometimes spatially
diffuse, form of industrialisation, where labour
intensive production is important in both modern
and traditional sectors. Spatially decentralised
industrialisation closely tied to local raw materials and markets also characterises much of the
central region in distritos such as Leiria and
Coimbra.

In terms of labour migration, these littoral
regions are affected by both the import and export
of people, receiving migrants from the interior and
sending emigrants to other countries (Arroteia,

107

1983). The precise balance between inflow, outflow
and return flows is spatially and historically variable with considerable differences even between
neighbouring concelhos[1]. There are also demographic
differences between the interior and littoral regions in line with these economic differences. In
the 1960s, the total population of the country fell
by about 175,000, and all the interior distritos
experienced population losses, ranging between -24
per cent (Guarda) and -9 per cent (Viana do Castelo).
Even some of the littoral regions lost population,
and only the five distritos in, or immediately
adjacent to, the two metropolitan areas recorded
population increases. The 1970s, however, were
marked by something of a shift in demographic trends
and the country as a whole experienced a population
gain of some 1,200,000, not least because of the
number of returning emigrants. Again, regional differences were evident; although population losses
have been stemmed in most of the interior distritos,
population growth was still greatest in the two
metropolitan regions (Lewis and Williams, 1985).
Consequently, between 1970 and 1981, the littoral
region's share of total population increased from 65
to 69 per cent.

A CASE STUDY OF THE ECONOMIC IMPACT OF RETURNED
EMIGRANTS IN THE REGIÃO CENTRO

Research Framework
Given the paucity of published statistics on returned migrants in Portugal, it is only possible to
proceed with any detailed research on their economic impact through field surveys. This is the
approach taken here, drawing on surveys undertaken
in 1982 in the região centro[2]. The study sought to
compare the determinants of the economic behaviour
of regressados, retornados and non-emigrants in contrasting economic environments. While there have
been several previous and subsequent studies of
regressados (for example, Brettell, 1979; Silva et
al, 1984; Trinidade, 1976), enabling obvious comparisons with returnees from Northern Europe in
similar countries, the retornados have, somewhat
surprisingly, been largely ignored, even by Portuguese researchers. Given the magnitude of this
group, their very different experience whilst 'abroad'
and the popular impression that they have constituted
a largely positive economic force, they were

considered to be an important element in the project. Finally, in order to allow for 'natural'
change in the different economic environments, it
was essential to include a control group of non-
emigrants in the study. This research framework
allows the identification of the relative importance
in explaining economic behaviour of the individual
characteristics of economic agents (in particular
their age, sex, education, occupation and experience
as migrants) and of the economic structure to which
they return (not least the set of employment or
investment opportunities that are available to migrants and non-migrants).

The questionnaire surveys were conducted in
places in which some population growth -- a surro-
gate for economic development -- was evident over
the past decade, in order to allow a greater possibility of returned emigrants having a positive developmental effect, since so many previous case studies
of returnees have drawn negative conclusions from
remote rural communities which are in irreversible
decline. Three areas were selected to represent the
principal types of economic, political and social
environments found in the region: a rural, agricultural settlement, a small town with some industrial activities and a city with substantial service
and industrial opportunities. On the bases of the
available aggregate statistics and field visits, the
village of Fóios (in Sabugal concelho), the town of
Mangualde and the city of Leiria were chosen as
representative of these types. In Fóios and Mangualde interviews were conducted in the freguesias
(parishes) of that name but in Leiria, they were
conducted in both the central freguesia (which
covers the historic part of the city) and the adjacent freguesia to the west, the industrial suburb of
Marrazes, in order to provide a cross-section of the
city's population.

Introduction to the Three Sample Communities
Fóios freguesia had a population of 470 at the 1981
census indicating a slight increase (+7 per cent) on
the 1970 figure: a considerable contrast to the
decline of previous decades, which had reached a
rate of -41 per cent in the 1960s. There are still
villagers working abroad, and a few in Lisbon, but
the predominant movement at present is homeward.
Evidence of this can be found in the scatter of re-
built houses amongst the traditional granite block
buildings of the village core and the grander new

'Swiss' housing on the edge. The local economy is
still dominated by agriculture, chiefly the production of rye, maize, milk and potatoes for subsistence. There are signs of agrarian change in the
commercialisation of the forests on the schist
ridges and the planting of an apple orchard just
south of the village but these have less impact on
the village economy than remittances or the lucrative
smuggling trade over the nearby Spanish border.
Industrial and service activities in Fóios are
limited to a small sawmill, the dozen or so cafes
and shops and two schools.

The old market town of Mangualde has been
changed more profoundly in recent years, with the
economic heart of the community shifting from the
shops around the town hall to the new factory site
at the western end of the dusty main street. This
is where Citroën opened their Portuguese assembly
works in 1974, creating directly some 600 jobs in
the factory and offices, and contributing greatly to
the 125 per cent increase in manufacturing employment during 1970-81. Largely as a result of this
growth, the proportion of the concelho's population
employed in manufacturing has risen from 25 per cent
to 39 per cent over that period, while a static agricultural labour force now only accounts for 35 per
cent of jobs as against 49 per cent in 1970. These
relative shifts have taken place in an overall context of substantial population increase. The most
obvious indications of this expansion to a size of
almost 8,000 are the streets of new housing, including blocks of apartments, and the improved range of
services now available. But it is still possible to
find relatively unchanged agricultural practices
only a few kilometres away, down towards the Mondego
river, where small parcels of land frame the intensive cultivation of maize, beans, potatoes and vines.

The third sample locality, the city of Leiria,
is the administrative centre for both the distrito
and concelho of that name. Over recent years the
growth of the city to its 1981 population of 13,700
has meant a spread of building away from the plain
below the towering medieval castle and onto the surrounding ring of hills. Much of the new construction
is comparatively recent for the growth rate of the
population of the central freguesia was only 7 per
cent in the 1960s but accelerated to 72 per cent
between 1970 and 1981. Marrazes freguesia, covering
the old housing for the brickworks just west of the
old city but now also containing new manufacturing
investments such as the Portucel cellulose plant,

has also seen significant population growth since
the early 1960s. Recent economic change in the
concelho as a whole can be summarised by reference to
the employment structure, which showed a halving of
the percentage in agriculture since 1970 to 15 per
cent in 1981 while the shares of manufacturing and
services have risen to 49 per cent and 36 per cent
respectively. As in Mangualde, the agricultural
crops of the zone around the city are primarily
maize, beans and wine, produced on holdings averag-
ing only 2 hectares in size. Unlike the other
sample areas, however, agricultural mechanisation
and commercialisation are widespread, especially
along the line of the main road linking Oporto and
Lisbon. The traditional industries of the area --
ceramics, food processing and timber -- still account for half the manufacturing employment but
plastic goods and metal products are the most rapidly-
growing branches. However, a large part of the
recent wave of industrial investment has been located either along the by-pass or on small scattered
sites in more rural parts of the concelho, so that
the city itself has been most affected by the expansion of tertiary activities. New commercial and
entertainment centres, extra offices of education
and administration, have all contributed to the 62
per cent growth in tertiary employment during the
1970s.

Interview Strategy
The original objective had been to obtain random
samples of 50 each of the regressado, retornado and
non-emigrant households in each of the study areas.
In practice this proved impossible. In the first
place, there were insufficient retornados to constitute a meaningful sample in the rural area, so this
group was excluded from the rural study. Furthermore, there were logistical difficulties which made
it impossible to reach the target figures in the
urban areas. Hence, a total of 327 usable responses
were obtained -- 63 in Fóios (33 per cent of all
households there), 129 in Mangualde (6 per cent) and
135 in Leiria (2 per cent). In the following analysis we are excluding from consideration regressados
who had principally worked outside Europe (e.g.
Venezuela or USA) and any returnees who had finally
resettled in Portugal before the political and economic changes of 1974, so only 303 responses are
analysed below. These are split 84 : 100 : 119 between regressado, retornado and non-emigrant

households respectively.

The interviews with the emigrants covered a broad range of economic and social experiences of themselves and other members of the household before, during and after emigration, while the shorter schedule for non-migrants covered comparable themes concerning past, present and future activity where appropriate. A comprehensive summary of the survey is available in Boura et al (1984). Discussion here is limited to the features bearing most directly on the economic development of areas of return and, thus, on tendencies towards uneven regional development.

ORIGINS AND OCCUPATIONS OF THE EMIGRANTS

While it is not intended to review the demographic, economic, and social features of emigrants in any detail here, it is important first to note the principal differences which influence their economic behaviour. The remainder of this section then proceeds to a consideration of the geographical and occupational mobility of the emigrant groups, both of which profoundly influence the impact they may have on economic development in the differing conditions of the sample localities.

Three demographic and social features of the emigrants tell us about their origins. First, in overall terms, emigrants to northern Europe tended to be relatively young, single and male (although there have been periods in which female emigration has been dominant as family reunification abroad occurred). This is evident in the high proportions of males as respondents in the sample -- 59 per cent for regressados compared to 50 per cent for non-emigrants -- and reflects the gender balance amongst emigrants as a whole apparent in official statistics (Ferreira, 1976). In contrast, emigration to the colonies was more permanent and so family migration was more common; consequently, a more even balance of sexes is observed, with a figure of 49 per cent males amongst retornados.

Secondly, emigrants in the samples again conform to expectations with respect to their educational background. Aggregate statistics have suggested that it is the least educated who dominated the flow of 'guestworker' emigrants and this is borne out by the survey results: only 3 per cent of regressados had more than the bare minimum of education (defined as the first four years of primary school), compared to

112

18 per cent of non-emigrants. However, many emigrants to the colonies were recruited to fill administrative and commercial posts and so were more likely to be better educated than average; thus, in the sample, 28 per cent of retornados had received more than a basic education.

The third feature to note is the existence of systematic social and demographic differences between respondents -- both emigrant and non-emigrant alike -- from the sample areas. These can be illustrated by reference to educational attainment, which was lowest in Fóios (no respondents having proceeded beyond the fourth class) and highest (25 per cent) in Leiria, and to features such as the age of respondent -- with 86 per cent of Fóios respondents aged over 40 but only 56 per cent in the case of Leiria. Of particular significance to the following discussion is the difference in emigration experiences amongst regressados, for inter-concelho variation in the dominant destination country has some unexpected consequences. Whereas in Fóios all regressados spent their longest period working in France (though several subsequently moved to Switzerland) and 68 per cent of Leiria respondents did likewise, only 19 per cent of Mangualde's European emigrants worked in France while the majority went to West Germany. This is largely a reflection of the relatively late involvement of Mangualde in European migration, with only 5 per cent of regressados departing prior to 1961 compared with 50 per cent in Fóios, and the fact that this occurred at a time when West Germany rather than France had become the prime destination for legal emigrants. Hence, when large-scale return movements started in the mid-1970s Mangualde received regressados who had least experience of working abroad and smallest accumulated savings. While in Fóios 57 per cent of respondents had worked abroad for over 15 years, none of the Mangualde regressados could claim the same.

The extent to which existing inter-regional differences are modified as a result of international migration is heavily dependent on the pattern of geographical mobility of both returnees and non-migrants. If returning emigrants use their accumulated savings in their areas of origin then there could be benefits for the poorer areas which have relatively high levels of initial emigration. However, should the migrant treat a sojourn abroad as but a step in a chain of internal rural to urban migration, the possibilities of some 'spread' effects would be greatly reduced. There is a widespread view

113

in Portugal that a 'return to roots' is dominant.
The vast majority of the local officials and priests
questioned about this thought that most regressados
now lived in the freguesia where they had been born.
This is in marked contrast to the evidence of both
aggregate statistics and survey results in similar
countries such as Greece (Unger, 1983), Spain
(Castillo Castillo, 1981) and Turkey (Toepfer, 1985)
where 'urban drift' predominates. Our finding that
84 per cent of regressados, 43 per cent of retornados
and 81 per cent of non-emigrants are currently living in the concelho of their birth suggests that
both tendencies are perhaps operating simultaneously.
    Table 5.1 reveals considerable variation between
localities in the degree of geographical mobility.
Amongst regressados, only those who had been born
there went back to the village of Fóios and the proportion of local people amongst returnees to
Mangualde is not much lower. Yet in Leiria, only 62
per cent of regressados originated in the concelho
and 9 per cent had even moved there from outside the
região centro. While this indicates that some 'urban drift' is occurring, it does not appear to be
confined to regressados for the comparable figures
for non-emigrant households show that 45 per cent of
those now in Leiria have moved there, a level higher
than that amongst returning emigrants from Northern
Europe (38 per cent). What this suggests is that
returnees are using their additional wealth as much
to enable them to live in the villages and small
towns where they have family ties as to finance a
move to the city. It clearly does not lead to the
conclusion that experiences of urban life abroad
make returnees more likely to migrate internally than
those who have stayed in Portugal: the attraction
of the more prosperous and developed areas of the
country would seem to be marginally greater for
those unable to draw on savings or a foreign pension
to lift their living standards where they were
brought up.
    The peculiar circumstances of the retornados'
arrival in Portugal means that their patterns of
mobility have been far more obviously affected by
the changing spatial distribution of opportunities
in the country. The generally low level of return
to areas of origin (43 per cent) is evidence of their
lack of personal ties within the country after years
as colonists and the fact that 10 per cent had been
born 'abroad'. Mangualde had over one-third of its
retornado population born outside the concelho,
while in Leiria this proportion was over three-

Table 5.1: Geographical and Occupational Changes for Regressados, Retornados and Non-Migrants (all data %)

	Respondents' Birthplace:		Respondents Employed:		Percentage of Employed who are Employees or Work on Family Farms:	
	Same concelho as current residence	Elsewhere	Before emigration	Now	Before emigration	Now
FÓIOS						
Regressados	100	0	93	75	77	23
Non-emigrants	97	3	-	94	-	14
MANGUALDE						
Regressados	89	11	81	76	89	57
Retornados	62	38	53	51	85	35
Non-emigrants	90	10	-	80	-	56
LEIRIA						
Regressados	62	38	83	74	76	31
Retornados	24	76	60	79	86	56
Non-emigrants	55	45	-	97	-	62
TOTAL						
Regressados	84	16	86	75	79	37
Retornados	43	57	57	65	86	46
Non-emigrants	81	19	-	90	-	44

Source: Authors' questionnaire survey.

quarters, which clearly indicates that this group of
returning migrants have been a significant cause of
the rapid growth of the larger urban centres during
the 1970s.

These patterns of spatial mobility are clearly
tied to changes in the occupation of individual members of the household as movement between different
economic environments may open up new employment
opportunities. Table 5.1 provides a simple summary
of trends in occupational mobility by indicating the
proportions of the samples working outside of the
household and the percentage of those working who
were employees (or in a subordinate position in a
family farm). Regressados are now less likely to be
employed than prior to their emigration with a fall
from 86 to 75 per cent employed overall, reflecting
both their ability to survive on savings or foreign
pensions and the age and gender composition of the
samples. This withdrawal of regressados from the
formal labour market is found in each of the study
areas and in all cases the proportion not working is
higher than for non-emigrants. Amongst retornados,
though, the picture is more complex for while more
are now employed than before emigration (65 per cent
up from 57 per cent), this proportion is still low
compared with non-emigrants. In this case it is not
so much a case of voluntary retirement or the withdrawal of women from waged work but a sign of the
unemployment problem facing retornados nationally.
The best available measure of this for our sample
comes from a comparison of the current level of employment (65 per cent) with the percentage who intended to seek employment on arrival in Portugal (82
per cent), a discrepancy that is especially marked
in Mangualde where 77 per cent intended to work but
only 51 per cent have been able to.

Amongst those who are employed, there has been
a decrease in the proportions of regressados working
in the agricultural, industrial, transport and public service sectors when comparing jobs before and
after emigration, with a corresponding increase in
commercial employment (up from 11 to 30 per cent
overall). There are obvious similarities between
these results and evidence from elsewhere in Southern Europe (e.g. King, 1984) but it is worth drawing
particular attention to the net shift out of industry. Before emigration 32 per cent of those employed
were in manufacturing jobs but, despite the fact that
over 40 per cent were so employed whilst abroad,
there is little sign of any transfer of acquired
skills as only 20 per cent of regressados now work

in this sector. In terms of employment position,
the contrast between pre- and post-emigration patterns is more marked, for while 79 per cent of
regressados in employment had been employees (or
family labourers) prior to their years away, on return this share fell to 37 per cent -- lower than
the 44 per cent recorded amongst non-emigrants. The
precise reasons for this change differ between areas;
in Fóios this shift was largely due to a growth in
self-employed farmers, but in both Mangualde and
Leiria it was the increasing number of owners of
other types of enterprise that dominated. In each
case, though, there has been undoubted upward mobility amongst regressados, relative not only to their
previous occupational positions but also to those
who did not emigrate.

Retornados show a similar set of shifts in
terms of the type of employment held before and
after emigration. Agriculture and industry now account for less than half their pre-migration share
of those in work (2 and 13 per cent respectively
now), whilst the proportion in commerce has doubled
to 56 per cent and that in public service risen
sharply to 23 per cent. Retornados have also been
occupationally mobile in the urban economic environments studied. As Table 5.1 shows, the percentage
of employees and similar has fallen from 86 per cent
before working in Angola or Mozambique to 46 per
cent at the time of interview. This, too, is below
the 58 per cent recorded for non-emigrants in the
same areas, so that, for those who have employment,
emigration would appear to have been beneficial in
spite of the unintended nature of return. Of course,
retornados might be expected to have a considerable
business advantage over the other two groups, because of their educational background and experience
'abroad', but the remarkably high share of owners
(55 per cent) and of commercial sector employment (75
per cent) amongst retornados in Mangualde is also
partly a response to the difficulties of finding alternative employment in this town. As there is no
guaranteed future for the plethora of economically
marginal bars and cafes that have been created there,
a note of caution about the permanence of the upward
mobility observed thus needs to be recorded.

It would appear from this review of different
types of mobility that international migration is
generally beneficial in economic terms for the households involved. Individuals seem better able to live
where they wish and to work or not, almost as they
choose. Those that do work are less likely to have

menial jobs in agriculture or industry than before they emigrated and are more likely to run their own businesses than those who have not emigrated. While this generally positive economic picture may not hold for all returnees -- and especially not for all retornados -- there is sufficient support here for the commonly-held view amongst emigrants that the sacrifices of the years abroad will be rewarded by self-advancement. To see how far these individual improvements after return contribute to the development of the regional economy, it is necessary to turn to returnees' expenditure and investment patterns.

RETURNEES' CONSUMPTION AND INVESTMENT: MOTORS OF A REGIONAL ECONOMY?

The importance of emigrant remittances and accumulated savings in their special bank deposits at a national level has already been noted. However, the ability of this injection of cash to transform the economic structure of a region is very much dependent on its subsequent use. For this reason our survey sought to establish both the balance between consumption and investment in returnee expenditure and the possible impact of this beyond the household concerned. In view of the differences already established between the two groups, it is most straightforward to treat the regressados and retornados in turn.

Specific forms of investment by regressados and non-emigrants are compared in Table 5.2. Answers have been simplified into a yes/no format in each case and no account is taken of actual amounts of money involved. The high priority attached to housing by returnees (76 per cent) is familiar enough from studies such as Rhoades (1978) and Connell (1980) but it is unwise to single them out since it also dominates the expenditure of non-migrants. Nor is it that easy to dismiss housing as simply a consumption expenditure for there are often supply linkages into the local area, which have helped to encourage a wave of industrial investments in brick, beam and block works even in the interior of the country. A car is also an important call on the funds of regressados and non-migrants alike but land -- for agriculture in Fóios or Mangualde and for building in Leiria -- is a much more common choice amongst regressados. In terms of changing the existing economic structure, neither group seems

118

Table 5.2: Specific Forms of Investment by <u>Regressados</u> and Non-Emigrants (%)

	Land	Housing	Business	Car	Repay Loan
Fóios					
Regressados	56	64	28	32	32
Non-emigrants	33	83	6	6	0
Mangualde					
Regressados	29	76	19	57	0
Non-emigrants	5	62	31	72	0
Leiria					
Regressados	53	88	34	47	9
Non-emigrants	21	48	34	72	0
Total					
Regressados	46	76	27	45	14
Non-emigrants	20	64	24	50	0

Source: Authors' questionnaire survey.

especially attracted to business investment overall but there are important inter-community variations. In Fóios, the different propensities to invest in business -- 28 per cent of <u>regressados</u> but only 6 per cent amongst the rest -- is a reflection of the differing levels of wealth within the community but in Mangualde the position is reversed, as the returnees generally had limited savings so the 19 per cent investing in business is well below the level amongst non-emigrants.

How these investments affect the local economies is explored more fully in the next paragraph but first we need to consider the wider range of consumption expenditures summarised in Table 5.3. Even though the levels of ownership cannot match those recorded in neighbouring Spain by Castillo Castillo (1981), the <u>regressados</u> generally are more likely to own basic consumer goods than non-migrants. The contrast between the proportion of returnee households owning, say, a fridge, which has gone from 9 per cent before emigration to almost 90 per cent nowadays, is clear testimony to the role of savings from remittances in financing this consumption. It is also important to note the consistent rural-urban gradient in ownership levels which cuts across the emigrant/non-emigrant divide. However,

Table 5.3: Ownership of Selected Consumer Goods (%)

	Motorcycle	Washing Machine	Car	TV	Fridge
Fóios					
Regressados:					
Before	0	0	0	0	4
After	19	35	39	81	89
Non-emigrants	7	10	7	32	45
Mangualde					
Regressados:					
Before	5	5	5	14	10
After	43	38	62	76	86
Non-emigrants	30	36	47	81	85
Leiria					
Regressados:					
Before	6	0	12	3	15
After	32	62	76	91	91
Non-emigrants	16	63	68	83	89
Total					
Regressados:					
Before	4	2	6	5	9
After	34	45	59	82	88
Non-emigrants	17	36	40	66	73

Source: Authors' questionnaire survey.

the secondary effects of the increased consumption by regressados are not confined to the locality, or even the country, as a large proportion of these goods are imported. For example, 60 per cent of regressados with televisions have imported sets compared with 50 per cent of non-migrants, and with motorcycles the difference is between 42 per cent imports amongst regressados and 27 per cent for other households.

If the general expenditure by returnees is apparently limited in its effects on regional development, many of the hopes that regressados can counter the increasing disparity between littoral and interior Portugal hang on the transformative power of their business investments. Hence Table 5.4 sets out details of the enterprises run by regressados in the sample for comparison with those of non-emigrants. The relatively high proportion of employers amongst

Table 5.4: Number, Employment Creation and Sectoral Distribution of <u>Regressado</u> Employers

	Employers as % Respondents	Total Employment	Mean Employment	Sectoral Distribution (%): Agriculture	Construction	Industry	Commerce
Fóios							
<u>Regressados</u>	21	11	1.8	50	17	0	33
Non-emigrants	6	3	1.5	--	--	--	--
Mangualde							
<u>Regressados</u>	16	11	1.8	17	0	0	83
Non-emigrants	10	12	2.4	--	--	--	--
Leiria							
<u>Regressados</u>	40	38	2.5	13	7	27	53
Non-emigrants	11	11	2.7	--	--	--	--
Total							
<u>Regressados</u>	29	60	2.2	22	7	15	55
Non-emigrants	9	26	2.4	--	--	--	--

Source: Authors' questionnaire survey.

Table 5.5: Specific Forms of Investment by Retornados and Non-emigrants (%)

	Land	Housing	Business	Car	Repay Loan
Mangualde					
Retornados	4	28	34	79	0
Non-emigrants	5	62	31	72	0
Leiria					
Retornados	21	67	38	55	7
Non-emigrants	21	48	34	72	0
Total					
Retornados	12	47	36	67	3
Non-emigrants	13	55	33	72	0

Source: Authors' questionnaire survey.

regressados, rising to 40 per cent in Leiria, has already been commented upon and is an initially encouraging sign. Yet if attention is turned to the number of jobs involved in each enterprise, the record is less impressive. Amongst both regressados and non-migrants the mean size of enterprise is little over 2 persons, usually meaning the owner and spouse. Furthermore, the type of business created by regressados tends to be in commerce or conform with the existing activity mix. Only in Leiria is there any investment in industrial production or in larger-than-family establishments, which suggests that the objective circumstances facing returnees in rural and small town economic environments are such that an industrial investment would not be viable.[3]

By and large the results of retornados' expenditure appear to be the same. Their general investment pattern (Table 5.5) has more similarities with that of the control group than differences. The obvious divergence between localities over housing investment, low (28 per cent) in Mangualde but high (67 per cent) in Leiria, is readily explained in terms of the extent of housing available through families to each set of returnees. Cars are more important to retornados that regressados, in keeping with the big difference in status while the two groups were emigrants, and the higher proportion of retornados investing in business also makes sense in light of their experiences prior to return.

Table 5.6: Number, Employment Creation and Sectoral Distribution of _Retornado_ Employers

	Employers as % Respondents	Total Employment	Mean Employment	Sectoral Distribution (%): Agriculture	Construction	Industry	Transport	Commerce
Mangualde								
Retornados	17	16	2.0	0	0	0	12	87
Non-emigrants	10	12	2.4	-	-	-	-	-
Leiria								
Retornados	32	55	3.2	0	6	35	0	59
Non-emigrants	11	11	2.8	-	-	-	-	-
Total								
Retornados	25	71	2.8	0	4	24	4	68
Non-emigrants	10	23	2.6	-	-	-	-	-

Source: Authors' questionnaire survey.

Unfortunately the detailed data collected on consumption goods for <u>retornados</u> is unreliable because so much was lost by some of them in the flight from Luanda, so the examination of their economic impact has to continue with a closer look at their business investments (Table 5.6). Once again, a high proportion of returned emigrants (25 per cent) appear to have become employers, as against the 10 per cent of non-migrants, and the bulk of the jobs associated with their enterprises are also in Leiria. The impact of <u>retornados</u>' investments, in some cases helped by special credit from the government, is greater in the area which is already growing more rapidly, for the limited number of Mangualde employers are concentrated in small-scale commercial activities while in Leiria there is investment in industry (35 per cent of <u>retornados</u>' firms) and a higher mean size of establishment.

Neither the <u>regressados</u> nor <u>retornados</u> seem to be significantly changing the development prospects of the regions to which they have returned. Some consumption linkages do exist, especially to the construction industry, but these are reduced by the high import content of expenditure on goods. The other obvious mechanism of 'spread' from the emigrants' households is their investment in business and, although this is at a higher level than amongst non-emigrants, this does not effect a transformation in the productive structure nor affect a large number of job seekers. Despite the changes in the banking system aimed at encouraging the productive use of migrant remittances in the regions of origin in Portugal, there is still a long way to go before their full potential is realised.

CONCLUSIONS

Both international emigration and regional inequality are long-standing features of Portuguese economy and society and the evidence reviewed here indicates that they continue as mutually reinforcing trends. The lack of opportunity in the poorer regions of the North and Centre of the country has meant that emigration provides one of the few means of self-advancement, but the beneficial effects of this for the households involved are not dispersed widely enough to present sufficient opportunities for the next generation. Even with the current inflow of remittances into the interior of the country, it is difficult to see this long-standing pattern changing for returnees, quite understandably, place the comfort and financial security of their household before that of their community. This means that their economic instincts are to 'swim with the tide' by recognising what is realistic in a given economic environment and behaving much as non-emigrants in the locality. For those regressados or retornados who plan to use their experience and savings in more original ways than the circumstances of a village or small town permit, there is clearly the option of migration to one of the more dynamic environments in the littoral region.

In this respect Portuguese returned emigrants are little different from those studied in other parts of the world; but it is important -- to return to the point made in the introduction to this chapter -- to recognise the variety that lies beneath such generalities. In particular, it is clear that the type of emigration that has been undertaken is an influence on subsequent behaviour, as several of the comparisons between retornados and regressados have shown. This suggests that some caution is needed in transferring lessons on return migrant behaviour from the Southern European evidence to, say, Central American or South Asian labour-exporting countries. Secondly, at a number of points we have drawn attention to the economic similarities between returnees and non-emigrants and it is important to recognise these for they reveal the limitations of treating all returnee behaviour as if it is affected by emigration. A closer specification of these similarities (e.g. in expenditure patterns) and of the differences (e.g. in terms of enterprise ownership) will help reduce the expectations that have been placed on regressados and retornados in areas with already poor economic prospects. Finally, there is the importance of the locality as an influence on the impact of returned emigrants. Even though areas with some dynamism were chosen for this study, it is evident that the positive contribution to the development of the regional economies was greatest in the city (Leiria) which was already growing rapidly. It should come as no surprise that regressados return to their village essentially to retire or run their small farms, while others prefer to invest in industrial firms only where there is an expanding market. Yet without a recognition of the influence of the existing structure on individuals' economic behaviour (and the other types of variety noted above), the well-intentioned policies to harness the economic potential of returning emigrants

in the development of the poor regions will have no
more effect in the future than they have so far.

NOTES

    1. The concelho is the basic unit of local
government in Portugal. The 274 concelhos of mainland or continental Portugal have populations ranging from some 2,000 (Barrancos) to over 800,000
(Lisbon). The distrito is the administrative unit
between the concelhos and central government. There
are 18 distritos in mainland Portugal, each approximately the size of an English county and with between 140,000 (Portalegre) and 2,060,000 (Lisbon)
inhabitants.
    2. The study is limited to the administrative
area of the região centro as it was funded by the
Comissão de Coordenação da Região Centro. Invaluable support was given to us by its President,
Dr. Manuel Porto, and by our co-directors, Drs.
Isabel Boura and Rui Jacinto.
    3. During a pilot survey near Fóios we did
interview a regressado who had brought back from
Paris the equipment he had built up in his business
supplying car parts to Renault. His new business
involved the fabrication of the same parts under sub-
contract to one of Renault's Portuguese assembly
works a few kilometres away in Guarda. However,
this example of a kind of rural industrialisation
was not repeated.

REFERENCES

Arroteia, J.C. (1983) A Emigração Portuguesa,
    Instituto de Cultura e Lingua Portuguesa.
Baklanoff, E.N. (1979) 'The political economy of
    Portugal's old regime: growth and change pre-
    ceding the 1974 Revolution', World Development,
    7, pp. 799-811.
Boura, I.M.R., Jacinto, R., Lewis, J.R. and
    Williams, A.M. (1984) 'The economic impact of
    returned emigrants', in Emigração e Retorno na
    Região Centro, Comissão de Coordenação da
    Região Centro, Coimbra, pp. 63-116.
Brettell, C.B. (1979) 'Emigrar para voltar: a
    Portuguese ideology of return migration',
    Papers in Anthropology, 20(1), pp. 1-20.
Castillo Castillo J. (1981) La Emigración Española
    en la Encrucijada, Centro de Investigaciones
    Sociologicas, Madrid.

Castles, S., Booth, H. and Wallace, T. (1984) Here
    for Good: Western Europe's New Ethnic Minori-
    ties, Pluto Press, London.
Connell, J. (1980) Remittances and Rural Development:
    Migration, Dependency and Inequality in the
    South Pacific, Australian National University,
    Development Studies Centre, Occasional Paper
    22, Canberra.
Ferrão, J. and Jensen-Butler, C. (1984) 'The centre-
    periphery model and industrial development in
    Portugal', Society and Space, 2, pp. 375-402.
Ferreira, F.S. (1976) Origens e Formas da Emigração,
    Iniciativas Editorias, Lisbon.
Gilani, I., Khan, M.F. and Iqbal, M. (1981) Labour
    Migration from Pakistan to the Middle East and
    its Impact on the Domestic Economy, Pakistan
    Institute of Development Economics, Research
    Reports 126-128, Islamabad.
Hudson, R. and Lewis, J.R. (1985) 'Recent economic,
    political and social change in Southern Europe',
    in R. Hudson and J.R. Lewis (eds.) Uneven
    Development in Southern Europe, Methuen,
    London, pp. 1-53.
King, R.L. (1984) 'Population mobility: emigration,
    return migration and internal migration', in
    A.M. Williams (ed.) Southern Europe Transformed,
    Harper and Row, London, pp. 145-178.
Lewis, J.R. and Williams, A.M. (1981) 'Regional un-
    even development on the European periphery:
    the case of Portugal 1950-1978', Tijdschrift
    voor Economische en Sociale Geografie, 72,
    pp. 81-98.
Lewis, J.R. and Williams, A.M. (1985) 'Portugal:
    the decade of return', Geography, 70, pp. 178-
    182.
Macedo, J. and Serfaty, S. (eds.) (1981) Portugal
    since the Revolution, Westview Press, Boulder.
Porto, M. (1984) 'Portugal: twenty years of change',
    in A.M. Williams (ed.) Southern Europe Trans-
    formed, Harper and Row, London, pp. 84-112.
Rhoades, R.E. (1978) 'Intra-European return migration
    and rural development: lessons from the
    Spanish case', Human Organization, 37, pp. 136-
    147.
Silva, M., Amaro, R.R., Clausse, G., Conim, C.,
    Matos, M., Pisco, M. and Seruya, L.M. (1984)
    Retorno, Emigração e Desenvolvimento Regional
    em Portugal, Instituto de Estudios de Desenvol-
    vimento, Lisbon.

Toepfer, H. (1985) 'The economic impact of returned
    emigrants in Trabazon, Turkey', in R. Hudson
    and J.R. Lewis (eds.) Uneven Development in
    Southern Europe, Methuen, London, pp. 76-100.
Trinidade, M.B.R. (1976) 'Comunidades emigrantes em
    situação dipolar', Analise Social, 48, pp. 983-
    997.
Unger, K.(1983) Die Rückkehr der Arbeitsemigraten,
    Brietenbach, Saarbrucken and Fort Lauderdale.
Williams, A.M. (1984) 'Introduction', in A.M.
    Williams (ed.) Southern Europe Transformed,
    Harper and Row, London, pp. 1-29.

Chapter Six

RETURN MIGRATION AND REGIONAL CHARACTERISTICS: THE
CASE OF GREECE

Klaus Unger

As emigration (especially the European case of
labour migration) can primarily be defined as a reaction of the individual towards certain factors of
his or her surroundings, it is worthwhile seeing to
what extent the pattern of return migration is being
affected by the areas of destination (of the returnees) and of origin (of the out-migrants).   The
secondary data reported in this chapter were collected from the different sources of the National
Statistical Service of Greece (especially the Popu-
laton and Housing Census in 1971), whereas the primary
data were generated from a field work period in
Greece in 1980 during which 574 male, married returnees from West Germany were interviewed in the
three cities of Athens (226), Salonica (217) and
Serres (131).[1]   The chapter is divided into three
sections.   I begin with an analysis of the secondary
data with respect to the various types of migration
(emigration, return migration and internal migration).   Secondly, aspects of the regional redistribution of the population through return migration
will be discussed on the basis of some of the
primary survey data.   Thirdly, the returnees interviewed will be classified on the basis of the
secondary data according to their place of origin,
and it will be shown in which way structural conditions in these places of origin are determining the
individual migration biographies.

EMIGRATION, RETURN AND THE REGIONAL STRUCTURE OF
GREECE: AN ANALYSIS OF SECONDARY DATA

According to official sources, a total of 296,789
migrants left Greece during the period 1970 to 1977,
58.1 per cent of them migrating to West Germany.

During the same period 189,512 migrants returned to
Greece, 61.5 per cent coming from West Germany.[2]
Looking at the shares of the various districts of
Greece in the total emigration and return migration
of the country, only a few districts show a share
equivalent to the share of the population of total
Greece. Districts in northern Greece and Epirus
have proportionately more emigrants than their
share of population. For example, the district of
Thesprotia has a share of only 0.4 per cent of the
total Greek population whereas 3.2 per cent of the
emigrants to West Germany during the period 1970-71
migrated from this district. In a quarter of the
districts the share of total returning migrants was
greater than their proportionate share of national
emigrants: thus, for example, Athens accounted for
7.3 per cent of emigrants to West Germany but 11.5
per cent of returnees from that country, and
Salonica's respective figures were 7.4 per cent and
12.8 per cent.
    Examination of the intensities of emigration
and return migration (i.e ratio of migrants 1970-77
in relation to the total population in 1971) shows
that the main areas of origin for emigrants to West
Germany are in northern, western and central Greece.
The highest figures are recorded in the northern
districts of Thesprotia (13.5 per cent for emigrants,
6.6 per cent for return migrants) and Drama (11.6
per cent for emigrants and 8.3 per cent for return
migrants). By contrast, most districts in southern
Greece and the islands recorded figures below 0.5
per cent for both out-movement to West Germany and
return. This regional picture remains substantially
unchanged when the figures and ratios for total
emigration (i.e. to all destination countries) and
total return are examined; this indicates that West
Germany was the most important element in the pattern of Greek external migration during the 1960s and
1970s. The only exception is that in the south (where
emigration intensity is low anyway) other destinations, primarily overseas, have greater importance
vis à vis West Germany.
    A 'remigration ratio' (the quotient of return
migration and emigration) was computed to characterise the regional choice of the returnees and to
indicate the migratory attractiveness of a district.
As regards the German migration stream, only three
of the total 52 districts (Athens, Salonica, and
Phocis) experienced more returnees than emigrants.
For all the other districts the migration process of
the 1970-77 period resulted in a net loss of

population. This result would be even clearer if
the figures for the 1960s were taken into account,
for then emigration to West Germany was much higher
than return migration. The mean remigration ratio
for all 52 districts is 66 returnees per 100 emigrants with respect to migration between Greece and
West Germany. For the total Greek migration the
ratio is only 54 returnees per 100 emigrants.
Migration not leading to West Germany (normally
transoceanic migration) normally implies a later or
more rare return whereas the German migration of the
1960s and 1970s shows a certain temporary character.
With respect to total migration no district experienced a return higher than the emigration!
    A study of the internal in-migration ratio
regional pattern tends to reveal a similar distribution to the external remigration ratio (especially
that from West Germany): the two big cities of
Athens and Salonica and their surroundings are the
districts which attract both international returnees
and internal in-migrants to the greatest extent.
    The following results are presented without
quoting the correlation coefficients to provide the
reader with a readable text. All the correlations
mentioned are significant on at least the 5 per cent
level; the reader is referred to Unger (1983) for a
detailed description of the coefficients. Several
indices of migration were computed:

EMITOT   - the intensity of emigration for total
           emigration, and for the German migration
           flow (EMITOTG);

REMTOT   - the remigration ratio (return migration in
           relation to emigration) again for total
           migration and for the German subcomponent
           (REMTOTG);

IMOUT   - the internal out-migration intensity;

IMRATIO - the internal in-migration ratio (in-
           migrants in relation to out-migrants)

The computation of the return migration intensity is
omitted because there is a high correlation with the
intensity of emigration.
    It was found that a high intensity of total
emigration is related to a high intensity of emigration to West Germany. This shows the importance of
West Germany for the Greek emigration process. As
there is a low remigration ratio from Germany in
districts with a high emigration intensity it can be

131

assumed that the districts of origin have a low
attractiveness for the returnees. This explanation
is supported by the fact that there is a low
internal in-migration ratio, too, in these districts.
Correspondingly, there is a strong and positive
correlation between the internal in-migration ratio
and the return migration ratio: districts with
strong attractiveness for internal migration have a
similar attraction in the course of the international
migration process. Thus it can be suggested that
internal in-migrants react towards the same characteristics of these districts as the external returnees.

On the other hand, a high international emigration intensity does not correlate with a high
internal out-migration intensity. This means that
different regional factors are responsible for these
two migration processes because there is no correlation between these two variables as far as a bivariate correlation is considered. Up to now, then,
there is no clear evidence for the hypothesis that
internal out-migration and international migration
are alternatives for the migrants. The results of
the field survey, however, show that internal out-
migration quite often was a step before migrating
abroad. When it is remembered that the survey was
carried out in cities, this suggests that emigration
abroad is only a step during a longer migration cycle
which starts by internal migration directed to the
cities.

The indices of migration, functioning as dependent variables, were then correlated with a
selection of 34 independent variables characterising
the following seven dimensions of the Greek regional socio-economic structure: regional distribution
of the population; urbanisation; housing; education;
standard of living; occupational structure of the
population; economic development. Unless explicitly
noted, all the following statements refer to the
indices of the total Greek migration as well as to
the German migration stream.

Those districts which experienced a higher increase of population during the period 1951-61 and a
higher decrease during the 1960s are characterised
by a higher intensity of emigration during the period
1970-77. This means that there was no real change
in the migration structure during the 1960s and 1970s
as the loss of the 1960s was primarily caused by
emigration. There is a higher emigration in districts with larger households but there is no direct
correlation between the intensity of emigration and
either the degree of urbanisation or the rural

132

character of a district. The age structure of the
population in districts with a higher intensity of
emigration shows the following characteristics: a
higher proportion of those aged under 15; a higher
proportion of those aged 15 to 24; a lower proportion of those aged 25 to 44; a lower proportion of
those aged 45 to 64 (only total emigration); a lower
proportion of those over 60.

A higher percentage of illiterates and persons
not having finished school as well as a lower proportion of persons with secondary education are the
essentials regarding the educational situation in
districts with heavy emigration. However, the standard of living and the housing conditions are generally not significant factors for emigration; only a
lower consumption of electric energy by private
households and a poor supply of teachers at secondary schools are relevant for districts with stronger
emigration.

The most important variables related to emigration are those on the occupational structure and
economic development of the districts. Thus we find
a higher rate of emigration in districts with a
lower proportion of dependent labour and employers.
Unemployment and underemployment are especially important factors for emigration and show that it is
a reaction towards the local labour market (Botsas
1970). Higher rates both of unemployment and underemployment of the male population and of all unemployed and underemployed together result in a
stronger emigration of people from the 'labour
reserve'. The same relationship holds where there
is heavy employment in the primary sector of the
economy and a lower proportion employed in the
secondary and tertiary sectors.

Only seldom is it necessary to differentiate
between the total and the Greece-Germany emigration.
This shows common factors influencing emigration in
general. With return migration, however, a common
pattern does not exist in all relationships.

Districts with a higher return migration ratio
during the period 1970 to 1977 are characterised by
a lower population decrease or a higher population
increase through the three decades 1951 to 1981 as
well as by a higher population density. A higher
Germany-Greece remigration ratio exists for districts
with larger households and a more urban population
(cf. also Lianos, 1975). As regards the age structure the high remigration districts show a lower
proportion of those under 15 years of age, but there
is no systematic pattern for the other age groups

either among total or Greece-Germany migration. A
higher total remigration ratio can be found along
with a higher proportion of those aged 15-24 and
25-44, whereas for the Germany-Greece remigration
there is no such significant correlation. However,
there is a higher percentage of those aged 45-64 in
districts with a higher remigration ratio from
Germany.

The appeal of different districts as possible
return migration destinations is shown, for instance,
by the educational situation; the remigration ratio
rises where the percentage of illiterates and persons not having finished school is less and where
the percentage of persons with completed secondary
education is higher. Living and housing conditions
of a district are also of great importance with
respect to the remigration ratio. This ratio is
found to rise when the percentage of households with
water-tap in the dwelling, with sewerage and with
electricity supply is higher; when the consumption
of electricity of the households is higher; when
more private cars are registered in a district; when
the supply of secondary school teachers is higher
(but only for Greece-Germany remigration); and when
the supply of physicians and hospitals is better.
These correlations show the importance of the infrastructural conditions of the districts in the course
of the return migration process.

Further, there is a correlation between the
remigration ratios and the occupational structure of
the districts. Return migration is stronger when
the percentage of dependent labour and of employers
is higher and the percentage of own-account workers
is lower. All these are characteristics of districts with a higher degree of urbanisation. There
is no significant relevance of unemployment and
underemployment as far as the total remigration
ratio is concerned, but there is a tendency for
districts with lower unemployment and underemployment (of the male population) to attract returnees
from West Germany.

Moreover, higher remigration ratios can be observed for districts with a higher intensity of
building activity and a lower percentage of economically actives in the primary sector and a higher
percentage in secondary and tertiary sectors of the
economy. Again, these are characteristics of urbanised districts.

As a result, on the basis of the bivariate
correlation analysis it can be formulated that returnees are attracted by more urbanised districts.

If internal migration is analysed as a special case,
then the same factors of the regional structure are
found to be determinant. This is perhaps obvious in
the fields of education standards and economic development. These two fields and the occupational
structure have the greatest impact on the emigration
intensity whereas for the remigration ratio and for
internal migration living and housing conditions
have to be added. The total remigration ratio and
the internal in-migration ratio show the same significant correlations with the structural variables.
On the other hand, it is obvious that different
correlation coefficients will result from splitting
the migration indices into the total migration and
the Greece-Germany migration indices.

In order to further enhance the meaning of the
factors so far identified as determining migration
processes, a multivariate analysis was carried out.
The set of 34 variables was first reduced to 26 to
provide a similar weighting of the seven dimensions
within the data set (viz. regional population distribution, urbanisation, housing, education, standard of living, occupational structure and economic
development). Indices of migration were not included in the analysis as the migration processes
are strongly represented in the variation of population (1951 to 1981), and such an inclusion would
have resulted in an overweighting of the dimension
'regional distribution of the population'. A
factor analysis, carried out according to the
varimax method, led to an extraction of five factors
and to a factor matrix which is documented in Table
6.1. The factors explain 77.7 per cent of the total
variance of the variables. Although factor V yields
a value below 1 the factor was left in the matrix,
following the rule that in case of doubt it is
better to include more factors than less.

The first factor represents 63 per cent of the
variance of the factor matrix and is characterised by
the variables of economic development and occupational structure. This factor is applicable for
districts with a higher intensity of building activity, a higher percentage of economically actives in
the secondary and tertiary sector and a lower percentage in the primary sector, a higher percentage
of dependent labour and employers and a lower percentage of own-account workers, a higher ratio of
registered private cars, a lower decrease of the
population during the 1960s and a higher increase
during the 1970s, and a higher proportion of persons
with secondary education. Thus this most important

135

Table 6.1: Varimax-rotated Factor Matrix with 26 Variables for 52 Districts of Greece (only loadings 0.40 and higher)

Variables	I	II	III	IV	V	h²
1. Regional Distribution						
POP5161			.82			.81
POP6171	.51		.51			.88
POP7181	.64		.40			.71
DENSITY		.74				.64
2. Urbanisation						
HHSIZE			.72			.61
URBAN		.61				.78
AGE1524			.73			.70
AGE65+			-.92			.91
3. Education						
NOEXAM					-.68	.65
SECEXAM	.46	.76				.96
SECPUPIL		.51			.74	.89
4. Housing						
WATERTAP				.76		.87
SEWERAGE				.57		.55
ELECTRIC				.78		.79
5. Standard of Living						
ENERGY		.76				.84
CAR	.49	.70				.93
SECTEACH			-.52		.59	.75
DOCTOR		.80				.81
6. Occupational Structure						
WAGE	.82	.46				.95
OWNACC	-.49	-.51				.77
EMPLOYER	.52					.39
LABRESERVE					-.59	.58
7. Economic Development						
BUILDING	.53		.50			.70
PRIM	-.85	-.43				.97
SEC	.85					.90
TERT	.64	.61				.86
Factor values	12.74	4.07	1.42	1.04	.92	
Variance explained	49.0	15.7	5.5	4.0	3.5	

List of Variable Names:

AGE1524   Proportion of population aged 15-24 in 1971

AGE65+   Proportion of population aged 65 and over in 1971

BUILDING   Change in the number of buildings 1961-71

Table 6.1 (cont'd)

CAR	Private cars in 1976 per households (1971)
DENSITY	Inhabitants per km² in 1971
DOCTOR	Physicans per inhabitant 1971
ELECTRIC	Proportion of households with electricity in 1971
EMPLOYER	Proportion of employers in economically active population in 1971
ENERGY	Consumption of electricity per household 1977
HHSIZE	Size of households (persons per household) 1971
LABRESERVE	Labour reserve (unemployed and underemployed as per cent of economically active population) 1971
NOEXAM	Proportion of persons not having finished school 1971
OWNACC	Proportion of own-account workers in economically active population 1971
POP5161	Population change 1951-61
POP6171	Population change 1961-71
POP7181	Population change 1971-81
PRIM	Proportion of economically active population in the primary sector 1971
SEC	Proportion of economically active population in the secondary sector 1971
SECEXAM	Proportion of population with secondary education 1971
SECPUPIL	Proportion of pupils at secondary schools 1975/76
SECTEACH	Secondary school teachers per population under 15 years old (1975/76)
SEWERAGE	Proportion of households with sewerage facilities 1971
TERT	Proportion of economically active population in the tertiary sector 1971
URBAN	Proportion of population living in places with 10,000 inhabitants and more (1971)
WAGE	Proportion of wage-earners (employees) in economically active population in 1971
WATERTAP	Proportion of households with running water inside their dwelling in 1971

factor of the Greek regional structure is named
socio-economic standard of development and the
variables under discussion are relevant for more
urbanised districts.

The factor yielding a further 20 per cent of
the variance can easily be identified as urbanisation as this factor shows high loadings on the
variables of population density and degree of urbanisation. Factor II also applies to districts characterised by a higher standard of living (as
measured by private consumption of electricity,
registration of private cars and medical standards),
a higher standard of education, and partly by some
of the variables which are already represented by
factor I.

Compared to the first two, the remaining
factors are clearly less important. Factor III
explains only 7 per cent of the variance and represents the demographic dimensions. This factor
includes a higher increase of population growth for
all three decades, large households, and a higher
percentage of people aged 15-24 and a lower percentage of those over 64. Together with the increase of
population a higher intensity of building activity
can be identified. Thus factor III can be named
population development; again the variables indicate
urbanisation.

Urban characteristics are also clearly represented by factor IV which describes the standard of
housing of the districts. Only the three variables
of this dimension show loads on this factor -- and
only on this factor.

The fifth factor, like factor IV, representing
only 5 per cent of the variance explained, describes
the educational and employment opportunities. A
greater labour reserve, less secondary school teachers, a higher percentage of persons not having
finished school, and a lower percentage of secondary
school pupils are the relevant variables here.

The matrix of factors presented shows the
strong determination of the Greek regional structure
by variables of socio-economic development and urbanisation. Four of the five factors identified are
clearly related to urban conditions. As the first
factor represents the most important details of the
regional structure in Greece (including urbanisation)
only this factor and factor V will be considered for
the purposes of the survey analysis (see below). To
confirm the results presented so far the set of
variables was reduced once again and a multiple
regression analysis of the migration processes was

computed.

This last step of the analysis of the secondary data will present regression equations for the different migration processes discussed so far. Fourteen variables from the total set were considered independent variables whose selection was determined by the intention to represent the several dimensions of the regional structure and the five factors of the matrix to a most typical extent. These fourteen variables were as follows (for the explanation of the variable names see Table 6.1): POP5161, URBAN, AGE1524, AGE65+, NOEXAM, SECPUPIL, ELECTRIC, CAR, SECTEACH, DOCTOR, WAGE, LABRESERVE, BUILDING, and PRIM.

The different indices of migration were correlated stepwise in a multiple regression analysis with the 14 independent variables; various variables were eliminated from the model on the basis of significance criteria (standard deviation of the regression coefficient, F-value, multiple collinearity); and the regression equations were calculated again until the procedure resulted in statistically valuable expressions. The equations presented below are significant at the 1 per cent level and exceed the critical value (r^2) for multiple correlation at the same significance level. The coefficients of the regressors represent the weighted beta-coefficients.

The calculations resulted in the following equation for the total emigration intensity:

$$\text{EMITOT} = -1.73 \text{ WAGE} - 1.66 \text{ PRIM} + 0.67 \text{ NOEXAM} + 0.37 \text{ POP5161}$$

(F = 10.57, df. 4/47, multiple collinearity 0.06, r^2 = 0.47)

Correspondingly the intensity of emigration in the 1970s rises with a lower proportion of wage earners and a higher proportion of persons having finished school and a higher increase of population during the 1950s. These characteristics are also true for districts with a higher labour reserve which means that this variable, which had to be eliminated because of high multiple collinearity, is represented meaningfully in the equation. The surprising result -- that a lower proportion of those economically active in the primary sector leads to a higher intensity of emigration -- can be explained by the circumstance that districts with a lower proportion of farmers are also affected by emigration, and by the fact that such districts are not clearly identified by other variables. By the way, there is no significant bivariate correlation between the

the variables URBAN and EMITOT, which also means
that it is not only rural districts that are affected by emigration. The regression equation for the
Greece-Germany emigration intensity shows only
slight differences from that just described:

EMITOTG = -1.69 WAGE - 1.55 PRIM + 0.62 NOEXAM + 0.52 POP5161

(F = 14.18 df. 4/47, multiple collinearity 0.05, r^2 = 0.55)

Unlike the case of the emigration intensity
where the direction of the bivarate correlation with
the variable PRIM changed, the regression equations
of the remigration ratios are consistent with the
bivariate correlations. The two equations read as
follows:

REMTOT = 0.50 ELECTRIC + 0.40 DOCTOR - 0.27 SECTEACH

(F = 16.55, df. 3/48, multiple collinearity 0.11, r^2 = 0.52)

REMTOTG = 0.49 ELECTRIC + 0.40 AGE65+ + 0.34 DOCTOR

(F = 16.55, df. 3/48, multiple collinearity 0.04, r^2 = 0.51)

Both equations demonstrate the higher attractiveness
of districts with good housing infrastructure (as
measured by electricity supply) and supply of doctors, whilst the negative value for secondary school
teachers in the total remigration ratio equation
indicates that in some cases returnees go back to
unfavourably developed areas of origin.

The multiple regression analysis with the indices of internal migration being the dependent
variables resulted in the situation noted earlier
that internal migration is determined by the districts' living standards. Thus, while international
emigration is mainly caused by factors of the local
labour market, the internal out-migrants are mainly
interested to move to a district with a higher
standard of living. A higher car registration
index and better medical and energy supply in a
district imply a lower intensity of out-migration and
a higher internal in-migration ratio. On the other
hand, a better supply of secondary school teachers
may result in a higher out-migration intensity.
This can be explained by the fact that in areas of
poor infrastructure the teacher-population ratio for
those aged under 15 is quite favourable because of a
lack of those under this age (this interpretation
might also be used for the impact of this variable
in the equation of the remigration ratio noted
above). As regards the internal in-migration ratio
a strengthening effect can be found through an

increase of population during the 1950s which shows
that the structure of the internal Greek migration
process did not basically change. Thus the following
two regression equations were computed:

IMOUT = -0.46 ELECTRIC - 0.37 CAR + 0.29 SECTEACH

(F = 18.08, df. 3/48, multiple collinearity 0.19, r^2 = 0.53)

IMRATIO = 0.52 CAR + 0.36 DOCTOR + 0.11 POP5161

(F = 65.63, df. 3/48, multiple collinearity 0.91, r^2 = 0.80)

Although the last equation delivers plausible ex-
planations it has to be rejected because of substantial multiple collinearity: the variable CAR
would itself explain 75.1 per cent of the variance
of the in-migration ratio and the variable DOCTOR
by itself would explain 66.8 per cent. This means
that computing multiple correlations in this case
does not result in a significant benefit of explanation in comparison to the variable CAR alone. Apart
from this rejection it should be pointed out that
all the other equations show very little multiple
collinearity.
     Summarising this analysis of the secondary data
on Greek migration and regional economic structure,
it can be stated that Greek emigration is primarily
a reaction of the migrants towards conditions of the
local labour market, whereas the return from abroad
and also the internal migration are determined by
the standard of living in a district. These characteristics are clearly related to the degree of
urbanisation of the districts and internal in-
migration as well as international return migration
are influenced in the same way by the various
factors. Thus the following two hypotheses are
supported: that the return from abroad may be the
last step of a combined internal-international
migration cycle originally directed into the cities;
and that the Greek migration of the 1960s and the
1970s has worked to strengthen the process of
urbanisation of the country.

PRIMARY SURVEY DATA

It is now obvious that in the course of the migration cycle, a regional redistribution of the population takes place as the return to Greece is often
the final step in what is primarily a rural-urban
migration. Switching over to the survey results and

Table 6.2: Domicile during First 15 years of Life and Prior
to Emigration, by Current Domicile (figures column per cent)

	Current Domicile		
First 15 years of life	Athens	Salonica	Serres
Athens	15.7	--	--
Salonica	0.5	21.3	0.8
Serres	5.1	1.9	60.3
other urban places	13.4	16.7	3.1
semi-urban places	16.1	19.9	16.8
rural places	49.3	40.3	19.1
(n =)	(217)	(216)	(131)
Prior to emigration			
Athens	48.6	0.9	5.3
Salonica	1.4	42.6	2.3
Serres	2.3	0.9	71.8
other urban places	7.7	13.0	0.8
semi-urban places	10.9	14.8	11.5
rural places	29.1	27.8	8.4
(n =)	(220)	(216)	(131)

Note: urban places: 10,000 and more inhabitants
       semi-urban places: 2,000 - 9,999 inhabitants
       rural places: less than 2,000 inhabitants

Source: Author's survey.

examining the origin of the returnees interviewed,
the significant differences between Athens and
Salonica on the one hand and Serres on the other are
obvious. Only 15.7 per cent of those returning to
Athens had spent most of their first 15 years of
life there. In Salonica the proportion was 21.3 per
cent but in Serres it was 60.3 per cent (see Table
6.2). Nearly half the emigrants returning to Athens
grew up in a rural area, and prior to emigration 29.1
per cent had lived in communities with less than
2,000 inhabitants. The proportion of respondents in
Athens who had already lived in Athens prior to emigration is 48.6 per cent. In Salonica 42.6 per cent
had already lived there. But in Serres only 28.6
per cent of the returnees had not lived there before.
Of Table 6.2's total of 567 returning migrants, 51

per cent returned to the place they had left, but
this overall figure is somewhat misleading due to
the above-mentioned differences between the large
cities and Serres.

The noticeable increase of those living in the
three cities prior to emigration in comparison with
those who had grown up in the cities supports the
chain migration hypothesis of the 'rural-urban-
abroad-urban' migration process. Even Serres, as a
medium-sized town, exercises a certain attraction
towards people from rural and semi-urban areas,
though this attraction remains largely confined to
the surrounding area: of the 47 emigrants returning
to Serres who had not grown up in an urban area, 34
spent their first 15 years of life in the district
of Serres (though not in Serres town itself); and of
26 returnees now living in Serres who prior to emigration had not lived in urban areas 20 had lived in
the district of Serres. Grouping all this together
for the entire district, 87 per cent of the respondents in Serres had lived in or around Serres prior
to emigration! It is also interesting to note that
7.6 per cent of respondents in Serres had lived in
Salonica or Athens prior to emigration, whereas only
0.8 per cent had lived in these cities during their
first 15 years of life. This points to a further
variation of the migration process, namely the case
of migration from smaller cities or rural areas to
the big cities, followed (perhaps after experiencing
failures there) by emigration abroad and then a
return to the home town or district.

Numerous migrants also initially return to
their rural villages and then move on to a Greek
city after experiencing problems of reintegration in
a small settlement. Of all respondents 39.3 per
cent mentioned that they had heard of such cases in
their city and 8.4 per cent explained that relatives
of theirs had undertaken such a migration path. In
Serres, especially interesting in this context because of its rural surroundings, the figures rose to
60.3 per cent and 12.2 per cent respectively. On
the other hand, due to the design of this survey,
based primarily on records of returnees re-entering
the three cities directly from abroad, only 2.1 per
cent of the respondents claimed not to have moved to
their current domicile immediately after their
return.

Considering the regions from which non-native
returnees to Athens and Salonica originated (and who
therefore came to these cities either as internal
migrants prior to emigration or in the course of

Table 6.3: Choice of Domicile after Return, by Length of Stay
Abroad (figures row per cent; n = 574)

| | Current Domicile | | |
Length of stay	Same as prior to emigration	Other than prior to emigration	n
below 9 years	69.4	30.6	(170)
9 to 13 years	46.6	53.4	(178)
above 13 years	40.7	59.3	(226)

chi-square = 34.00, d.f. 4, p < 0.001

Source: Author's survey.

their return from Germany), a noticeable difference
between the two cities becomes apparent. Of 170
respondents who had not grown up in Salonica but who
live there now, 80.6 per cent came from Macedonia
and a further 13.5 per cent from Thrace. By contrast, the distribution of the origins of the 188
returnees who had not grown up in Athens is spread
all over Greece though there are concentrations from
Epirus (23.9 per cent), the Peloponnesos (18.1 per
cent), and Macedonia (17.6 per cent) which correspond with the tendencies of regional movements shown
in internal Greek migration.
      It can also be observed among migrants return-
ing to their pre-emigration domicile that 46.1 per
cent were emigrants from the wave following the
1966/67 West German recession. This group represents only 25.6 per cent of the total sample who
changed domicile. This points to the relationship
that the longer the stay abroad, the less likely the
migrant is to return to his pre-emigration place of
residence (see Table 6.3).
      The problem of regional redistribution of the
population through return migration can be summarised as follows:

   1.   Barely half the returnees in Athens and
        only 42.6 per cent of those in Salonica had
        ever lived in these cities prior to emigra-
        tion. The return migration process in
        Greece therefore stresses urbanisation, at
        least in these two cities.

2. Smaller cities (e.g. Serres) mainly take in returning migrants who had lived there before.
3. Athens draws returnees who have emigrated from all parts of Greece (similar to its attraction for internal migration). One in five returnees in Athens originally came from Epirus. The Peleponnesos and Macedonia are also areas of special relevance.
4. Salonica's attraction is limited almost exclusively to the surrounding regions of Macedonia and Thrace.
5. Smaller cities such as Serres are actually only significant as a place of return among those coming from the surrounding region and from that district (nomos) specifically.

The following facts must also be stressed: among respondents in Athens and Salonica none had lived or grown up in any one of the other five cities in Greece with a population (in 1971) of more than 50,000 (Patras, Volos, Iraklion, Larissa, Chania). This may indicate that cities with populations greater than 50,000 are in a position to draw back emigrants from those cities upon their eventual return and not to 'lose' them to other cities. Athens, Salonica, and the five cities mentioned above made up 75.3 per cent of Greece's urban population in 1971 and there does not seem to be any 'competition' among them in terms of attracting returning migrants who had lived there prior to emigration.

CONCLUDING DISCUSSION

At this point reference is again made to the results of the factor analysis presented earlier. Factor values of Greece's 52 districts including factor I (socio-economic development) and factor V (educational and employment opportunities) were computed to establish a classification of the migrants according to where they lived prior to emigration. Prior to emigration, 39.4 per cent of those surveyed lived in districts with a low, 19.4 per cent in medium, and 41.2 per cent in high levels of socio-economic development. In terms of the educational and employment situation, 37.3 per cent of the respondents emigrated from places with a low level, 18.5 per cent from middle and 44.2 per cent from high. The

Table 6.4: Educational and Employment Opportunities, by
Socio-economic Level of the Migrants' Districts of Origin
(figures row per cent; n = 573)

Level of Socio-economic Development	Educational and Employment Opportunities		
	low	medium	high
low	83.6	25.5	7.9
medium	13.6	71.7	2.4
high	2.8	2.8	89.7
(n = 573)	(214)	(106)	(253)

chi-square = 625.49, d.f. 4, p < 0.001.

Source: Author's survey

distribution leads to the assumption that these
factors are correlated. Table 6.4 confirms this.
The two variables will now be correlated with a
selection of variables to study the meaning of the
structural conditions in the area of origin in the
light of the characteristics of the returnees (keeping in mind that the two variables are correlated to
each other as documented in Table 6.4).

      Among respondents who lived in districts of low
socio-economic development prior to emigration, the
father more frequently (52.4 per cent of cases)
worked as a farmer. The percentage from middle
levels is 45 and from high levels 39. A similar
distribution is seen among the occupations practised
by the migrant himself prior to emigration. The
percentage of farmers among migrants in the least
developed areas was 18.1, in areas on a middle level
10.8, and only 1.7 in highly developed areas. Furthermore, a greater proportion of farmers were
amongst the migrants originating from districts with
poor educational and employment opportunities: 16.8
per cent for low, 12.3 per cent for medium, and 3.2
per cent for high levels. Among respondents having
statistically greater employment opportunities in
their district of origin, a substantially higher percentage had worked as wage-earners prior to emigration (83.8 per cent among the high, 76.6 per cent
middle, and 67.5 per cent low). This again points
to self-employment as a solution to the employment
misery. In areas with relatively better employment

146

opportunities, unemployment prior to emigration was significantly less frequent than in middle and low opportunity areas together (32.2 per cent versus 42.1 per cent). Not surprisingly, respondents from the latter two areas more frequently named unemployment as a reason for emigration. Those surveyed from districts with poor educational and employment opportunities did not have a clear picture of how long they intended to stay abroad: 51.5 per cent of them emigrated for an indefinite period compared with 43.3 per cent of those respondents from middle districts and 38.4 per cent of those from low ones.

Respondents emigrating from districts with low or medium socio-economic development were twice as likely to have worked in construction upon their arrival in Germany (12.9 per cent of respondents) as those coming from highly developed districts (6.4 per cent). This difference does not, however, exist for the last position held in Germany though emigrants from the most advanced areas were more often (13.1 per cent) represented in the service sector than those from the relatively less advanced areas (7.4 per cent). The tendency was for a migrant from a highly developed area to become a skilled worker or salaried employee (24.4 per cent compared to 15.2 per cent from least developed) rather than work as an unskilled worker (25.6 per cent versus 33.2 per cent). Furthermore, only two-thirds of the wives of those from the most developed districts worked during the entire stay abroad compared with over three-quarters of those from the less developed districts.

Respondents from areas with poor educational and employment opportunities sent savings home on a monthly basis less frequently (21.6 per cent as against 29.5 per cent for those from areas with the best opportunities) and were more likely to have left children in Greece for whose living expenses the remittances were intended. This also helps to explain why respondents from areas of high opportunity more frequently used their transferred funds to build or buy a house (49.7 per cent versus 35.3 per cent for low).

After having discussed some aspects of the period prior to emigration and of the stay abroad with reference to the structural conditions of migrants' districts of origin, the effects on return migration and reintegration can now be examined. As noted above, migrants from areas with poor educational and employment opportunities were more likely to have left their children in Greece. Children,

therefore, are also more frequently cited in these
areas as a reason for returning to Greece (28.5 per
cent, compared with 17.9 per cent for respondents
in middle opportunity areas and 11.5 per cent for
those in high opportunity areas). Migrants from the
least developed districts were more likely to judge
that their lives improved in the course of emigration (92.4 per cent) and since their return (38.5
per cent) than migrants coming from the most
developed areas (82.8 per cent and 25.8 per cent
respectively). Nevertheless, the latter group tends
to be somewhat more strongly inclined (58.5 per cent)
than those from the more developed areas (53.9 per
cent) to re-emigrate to Germany if given the chance.
This may be because although they were able to improve their plight it was not as much of an improvement as they had hoped for. Therefore a second,
limited stay abroad is thought necessary.[3]

Sixty-two per cent of those surveyed from areas
with high or middle employment opportunities work as
wage-earners (low level: 52.9 per cent), which may
partly be due to their being employed as such prior
to emigration as well. Respondents from high areas
work more frequently (41.7 per cent) within industry
other than construction (cf. 35.9 per cent middle
and 30.8 per cent low opportunity), and less frequently in private services (39.4 per cent; cf.
middle 43.5 per cent, low 48.1 per cent). Although
45.6 per cent of migrants from least developed areas
(compared with 32.1 per cent of those from more
developed areas) claim to have substantially improved their income in comparison to the time before
emigration, it was found that they are overrepresented among low income households and underrepresented
in high income households (which alludes to how low
their incomes must have been prior to emigration).

Though respondents from the least developed
socio-economic areas tend to have a lower household
income, it is important to note that their household is less likely to have less than 4 persons (21.2
per cent of cases) than those from a higher level
(32.6 per cent) and is more likely to have more than
4 persons (27.9 per cent, cf. high level 16.9 per
cent). This finding can be traced back to the
greater frequency of the 'extended family' (16.8 of
respondents in low level areas, 10.2 per cent in
high). These returnees do, however, live in larger
dwellings (as measured by number of rooms), but only
50.4 per cent of dwellings in low level areas have
central heating (cf. 72.3 per cent in high). This
situation is certainly influenced by the returnees

Table 6.5: Respondents' Place of Living, by Socio-economic
Level of the Migrants' Districts of Origin (figures row per
cent; n = 573)

Place of Living	Level of Socio-economic Development			
	low	medium	high	n
Athens	15.6	31.1	53.3	(225)
Salonica	33.6	18.0	48.4	(217)
Serres	90.1	1.5	8.4	(131)

Chi-square = 202.30, d.f. 4; p < 0.001

Source: Author's survey.

in Serres who prior to emigration already lived in
a low-level district and then returned to their
more spartan living quarters. Respondents from
least developed districts are also less likely to
own a car (42.9 per cent, as against 56.8 per cent
in high-level districts).
      Table 6.5 portrays the structure of the sub-
samples in the three cities according to the socio-
economic level of development of the districts
where the interviewees lived before emigration. The
data reveal that the sample in Athens has the smallest number of emigrants from least developed areas
whereas such persons play a more substantial role in
Salonica. The large percentage of migrants from
highly developed districts in Athens and Salonica
can mainly be explained by the large number of
emigrants who already lived in these cities prior to
emigration. This same explanation also accounts for
the high percentage of migrants from least developed
areas in Serres.
      In summary, the level of socio-economic develop-
ment and the educational and employment opportunities in the areas of the migrants' origin plays a
significant role influencing the current situation
of the migrant. Respondents from less developed
districts (who tend to have less schooling) more
frequently resort to self-employment. They also
have smaller incomes and live in larger, though less
fully equipped, dwellings than those respondents who
lived in highly developed districts prior to emigration. Therefore, it can be assumed that the return
is associated with more problems for the former

group. This assumption is reflected in the stronger tendency to probably emigrate again if given the
chance. A higher level of development in the area
of origin therefore assists the re-integration process of the returnee. The data presented in this
chapter clearly suggest that the regional structural
characteristics of Greece are affecting the biographies of the migrants to a larger extent than the
reverse process.

NOTES

1. The research, carried out at Bielefeld
University during 1979-81, was supported by the
Volkswagen Foundation. The full results of this
research, including details of research design, etc.,
are published in German in Unger (1983); for brief
English language accounts of certain aspects of this
research not covered in the present chapter, see
Unger (1981; 1984).
2. For the general background to postwar
Greek emigration see Lianos (1979) and Papademetriou
(1979).
3. In their biographical study of 15 returnees
in Athens, Bernard and Ashton-Vouyoucalos (1976)
find considerable ambivalence in returnees' views of
the relative desirability of staying on in Greece or
re-emigrating.

REFERENCES

Bernard, H.R. and Ashton-Vouyoucalos, S. (1976)
    'Return migration to Greece', Journal of the
    Steward Anthropological Society 8(1), pp. 31-
    51.
Botsas, E. (1970) 'Some economic aspects of short-
    run Greek labour emigration to Germany',
    Weltwirtschaftliches Archiv, 105, pp. 163-173.
Lianos, T.P. (1975) 'Flows of Greek out-migration
    and return migration', International Migration,
    13(3), pp. 119-133.
Lianos, T.P. (1979) 'Greece', in D. Kubat (ed.) The
    Politics of Migration Policies, Center for
    Migration Studies, New York, pp. 209-218.
Papademetriou, D. (1979) 'Greece' in R.E. Krane (ed.)
    International Labor Migration in Europe,
    Praeger, New York, pp. 187-200.
Unger, K. (1981) 'Greek emigration to and return mi-
    gration from West Germany', Ekistics, 290,
    pp. 369-374.

Unger, K. (1983) Die Rückkehr der Arbeitsemigranten:
    Eine Studie zur Remigration nach Griechenland,
    Breitenbach, Saarbrucken and Fort Lauderdale.
Unger, K. (1984) 'Occupational profile of returnees
    in three Greek cities', in D. Kubat (ed.) The
    Politics of Return: International Return
    Migration in Europe, Centro Studi Emigrazione,
    Rome, pp. 93-99.

Chapter Seven

THE READJUSTMENT OF RETURN MIGRANTS IN WESTERN
IRELAND

George Gmelch

This chapter examines the readjustment that Irish
return migrants experience in re-settling in small
communities in western Ireland.[1] Some students of
return migration have suggested that because returnees are familiar with their destination and are
likely to have friends and relatives living there,
the barriers to and psychic costs of returning will
be lower than for individuals arriving for the first
time (for a review see Bovenkerk,1974; Gmelch,1980).
Moreover, if there is a degree of learning-by-
experience associated with migration, then persons
who have emigrated at least once should find it
easier to move again. The Irish case described
below, however, presents a very different picture.
Some migrants do readjust quickly and encounter few
problems; even after many years' absence they appear
to pick up where they left off as though they had
never been away. But many migrants are unhappy and
disillusioned. While they are often economically
better off than their neighbours, they are disappointed and sometimes bitter about life in their
homeland.

THE SETTING AND OUT-MIGRATION

The eight western counties (Cork, Kerry, Clare,
Galway, Mayo, Sligo, Leitrim and Donegal) in which
this study was conducted constitute the poorest and
least developed region of Ireland. The area is predominantly rural with more than half the population
living on farms or in settlements of less than 1,500
population. Family farms, the majority under 30
acres in size and carved into small parcels separated
by hedgerows and stone fences, form a quiltlike
pattern across the landscape. The rural economy is

based largely on cattle and sheep farming. Special-
isation in the form of commercial livestock farming
is increasing, yet a sizeable proportion of the
population still practises mixed cottage farming
aimed at producing just enough to meet household
subsistence needs. For all but the large landowners,
agricultural opportunities are limited by low-
fertility soils, widespread blanket bog, and a wet
and windy climate.

The expansion of non-agricultural employment
has not been able to keep pace with the surplus
farm population or the natural population increase
of the towns. The lack of adequate economic opportunities at home coupled with a growing desire for
a higher standard of living has sent many young
people abroad. Emigration is a fact of life in the
west of Ireland; in some way it touches every family.
In the period 1951-71 net emigration from Ireland
totalled 543,000 or about half the Irish labour
force at the end of the period (Walsh, 1974). In the
last century the population of the rural areas and
small towns of the west has declined by roughly a
half. In the present study 59 per cent of the 2,206
men and 64 per cent of the 1,920 women in the
families in which the respondents or their spouses
were raised had emigrated.

A study of the attitudes toward emigration
among young people in one Irish county (Cavan)
found that 36 per cent of the youths surveyed defi-
nitely intended to emigrate and an additional 40 per
cent were seriously thinking of it (Hannan, 1970).
The primary reason was their belief that their home
region would not be able to satisfy their occupational and income aspirations. Among the return
migrants in my survey, 76 per cent of the men and 67
per cent of the women gave economic factors as the
main reason for their emigration from Ireland.
Several studies, however, point to factors other than
economic ones as also being important causes of Irish
emigration. In her work in the Gaeltacht areas of
western Ireland, Kane (1969) found emigration to be
a rite of passage -- one means by which young people
make the transition to adulthood. Emigration is also
an opportunity for a profitable, mildly adventurous
change. Bovenkerk (1973) in a study conducted in
one of our sample communities (Castleisland, County
Kerry) found that the desire for adventure -- 'to
see the world', 'to travel,' 'to see how other
people live,' and 'wanting change in life' -- was
nearly as important in promoting emigration as
economic motives. In other studies the lack of

153

social and recreational facilities was found to be
an important motive, especially for women (Hannan,
1970; Kane,1969).

Emigration from western Ireland has, however,
fallen in recent years as economic prospects have
improved and work opportunities for emigrants in
Europe and North America have tightened. Also,
western Ireland has recently entered a period of
comparatively rapid economic expansion and development. The State Industrial Development Authority
has lured many foreign industries with a resulting
increase in employment (nonetheless the rate of unemployment is still high, about 15 per cent in 1984).
Farmers are benefiting from higher prices and special subsidies brought by membership in the European
Economic Community. While young people are still
noticeably few in number on the streets and in the
fields, emigration is declining and the return flow
increasing.

According to official figures, emigration from
the western region dropped from an average 17.2 per
1,000 population in the 1950s to 5.07 persons returning per 1,000 population in 1971, a rate far
exceeding the 3.62 for the rest of the country.
County Donegal had the highest rate of return (6.4)
in the country, while the other Atlantic seaboard
counties of Clare, Sligo, Kerry, and Galway ranked
third, fourth, fifth and sixth. The only county
outside the survey area with a comparable rate of
return migration was Wicklow (6.0), which borders
Dublin on the east coast of Ireland. If present
economic trends continue, net immigration (the
number of people entering the country for the first
time plus return migrants minus the number of people
leaving) should continue to increase in the future.

METHODS

The fieldwork on which this study is based was
carried out over two summers in 1977 and 1978. Data
were gathered principally through questionnaire
survey and open-ended interview. The questionnaire
contained 98 items and was divided into four main
parts: the circumstances of the migrant before emigration, the emigration experience, the reasons for
return, and the post-return adjustment.

A sample of 606 migrants were interviewed by a
team of twelve interviewers in communities along the
western seaboard, beginning in County Cork in the
south and stretching to County Donegal in the north.

The sample was selected opportunistically with the names and addresses of return migrants being obtained from postmen, shopkeepers, clergy, teachers, and from the returnees themselves who at the conclusion of each interview were asked to provide names of other migrants in their neighbourhood. In small communities an attempt was made to interview all the known migrants in the locale. Most migrants were interviewed at home, although some interviews were conducted in the work place. The response to the survey was good: about 85 per cent of the migrants approached agreed to be interviewed. Only in areas of heavy tourism such as the Ring of Kerry and Connemara were there many refusals. As a general rule, the more remote a community was from the major tourist routes the more cooperative were the returnees and the higher the response rate.

In-depth interviews, some tape recorded, were conducted with about 15 returnees. Also interviewed were staff at the United States Embassy, the organisers of two American-Irish associations, and other individuals who had regular dealings with returnees and who were familiar with their situation.

SOME CHARACTERISTICS OF THE SAMPLE

Fifty-one per cent of the respondents were men and 49 per cent were women. Most of the migrants had emigrated from Ireland in their early twenties; the mean departure age was 22 years. At the time of their emigration all but 11 per cent were single. By the time they returned, 58 per cent of the men and 55 per cent of the women had married. Ninety per cent married other Irish. In one-third of the marriages both partners were from the same parish; another 12 per cent were from the same county. Thus almost half the emigrants who married while abroad selected a mate from close to home.

The average period of time spent abroad by the sample was 17 years, with a range of 2 to 55 years. There are several indications that the respondents in the sample had been away longer than most Irish return migrants. First, Brannick (1977) found in a survey of a single parish in County Clare that the local returnees had been away an average of 6.4 years. Secondly, my decision to omit from the sample returnees who had been away less than two years eliminated many migrants who had been away for only short periods. Third, post office employees from whom we solicited many names of returnees were most likely to forget emigrants who had not been away very long.

A comparison of the place of residence of the migrants before and after their return reveals that return migration for the majority was essentially an urban to rural movement. Over 74 per cent of the Irish had left cities in the United States and Britain with populations of more than one million. Of those returning from the United States 58 per cent had left New York City, while 51 per cent of those returning from the UK had come from London. A majority of the household heads in the sample had returned to their home communities. This pattern is less true of white-collar migrants who are inclined to resettle in urban areas where the employment opportunities they desire are based. The migrants' reasons for returning to western Ireland have been discussed at length elsewhere (see Gmelch, 1983).

RETURN MIGRANT READJUSTMENT

How well do the Irish returnees readjust to rural life after having spent many years away in an urban-industrial society? What problems, if any, do they experience? The experiences of many of the returnees surveyed suggest that readjustment may be difficult. When asked how satisfied they were with their lives in Ireland during their first year back, over half (51 per cent) of the returnees said that they were not satisfied and would have been happier had they stayed abroad. The first year appears to be particularly difficult; it is a time when many returnees wonder if they have made the right decision. Most individuals eventually do learn how to cope with the problems they experience upon returning; among the returnees surveyed just one in five still regretted their decision to return at the end of their second year at home in Ireland.

Problems in Readjustment

What poses the greatest difficulty for the return migrants when they first come back? Fully one fifth (21 per cent) of the returnees interviewed said that readjusting to the slow pace of life in Ireland and coping with widespread inefficiency had been their biggest problem. Everything seemed to happen so slowly or take so long to accomplish that they often became impatient and frustrated. Most respondents expressed this problem in concrete terms. Clerks and check-out girls, for example, were described as

moving at a snail's pace compared to their counterparts in America and England. In the larger stores
there were long waits in the check-out aisles as
checkers casually carried on conversations with other
customers and employees. Plumbers, electricians,
carpenters, and other workmen failed to come at
appointed times or did not come at all. A two-year
delay in getting a telephone was not unusual. The
paper work and legal delays in buying a house dragged
on for months, in some cases for years. One middle-
aged returnee whose husband had died of a heart
attack went so far as to attribute his death to the
frustrations and aggravations he had experienced in
trying to build his own home in Ireland.

Another exasperated returnee, the owner of a
launderette in a small town in County Mayo, encountered so many delays in ordering replacement parts
for his washing machines from Dublin that he now
orders from a firm in Cleveland. As an illustration
of the problems he feels are commonplace for returnees running businesses in Ireland he recounted how
he had ordered the same part, a small plastic cog,
from both the American and Dublin firms:

> Three weeks ago the part arrived from Cleveland.
> And do you know what I've heard from the people
> in Dublin? Nothing! Nothing for five weeks,
> till this morning. Would you believe, they
> want me to send them a money order before they
> will send the part? The part costs less than a
> pound, and they want a feckin' money order.
> Five weeks to tell me they want a money order,
> and the machine'd be out of use all that time.

Somewhat later in reflecting upon his situation he
explained:

> The problem is that I've seen another system,
> where people do their work and things get done.
> The people here that have never left Ireland
> don't know any better. And if you don't know
> another way, you're happy with what you have.

Another informant described his eventual adjustment as a process of slowing down to the Irish pace,
and radically changing his expectations:

> It took me two years to settle, the pace was
> too slow. Time doesn't mean anything to
> people here. If you wanted someone to paint
> the house, they'd say they'd come at ten o'clock

and not come till two or maybe they mightn't
come at all. At first I was angry but now I
don't mind. I don't expect them to carry
through with what they say, with what they
promise. That way, you're not disappointed.

The second most frequently mentioned readjustment problem involved relationships with local
people. Fourteen per cent of the returnees felt that
the attitudes and world view of local people had
been the single most difficult aspect of their
return. Local people were described as 'narrow-
minded' and 'backward', as inflexible and inward-
looking. They were criticised for being preoccupied
with the lives of others in the community. After
experiencing the anonymity of big city life in
America or Britain, these returnees felt that their
lives were being closely monitored by neighbours.
They felt that their actions -- what they wore, the
new piece of furniture they bought, or who their
daughter was seen holding hands with at a school
outing -- were always under public scrutiny and
gossiped about. Some returnees perceived this as a
loss of personal freedom.

In America you could do anything you want, and
nobody would bother you or take notice. In
Ireland people are gossipy, nosey, always
interested in other people's affairs. You don't
have that sense of freedom. Not freedom like
you find in America.

According to another repatriate:

People here are very cagey about what they say.
People here worry too much about what other
people think of them. Americans have more
freedom to say and do what they want. In
America people talk out loud in public, they
are free and easy in their talk. Here you have
to keep your voice down. You never know who's
listening.

Some return migrants also felt that they no
longer shared many interests with local people.
Their own interests tended to transcend the local
community and were more cosmopolitan in nature.
Local sporting events, for example, did not hold the
same fascination for them as they did for other community members. Having spent a good part of their
lives in America or Britain they remained interested

in the current events of their host countries and
were disappointed when their neighbours did not express the same interest or were openly disinterested.
    Other migrants had returned expecting to resume
relationships with friends and relatives at the same
level of intimacy they had shared years before. Not
infrequently they were disappointed. The first few
visits during which they reminisced and exchanged
memories were pleasant, but later visits revealed
that they no longer had much in common. A 35-year-
old school teacher who had been away four years
recalled some of the difficulties of meeting old
friends:

> Initially, in the first three months at home,
> you meet all the friends and acquaintances that
> you had and were friends of yours four or five
> years earlier. Some of them have been married
> and their partner is less obviously going to be
> a friend. Or they have changed circumstances
> enormously or changed interests enormously.
> You've got to realise that you've changed and
> that they've changed, you can't just pretend
> that four years didn't exist.

    The problems encountered in re-establishing
former relationships increase with the amount of
time returnees have spent abroad. And it is partly
because of the difficulties returnees face in trying
to resume past relationships that they come to realise just how much they have changed during their
years abroad. We asked returnees if they felt they
were different from Irish people who had never lived
abroad and, if so, how? Fully 85 per cent felt that
they were different; some felt that they had been so
changed by the overseas experience that they now had
more in common with citizens of the host country
than with their own countrymen. Seventy per cent
believed that they were 'broader in their outlook'
than those who had never left Ireland. They had been
exposed to many different ethnic groups and lifestyles and had come to understand, to a certain extent, that culture is relative, that the Irish way
of doing things is only one of many ways and that
others are equally valid. As one informant explained
about returnees.

> They have experience of a different society,
> whether it's successful or unsuccessful doesn't
> matter. They have experienced a different kind
> of way of life, different kind of environment

and they've got to bring that back with them.
It just widens the world view, so you've got to
be different...For me, it gives me much greater
understanding and tolerance for the ambiguities
of people.

Returnees also felt that they were better educated
(35 per cent) than non-migrants and that they worked
harder or were more ambitious (28 per cent).

Closely related to the problem of divergent attitudes and interests was that of developing a satisfactory 'social life'. Over 13 per cent of the
respondents cited this as the single most difficult
aspect of their readjustment. The difficulty in
making friends was mentioned most often by women (17
per cent versus 9 per cent for men). This is partially explained by the fact that few married women,
especially those living in rural areas and small
towns, are able to find jobs in Ireland. Women who
worked while living abroad and who had made many
contacts through their jobs were now stuck at home.
Also, many of them did not have a car, which would
enable them to get out and visit. Some younger women
returnees complained that neighbouring women who
they might have been able to socialise with were
overly family-oriented and were not interested or
did not make time for activities outside the home.

Since the failure to achieve a good social life
is closely related to the lack of shared interests
and the perceived 'narrow-mindedness' of local
people, the two variables could be lumped together.
When this is done it becomes the single most important adjustment difficulty faced by return migrants
(27 per cent compared to 21 per cent citing the slow
pace of life).

The Irish climate also posed a major problem
for 14 per cent of the sample, particularly the
elderly and those who had returned from America.
Irish winters are damp, the sky is grey much of the
time, and daylight hours are short. Due to the damp-
ness and the absence of central heating in many homes,
the cold is penetrating. Although the temperatures
do not dip below freezing for long and there is very
little snow, older returnees find the weather more
uncomfortable than the bitter but less humid winters
of the northern US cities -- New York, Boston and
Chicago -- which most of the American returnees had
left. The psychological effect of the dreary Irish
winter is compounded by the fact that most returnees
while living abroad had only visited Ireland during
the pleasant months of summer. Thus many had

forgotten what the climate is like during the rest
of the year. We interviewed several returnees who
were considering re-emigrating to a sunnier and drier
climate. One returnee advised emigrants thinking of
re-settling in Ireland:

> Take time off and really see the country and
> spend a winter here. They must spend a winter
> here before they give up their homes. When
> they come on a vacation during the summer the
> weather is beautiful, and you think the weather
> is always good. We lived here last winter, and
> it wasn't the same Ireland we saw on our visits.
> It was very depressing. It was cold and the
> dampness seeps into your bones.

One-tenth of the returnees found the unfavourable economic situation the most difficult aspect of
their readjustment. Some who had set up their own
businesses, most commonly pubs and small construction firms, had been overly optimistic when estimat-
ing the income they would be able to earn from these
enterprises. Publicans, for example, often found
that they were making less money owning and running
their own pub in Ireland than they had made tending a
bar for someone else in New York City. To make
matters worse, the hours were longer. Instead of
working an eight hour day, most returnees with businesses were working twelve hours a day, six days a
week.
Other factors mentioned by returnees, but of
less consequence, were the absence of modern conveni-
ences ranging from household appliances such as dish-
washers to public transport. The lack of variety in
shopping, which had become a favourite pastime of
some women while abroad, was also missed.
In many cases the problems of readjustment,
especially during the first year back, can be attributed to the returnees' false or unrealistic expectations about life in Ireland. Many returned without
up-to-date information on living conditions, the
economic climate, and other factors which impinge
upon their lives. Some basic fact-finding and more
thoughtful questioning would have in many cases
enabled returnees to avoid serious disappointment.
For example, if one elderly couple planning retirement in a remote part of Connemara had considered in
advance the infrequency of bus services in the area,
they might not have returned and found themselves
isolated and confined to home six days of the week.

Emigrants err in both directions in their expectations about Ireland. Most expect to find the
same level and range of amenities and services that
they enjoyed in America or Britain and are disappointed. Others expect to find Ireland as undevel-
oped as when they left many years before. They too
are disappointed when they discover that Ireland is
no longer the traditional, close-knit, folk society
of memory. One Mayo publican complained about
several of the returnee families in his community,
saying:

> They think it has stood still all these years
> they were away. They still believed the streets
> were unpaved, thatched cottages, and all...They
> should have been aware that Ireland today is a
> modern society.

To a large extent, the problems return migrants
experience can be attributed to differences in the
scale of the communities they have returned to.
Nearly three-quarters of the sample had left large
cities in Britain and America and returned to small
villages and towns in western Ireland. Their complaints that neighbours seem narrow-minded and
provincial would probably be the same had they moved
to rural areas within North America or Britain. In
other words, many of their complaints about life in
small communities in rural Ireland are true of small
communities everywhere.

While most returnees adjust to the changes demanded of them, some features of Irish life continue
to bother them well after the initial period of
readjustment. The returnees were asked what they
felt were the major disadvantages of life in Ireland.
Among the respondents who had been back three years
or more, 38 per cent considered low wages and poor
working conditions to be a major disadvantage of life
in Ireland. For some the difficulties of making a
good living in Ireland were not apparent during
their first year back when they had savings to fall
back on and were hopeful of new opportunities at
home. The excitement of being home and among old
friends and relatives and of planning for a new life
overshadowed early financial difficulties. By the
third or fourth year many who were still unable to
find a well-paying job, or any job at all, had begun
to discover the economic costs of return migration.
The 'bad' climate continued to be an annoyance for
nearly one-third of the migrants. About an equal
number complained that even after several years at

home they had still not developed a good social
life.

With time the majority of returnees learn to
cope with such disappointments; they learn to bring
their own expectations into line with the realities
of life in Ireland. While over half (51 per cent)
were dissatisfied during their first year back, only
21 per cent still felt that way after two or more
years at home. And among those who had been back
for more than five years, the number who were malad-
justed or felt dissatisfied dropped to 17 per cent.
Not included in this figure, however, are the
estimated 5 to 10 per cent who were so unhappy that
they had already re-emigrated.

Predictors of Readjustment
What factors are related to successful readjustment?
Is a person who spent many years abroad less likely
to adjust well than someone who has been away for a
shorter period of time? Do men adjust better than
women? In order to test these propositions and
others, the relationship between the level of adjustment and seven independent variables -- sex, age,
education, length of time abroad, job satisfaction,
housing satisfaction, and satisfaction with social
life -- were examined. Zero order correlations
between adjustment and each of the independent or
explanatory variables were computed. The results
are presented in Table 7.1. No relationship was
found between adjustment and education ($r = 0.01$).
A weak but statistically significant relationship
was found between sex ($r = 0.10$) and adjustment,
with men being more satisfied than women. Several
factors probably contribute to this. Married women
who enjoyed working abroad are often unable to find
jobs in Ireland, which eliminates an important arena
in which they can make friendships. Secondly, non-
working women in rural areas, particularly those
without cars, are confined at home much of the time.
Third, women more than men miss the modern conveni-
ences they had abroad which make housework easier.
And finally returnees more often return to the
husband's home community where the wife does not
have a support group or old friends. Given the dis-
advantaged position of returnee women in Ireland it
is somewhat surprising that the relationship between
sex and adjustment is not stronger.

The relationship between age and adjustment is
also weak ($r = 0.13$), and if we control for years
spent abroad this relationship is reduced to 0.00,

Table 7.1: Correlations of Variables with Readjustment

Variable	Correlations with Adjustment
Sex	.10*
Age	.13*
Education	.01
Length of time abroad	.18*
Job (satisfaction with)	.26*
Housing (satisfaction with)	.25*
Social life (satisfaction with)	.37*

*p <0.05 or better.

indicating that the reason older returnees are less satisfied is that they have been away from Ireland longer.

An inverse relationship was hypothesised between the length of time spent abroad and adjustment. It was reasoned that the longer the period spent in another society, the higher the level of acculturation in that society and the more divergent the migrant's attitudes and values would have become from those of his native society. The hypothesis was supported (r = 0.18); controlling for age reduces but does not eliminate the relationship (r = 0.12).

A moderate relationship was found between readjustment and both housing and job satisfaction (r = 0.25 and r = 0.26, respectively). That is, respondents who found their jobs and housing in Ireland better or about as good as what they had abroad tended to be well adjusted.

The variable most strongly related to adjustment was satisfaction with social life (r = 0.37). Returnees who felt their social life in Ireland was as good or better than what they had abroad tended to be better adjusted than those who do not feel this way. Here we see again the importance of developing friendships, of gaining acceptance among local people. And a key factor in gaining acceptance appears to be conformity. That is, returnees must not appear to think or behave too differently from local people, nor should they dwell on their life abroad. The factor that probably hinders the acceptance of returnees more than any other is their temptation to make comparisons between Ireland and the host countries they have left. Irish people are naturally

sensitive and at times defensive when their small
country is compared with America or Britain; they do
not wish to hear that wages, medical services, public
transport, or vegetables are poorer in Ireland.
They have heard it all before and do not wish to hear
it again. One informant's response to the question
'What advice would you give future returnees?' ex-
presses the sentiment of many:

> Settle down and get to know your neighbours.
> Answer their questions but don't keep talking
> about the country you came from. They don't
> like to hear it.

The term 'Return Yank' is applied, often derog-
atorily, to the returnee who has not changed his
foreign ways, who has retained his foreign accent,
idioms and expressions. At the opposite end of the
spectrum from the stereotypic 'Return Yank', however,
are a minority of returnees who have so successfully
embraced the traditional rural Irish lifestyle that
the outsider would never guess they have been out of
the country.

SOME OBSERVATIONS ON THE IMPACT OF RETURN MIGRANTS

Since this book is primarily concerned with the
economic and social implications of return migration
for the sending societies, it is only fitting that I
conclude with some observations on this issue for
rural Ireland.[2]
      One issue in assessing the impact of migrants
is whether they return with more work skills than
they had before they left, especially skills that
might be useful to a developing region. The migrants
surveyed were asked if they had acquired a skill or
trade during their stay abroad, and 37 per cent said
they had. However, when we look at some of the jobs
(e.g. labourer, bartender) that these returnees held
while abroad it is apparent that many either defined
skilled work loosely or exaggerated.
      For their foreign work experience to have a
beneficial effect at home the returnees must find
jobs which make use of their skills. The migrant
who learned welding in London and returns to the
family farm in County Kerry is likely to have little
or no work related impact. The industrial jobs that
many migrants worked at abroad appeared to have
little relevance to the agricultural economy of
rural Ireland.

A second area of potential impact concerns the migrants' repatriation and investment of foreign earnings. While the migrants were not asked how much money they had brought back, over half (58 per cent) said they had saved money while abroad for their use in Ireland. In addition to savings account deposits, many had cash from the sale of their overseas assets, including house, car, and furniture. Although some goods were shipped home, the bulk of the migrants' possessions were sold before returning. More important than the amount of money, perhaps, is how it is spent. Is it invested in capital improvements such as developing a new business which benefits the entire community? Or is it spent on consumer goods, home decoration, or drink? Buying a business or a farm was a high priority for many returnees. In fact, nearly a third (31 per cent) of the migrants were employed in their own businesses, most frequently in construction or as owners of public houses. In many small towns half or more of the pubs are owned by returnees; the publican's migration experience is sometimes reflected in their name of the establishment, such as 'The Chicago Bar', 'The American Dollar', and 'The Americano Lounge'. Some returnees had started small supermarkets, similar in size and function to the 'convenience marts' they had known in America.

But the purchase of a home appears to be the major use of the returnees' repatriated capital. One of the major changes in the appearance of rural Ireland in the past decade has been a flurry of new home construction. Even in the more depressed areas of the west, such as Dunbeg in County Donegal where fish catches have been dropping steadily over the past several years, new bungalows financed with savings from abroad are cropping up all over the landscape.

Appliances, furniture, and consumer goods for the home were also a major use of the migrants' savings. The migrants' homes were often noticeably better equipped with modern appliances such as washing machines and dryers than those of their non-migrant neighbours. They also contain many more ornaments and tourist curios. On the other hand, there is little excessive consumerism, 'conspicuous consumption run amok', that Rhoades (1978) describes among Spanish returnees from Germany.

The most noticeable differences in the Irish returnee home, particularly among those migrants who had returned from the United States, is not the quantity of consumer goods but the type of decoration.

In many rural Irish homes there is a strong preference for colour and pattern: carpets, wallpaper,
curtains and upholstery are all likely to be patterned. By contrast, in returnee homes solid colours
often replace patterned wallpaper, and muted or
neutral shades replace primary colours and bright
pastels. Houses which have been designed and built
by returnees from the USA are especially distinguish-
able from those of their non-migrant neighbours.
Some feature Spanish-style arches or colonial columns, picture windows, pine or oak panel doors, and
front lawns instead of gardens. This style is sel-
dome directly imitated by locals; however some
American architectural features are becoming common
in new Irish domestic architecture.

Irish returnees may also introduce new attitudes which they have acquired abroad into their
home communities. Brannick (1977) in a survey of
opinions concerning child-training practices, family
planning, divorce and the like in a rural parish in
County Clare found that returnees were considerably
more 'modern' in their outlook. My earlier discussion concerning the returnees' readjustment difficulties also supports the notion that returnees hold
certain attitudes and values which are different from
their non-migrant neighbours. But the key issue in
understanding the migrants' impact is the extent to
which their foreign-acquired attitudes influence
local people. Put differently, is Irish return migration an innovative influence promoting change or
is it basically conservative, promoting the status
quo?

We asked local people what innovations or
changes had been introduced into their communities
by return migrants. The query usually drew a blank,
even individuals who gave the question serious
thought were unable to think of any new ideas or
techniques introduced by returnees. There were, of
course, some exceptions such as the school teacher-
farmer in west Dingle who had introduced silage
making to his community. Some informants answered
the question by explaining that they were not really
interested in what returnees had to say. Others said
that whatever the returnees had learned in America
or Britain would be of little interest to local
people. From these conversations it seemed that few
of the returned migrant's foreign ideas or attitudes
rubbed off on local people. Or if they had, neither
returnee nor local was willing to admit it.

It must be remembered that rural Ireland is a
conservative society in which people are slow to

167

accept change. And many returnees in their desire
to gain acceptance are reluctant to push their ideas
on other people. As previously discussed, the best
hope returnees have of gaining social acceptance and
of successfully readjusting to life in Ireland is to
conform -- to not remind local people of their foreign experience, especially not to make unfavourable
comparisons between Ireland and the host countries.
Many returnees are sensitive to the problems inherent in suggesting that things be done another way.
In the words of one man at home for almost ten years:

> They (local Irish) want no part of our ideas.
> Even people who have come back from America and
> started a business here end up doing it the
> Irish way. Irish people just will not be
> changed. They have a certain way of living and
> nobody is going to change them. They feel that
> if things were good enough for my father, they
> are good enough for me, and that's that.

Arnold Shrier, writing about American Irish returnees before 1950, suggests that the returnees transferred very little of their American experience to
Ireland because they were not viewed by the Irish as
'genuine Americans':

> A group of strangers, if they do not represent
> a threat to a community, are generally respected
> for their differences, and over a period of
> years some of their customs or ideas might even
> infiltrate and become accepted by the society
> in which they have settled. But the returned
> Yank was at best an adapter, a hybrid whose
> roots were essentially in Irish soil, and he
> was not respected as the true bearer of new
> gifts (Shrier, 1955, p. 142).

One area in which returnees may affect their
community is in encouraging emigration. Most of the
migrants surveyed believed their emigration had been
a positive experience; and 58 per cent said they
would encourage young people to emigrate. But the
returnees probably encourage emigration more by
example than by verbal persuasion. Their presence
in the community -- more prosperous and more 'worldly'
than local people -- presents an attractive role
model for the young. In the eyes of many youth, the
returnees are living proof that it is possible to
have the best of both worlds: to live abroad for a
while and have adventure while holding a better job

168

and making more than one could in Ireland, and then
with savings in hand, returning home to the security
and companionship, at least ideally, of family and
old friends.

NOTES

1. The research on which this paper is based
was generously supported by the Irish Foundation for
Human Development, Earthwatch and the Center for
Field Research. I wish to acknowledge the assistance of Theresa Brannick and John Cullen in the
planning of the survey, the twelve Earthwatch vol-
unteers who helped conduct interviews, Larry
Delaney and Richard Felson in the data analysis, and
Jack Brady and Sharon Gmelch for comments on an
earlier draft of this paper.
2. I should make it clear that I did not
gather data on this issue in a systematic fashion.
There were, however, several questions in the survey
questionnaire concerning the migrants' impacts at
home, and I did record other data on this topic in
the course of doing in-depth interviews with return
migrants and in ethnographic research in several
County Kerry communities during the summer of 1977.
I also benefited from the observations of some of my
field school students who did ethnographic research
in ten communities in County Kerry.

REFERENCES

Bovenkerk, F. (1973) 'On the causes of Irish
    emigration', Sociologia Ruralis, 3, pp. 263-
    275.
Bovenkerk, F. (1974) The Sociology of Return Migra-
    tion, Martinus Nijhoff, The Hague.
Brannick, T. (1977) A Study of Return Emigrants in a
    Rural Parish, M.A. Thesis, University College
    Dublin.
Gmelch, G. (1980) 'Return Migration', Annual Review
    of Anthropology, 9, pp. 135-159.
Gmelch, G. (1983) 'Who returns and why: return
    migration behaviour in two north Atlantic
    societies,' Human Organization, 42(1), pp. 46-
    54.
Hannan, D. (1970) Rural Exodus, Geoffrey Chapman,
    London.
Kane, E. (1969) A Gaeltacht Report, Comhairle
    Gaeilge, Dublin.

Rhoades, R. (1978) 'Intra-European return migration
    and rural development: lessons from the
    Spanish case', Human Organization, 37(2),
    pp. 136-147.
Schrier, A. (1955) Ireland and the American Emigra-
    tion: 1850-1950, University of Minnesota Press,
    Minneapolis.
Walsh, B. (1974) 'Expectations, information, and
    human migration: specifying an econometric
    model of Irish migration to Britain', Journal
    of Regional Science, 14(1), pp. 107-120.

Chapter Eight

RETURN MIGRATION AND URBAN CHANGE: A JORDANIAN
CASE STUDY

Allan Findlay and Musa Samha

INTRODUCTION

Return migration must be studied in the context of
the entire migration process. The behaviour of many
foreign workers in the use of their earnings reflects their expectation of eventually returning to
their place of origin. Comparison of the characteristics of returned migrants and current migrant
workers shows, however, that the likelihood of return
is much greater for some persons than others.
Analysis of the geographical impact of the investment of migrant remittances also serves to show in
many instances the inappropriateness of migrant remittance expenditure to the long term needs of return
migrants seeking to reinsert themselves in their
community of origin. One of the most evident geographical consequences of international migration
within the Middle East has been the rapid growth of
cities in the labour exporting nations as a result
of the investment of remittances in house building
(Simon, 1982; 1984). This has resulted in a new
form of urbanisation and urban economy which is most
ill-suited to the reinsertion of returning migrant
workers.
    This chapter examines the nature of recent re-
turn migration to Jordan, with particular reference
to the capital city, Amman. It reports on some of
the results of a household survey undertaken in
early 1984, in which the authors sought to examine
the nature of the relationship between international
migration and urbanisation and to contrast the
characteristics of current and return migrants. The
survey results are of interest not only because of
the regionally specific geo-political implications
of Palestinian and Jordanian labour migration, but
also because of the broader issues identified. The

international migration process, in which return
migration forms the final phase, results in the
transfer between nations of labour skills, financial
resources, technology and lifestyles, all of which
have a marked geographical impact on the regions of
origin.

These transfers are very evident in Jordan
which has an estimated 40 per cent of its active
workforce employed abroad (Serageldin, 1983), which
depends on migrant remittances for over 20 per cent
of its gross national product, and which has recently been described by one commentator as a
'charity' state (Abu Lughod, 1984). Now there is
evidence that since 1979 opportunities for
Palestinian and Jordanian employment in the oil-
rich states have declined, and that the rate of
return migration has begun to accelerate. The
prospect that this trend will continue is an
immense threat to the dependent Jordanian economy.
The geographical impact at regional and local levels
of a decline in the receipt of remittances is likely
to be even more severe.

THE HISTORY OF JORDANIAN EMIGRATION

The 1948 Palestine war resulted in a substantial
refugee movement into the enlarged Kingdom of
Jordan. This in turn precipitated labour emigration
from Jordan on a new and increased scale since the
economy was unable to provide adequate domestic
employment opportunities, particularly for the
Palestinian population. At the same time the demand
for immigrant labour was growing in the oil states
of Saudi Arabia and the Gulf. By the time of the
1961 Jordanian census some 63,000 Jordanians were
resident abroad, 80 per cent of whom had emigrated
from the West Bank (Seccombe, 1984). Occupation of
the West Bank by Israel in 1967 led to further
refugee movements and further labour emigration to
the oil states. Following the oil price rises of
1973/74 opportunities for emigration from Jordan to
Saudi Arabia and the Gulf States were further enhanced as the oil states launched ambitious new
development projects financed by their oil wealth.
By the late 1970s an estimated 300,000 Jordanians
were working abroad (Hashemite Kingdom of Jordan,
1983, p. 20), while the 1979 census reported that
the Jordanian domestic labour market employed only
447,000 persons. The massive growth in emigration
during the 1970s was mirrored by an expansion in the

172

value of migrant remittances which rose from 7.4 million Jordanian dinars (3.4 per cent of GNP) in 1972 to 382 million JD (22.4 per cent of GNP) in 1982. Not only did the 1970s increase Jordanian dependence on foreign labour markets as a source of employment, but the economy also became dependent on the inflow of massive amounts of Arab aid from the oil rich states. In 1980 Arab aid totalled 399 million JD, equivalent to 46 per cent of the value of the country's GDP in that year. These inflows of capital from migrant workers and Arab aid helped to finance the rapid economic growth rate which Jordan experienced in the 1970s, despite the absence of a broad physical resource base on which to construct economic development.

Initially Jordanian emigration helped to absorb surplus manpower from the domestic economy through the emigration of persons unable to find work in Jordan and through the boost to the domestic economy which occurred as a result of remittance expenditure, but by the late 1970s labour shortages had begun to emerge in Jordan which could only be avoided through either a restrictive policy on further emigration or the importation of labour from other labour surplus economies. Samha (1984) has shown how the government, by favouring the second course of action, turned Jordan into a major labour importing nation, creating the interesting phenomenon of replacement migration. By 1980 there were 80,000 foreign workers in Jordan of whom 45,000 were employed in Amman City, indicating once again the urban bias both of foreign immigration and Jordanian emigration. Egyptians accounted for 70 per cent of immigrants in Jordan and 90 per cent of foreign immigrants to Amman.

The boom in Jordanian emigration came to an end in 1979, with a sudden loss of confidence in the world oil market and a decline in the demand for migrant labour. Seccombe (1984) has shown that after 1979 there was a substantial decline in the number of work permits issued to Jordanians for employment in Saudi Arabia and Kuwait, and that the number of permit renewals also fell. In addition the crude balance of passenger arrivals to departures at airports and border points indicated a net inflow of Jordanians to the East Bank from 1978 onwards. Not only have opportunities for emigration declined and return migration accelerated, but the character of emigrant and return migrant workers also changed, reflecting a modification in the quality of labour required in the oil states. The Jordanian Royal

Table 8.1: Distribution by Occupation Group of Current and
Returned Migrants (%)

	Current Migrants	Returned Migrants	
		Main Job Abroad	Current Job
Professional	44.5	36.9	28.5
Clerical	18.2	8.8	7.6
Sales and services	5.3	7.0	12.1
Production, transport, manual	27.0	39.2	35.9
Armed forces	2.8	5.7	3.9
Other, unclassified, unknown	2.3	2.5	12.0

Source: Royal Scientific Society (1983, pp. 75-76).

Scientific Society (RSS), which carried out a household survey in Amman in 1980, found that emigrants
were much more highly skilled and were more likely
to be employed in professional and technical occupations than had been the case in the mid 1970s
(Royal Scientific Society, 1983). Table 8.1 shows
that return migrants were less likely to have been
employed in professional and clerical jobs while
abroad and more likely to have been production or
manual workers than was the case for current migrant
workers. This suggests that there may have
been a selective return migration of the less
skilled workers, a trend which is consistent with
the tendency for the oil-rich states to reduce their
emphasis on investment in infrastructural projects
from the late 1970s onwards, and to assign many of
the construction projects to companies bringing
workers from the Far East. The RSS survey also
indicated that return migrants had to accept slightly lower status employment on their return to Jordan.
     Since the RSS survey in 1980 pressure to return
has grown, while opportunities for further emigration
from Jordan have narrowed, resulting in some marked
changes in labour market conditions by the time of
the present authors' 1984 survey. In addition, the
vulnerable 'charity' status of the Jordanian
economy had become increasingly apparent, with many
of the Arab oil states reneging on their commitments
to give aid to Jordan, because of their own economic

problems arising from oil sales. In 1984 the
Jordanian government claimed to have received only
67 per cent of the 183 million JD in aid for which
it had budgeted (Dougherty, 1985). Thus at the very
time when external financial assistance to boost the
domestic economy has been squeezed, the threat of
substantial return migration to the Jordanian labour
market has also risen. Analysis of the impact of
emigration and return migration is therefore a very
important issue in the context of the Jordanian
economy.

CHARACTERISTICS OF THE SAMPLE

The authors' 1984 sample survey was carried out in
five different and socially contrasting districts
of Amman. The purposive sample sought to compare
and contrast households containing migrants currently working abroad with homes where the head of
household had formerly worked abroad. In total 173
households were identified in the former category
and 77 in the latter, but the ratio of return to
current migrants varied considerably between the
five different sample areas. Return migration was
highest in the eastern and north-eastern sample
areas of Russeifa and Nuzha, in which almost as
many households were identified with return migrants
as with current migrants working abroad. The eastern
parts of Amman are generally characterised as being
the poorer and more densely populated areas of the
city, while the west and north-west of the city is
considered a higher status zone. In the other
three sample areas there was only one return migrant
household for every four current migrant households
identified. The results of the survey of 173 households in which a member of the household was absent
due to working abroad have been reported elsewhere
(Findlay and Samha, 1985). The results discussed
below relate specifically to the return migrant
population.
        Amongst return migrants 73 per cent were
Palestinian by birth, but had returned from Saudi
Arabia and the Gulf to live in Amman. As can be
seen from Table 8.2, the family members of return
migrant households had quite a different distribution of birth places from the heads of household.
This predominantly reflects the re-settling of
Palestinian refugees on the East Bank. While only
19 per cent of heads of households were native to
Amman, 48 per cent of household members had been

Table 8.2: Place of Birth of Returned Migrants

Place of Birth	Head of Household	Family Members
Amman	15	234
West Bank	44	119
Palestine '48	12	28
Other regions of Jordan	6	30
Abroad	0	72
TOTAL	77	483

Source: Authors' survey.

born in Amman. Many of the return migrants were therefore Palestinian refugees who, after the troubles of 1948 and 1967, chose to raise their families in Amman, while themselves emigrating to the oil states to earn a living.

A high proportion of return migrants were poorly qualified, 55 per cent being either illiterate or having received only elementary schooling. Unfortunately it was difficult to determine the occupation of the migrants before their initial departure from Jordan, 38 per cent of the sample being unwilling to respond to this question. Most of these were persons forced to leave Amman after the 1970 civil war.

Table 8.3: Date of First Emigration from Jordan

	Return Migrants	Current Migrants
Before 1965	14	18
1965 - 1974	26	42
1975 - 1979	32	73
1980 - 1983	5	40
Total	77	173

Source: Authors' survey.

Table 8.3 shows the timing of departure of the sample of households with return migrants. This reflects the general trend in Jordanian emigration outlined above, with the peak period of emigration

being the late 1970s. Only five of the return migrants had departed after 1980. The average length
of the return migrants' last trip abroad was of
relatively short duration with 43 per cent having
spent less than four years away. Most return
migrants had therefore worked for only a limited
period abroad in order to gain sufficient capital
to build a new house, buy a car or establish a small
shop or business.

DETERMINANTS OF RETURN MIGRATION

Comparison between the characteristics of households
with current and return migrants permits some assessment to be made of the factors encouraging return.
Clearly the survey design captures only those
migrant workers whose families remained in Jordan,
and fails to evaluate the forces influencing those
workers who succeeded in taking their families with
them to the oil states. Comparison of return
migrants with current migrants is also problematic
because of the great difficulty of differential
characteristics in the cohorts of migrants departing at different times. The sample data were carefully examined to identify time-specific variations
in the characteristics of Jordanian emigration, and
an attempt was made to control the temporal variations in migrant characteristics which might have
unduly influenced the conclusions concerning return
migration. Despite these precautions great difficulties remain in identifying the determinants of
return migration because of the apparently
insoluble problem of adequately defining the population of future potential return migrants. The
survey permitted five hypotheses concerning return
migration to be tested:

1. East Bank migrants would be more likely to
   be found in the return migrant sample
   because of the greater ease with which they
   could expect to be reinserted in the
   Jordanian economy.
2. Return migration would be more common
   amongst those who had emigrated at an early
   date than amongst more recent migrants,
   since more recent migrants would be less
   likely to have achieved their earnings
   target for house-building, etc.
3. Migrants would be more likely to have had
   to return from the Gulf economies than from

Saudi Arabia, because of the greater economic difficulties faced by the smaller Gulf
countries as a result of the downturn in
the world oil market during the 1980s.
4. Return migration was expected to be more
likely amongst migrants with smaller
families, since these families would have
been able to save and invest a higher proportion of remittances than larger families.

For each of these hypotheses statistical comparison was made between current and return
migrant households, in order to determine whether
return migrants differed from non-returning migrants
in the expected fashion. A major difficulty in
testing the first two hypotheses was the strong
association which existed between date of first
emigration and place of birth. As shown in the
earlier paper (Findlay, 1984), large-scale
Palestinian emigration preceded East Bank emigration
by several years. The separate effects of place of
birth and date of emigration on the likelihood of
return (and non-return) migration were examined using
a log-linear model for categorical data as outlined
by Bowlby and Silk (1982). Not surprisingly, it was
found that the date of emigration directly influenced the probability of return, but interestingly
no independent statistical association could be
found between place of birth and return migration.
It was therefore concluded that emigrants native to
Amman and the East Bank were no more likely to
return than were Palestinian workers. Consequently,
since Palestinians had emigrated at an earlier date,
they were also well represented amongst the return
migrant population.
The third hypothesis was rejected, statistical
analysis failing to detect any differences in the
countries of employment of current and return
migration. Hypotheses 4 and 5 concerning family
size and remittance use both proved statistically
significant. The average size of the households
with return migrants was 6.27 persons compared with
6.93 persons in households with current migrants.
None of the return migrant households had more than
ten members whereas more than a tenth of current
migrant households were of this size. Considerable
difficulty exists in interpreting the nature of the
relationship between return migration and the
propensity to invest remittances since investment
patterns can be seen to be both cause and consequence of a migrant's return. As Table 8.4 shows,

Table 8.4: Remittance Use by Return and Current Migrants
(proportion of persons investing in each category)

Remittance Use	% Return Migrants	% Current Migrants
Building	55	43
Car purchase	40	20
Land	31	21
Education	17	20
No investment or major purchase	5	20
Industrial projects	5	4
Agricultural projects	3	1

Source: Authors' survey.

return migrants were much more likely to have
purchased land as an investment or to have used
their remittances for house construction or altera-
tion than current migrants. As many as 20 per cent
of current migrants had not used their remittances
at all for investment either in property or in
purchasing major consumer goods such as a car.
Neither current nor return migrants showed much
interest in devoting their remittances to agricultural and industrial projects, but a similar
proportion of both groups had used their foreign
earnings to help fund the education of another
member of their family.

THE GEOGRAPHICAL IMPACT OF REMITTANCE INVESTMENTS IN AMMAN

As Table 8.4 shows, the direct investment of migrant
remittances in the productive sectors of the
Jordanian economy is minimal. This finding is
substantiated by other surveys of remittance use
(e.g. Saket, 1983). Nevertheless the geographical
impact of remittance expenditure has been very
considerable. The very rapid physical growth of
Amman between 1972 and 1982 can be in large part
traced either directly or indirectly to the influence of migrant capital being invested in the
construction sector. Fig. 8.1 shows the remarkable
spatial expansion of the city which has occurred

Figure 8.1: Location and Spatial Extension of Amman City

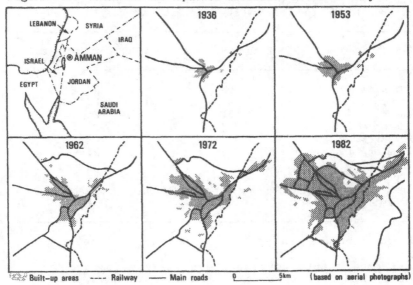

Built-up areas   ---- Railway   —— Main roads   0 _____ 5km   (based on aerial photographs)

Table 8.5:   Construction Activities in Amman and Zarqa,
1974-1982

	Number of Building Permits Issued	Area of New Construction for Permits Issued (M^2)
1974	1348	261
1976	n.a.	577
1978	3206	590
1980	3582	1118
1982	2830	887

Source: Findlay (1984, p. 213).

over the last decade, while Table 8.5 shows the
dramatic growth in the demand for building permits
which the Amman-Zarqa region experienced during the
same period. In 1972 the surface area was only
21km^2; by 1982 it had increased to 54km^2. This
doubling of the built area has occurred mainly
towards the north-west of the city with districts

such as Shmeisani mushrooming and with building
continuing rapidly along the routes towards
Suweileh and Wadi es Sir. The style of building is
characterised by four to five storey apartment
blocks built in a relatively anonymous cosmopolitan
style. Such architecture owes its form to twentieth
century building technology and shows little trace
of any Arab heritage. External influences on housing styles are even more apparent in the rich garden
suburbs of Amman, where large new villas with steep
sloping roofs suitable for Alpine or Scandinavian
winters have been built. Architectural styles
indicate that return migrants' aspirations for
'modernity' have apparently become confounded with
'westernisation'. New house designs have abandoned
the courtyard plan, which has proved so satisfactory
both in environmental and cultural terms for many
centuries, for an extraverted European house with a
central residential unit and a public garden.

Although the physical extension of Amman is the
most visible sign of the investment of migrant
remittances in the urban economy, more subtle
changes are also perceptible. The density of
buildings near the old centre has increased such
that there are virtually no vacant plots suitable
for further building. In the centre and in the
areas near the centre such as the inner part of
Jebel Hussein urban growth has resulted in a
vertical rather than horizontal expansion of the
built environment. Houses are frequently found with
an extra storey recently added or under construction.
In the poorer southern and eastern districts of the
city the perimeter of the city has not extended as
rapidly as the richer west, yet growth of the built
environment has been extremely rapid through the
infill of vacant plots and through the subdivision
of former garden areas to permit new housing stock
to be introduced. This typical response was found
for example in the district of Badr, where
Palestinian refugees from the camps in this area
have gradually begun to move out to new housing
built at high densities in the immediate vicinity.

Conversely in the west horizontal expansion of
the city has led to low density development, with
rapid urban sprawl leaping from hilltop to hilltop
as developers have sought out the most desirable
locations for new villas. The rate of urban growth
has stimulated rapid rises in land values to the
west of the city, encouraging speculative investment
in buildings and land. As a consequence in some
parts of Amman plots of underdeveloped land have

been engulfed within the city, while on the fringe
agricultural land has gone out of production as
speculators have bought up land ahead of building
demand, in the hope of reaping profits from an
inflationary spiral in land values.

The survey revealed that amongst return migrants
the modal lag between emigration and the purchase of
land for building was only two years. The actual
decision to buy land and build a new house was much
more common amongst those migrants who had departed
in the 1960s or early 1970s than amongst later
migrants. An interesting contrast existed between
current and return migrants in house building
habits. Amongst return migrants the proportions
investing in new houses or modifying existing
buildings was similar both for Palestinian (55 per
cent) and East Bank (52 per cent) households, but
amongst current migrant families, Palestinian
households were more likely than others to be investing in housing. It is highly significant from
a political and economic perspective that so many
Palestinian migrant workers either already have
returned or intend to return to live in Amman. If
the high level of fixed investment in the city's
housing stock can be taken as a measure of their
intention to settle there, then the large stock of
new empty houses around the outskirts of the city
suggests that in the future a great many migrants
currently working in the Gulf will return and settle
in Amman. The major problem facing the city, given
the likely prospect of the return of many Palestinians and Jordanians in the late 1980s and 1990s, is
not therefore one of housing since in this respect
the migrants have prepared their own programme for
reinsertion through house building investments.
The major problem lies in employment generation in
an urban agglomeration whose prosperity during the
1970s depended firstly on the tertiary sector as
retailing and service activies expanded to match the
new consumer demands being fuelled by migrant
remittances (Findlay, 1984) and, secondly, on the
booming construction industry which prospered
through the massive house building programme that
occurred. The 1980 RSS survey indicated that returning migrants had moved into the sales and
service sector from virtually every other job
category abroad. For example, about 16 per cent
of clerical workers abroad reported moving to sales
work in Jordan (RSS, 1983, p. 65). The RSS survey
also indicated that even in 1980 many return
migrants found that opportunities within the Amman

182

labour market were limited and almost 20 per cent
were actively seeking to emigrate once again,
especially those who were living in the 1948 refugee
camps.
    The current occupations of the return migrants
interviewed in the 1984 survey corroborate the
evidence of other return migration studies (King,
Mortimer and Strachan, 1984; Swanson, 1979) that
return migrants swell the ranks of tertiary employment and underemployment in urban areas, with
relatively few becoming industrial employees. Only
16 per cent of 'our' return migrants were involved
in some form of industrial production, while sales,
service, professional and administrative sectors
absorbed 51 per cent. The security of employment in
these tertiary activities is highly dependent on the
continued 'charity' status of the Jordanian economy
as a whole, and in particular on the continued
inflow of remittances and aid from other countries.
By 1984 the reduction in Arab aid had already begun
to force cuts in the Jordanian development plan,
and threatened retrenchment in the tertiary sector
of the economy.

CONCLUDING SUMMARY

This chapter has attempted to show that return
migration as part of the international migration
process is an extremely important force in generating urban change in Jordan. The specific circumstances of Amman and the Jordanian economy amplify
the importance of return migration, but there can
be little doubt that similar impacts are being
experienced on a smaller scale in other labour
exporting regions of the Arab world. The geographical impact of the process in the present physical
growth of cities is apparent, but only the future
will reveal whether this unusual form of urbanisation can be sustained in the absence of balanced
economic development within the urban system.

REFERENCES

Abu Lughod, J. (1984) 'Culture, "modes of
    production" and the changing nature of cities
    in the Arab world', in J. Agnew, et al. (eds.)
    The City in Cultural Context, Allen and Unwin,
    London, pp. 94-119.

Bowlby, S. and Silk, J. (1982) 'Analysis of quali-
    tative data using GLIM', Professional
    Geographer, 43, pp. 80-90.
Dougherty, P. (1985) 'Jordan's 1985 budget', Middle
    East Economic Digest, 29, pp. 12-13.
Findlay, A. (1984) 'Migrations, transferts de
    revenues et croissance urbaine à Amman, in G.
    Simon (ed.) Villes et Migrations Internationales
    de Travail dans le Tiers-Monde, Migrinter,
    Poitiers, pp. 205-224.
Findlay, A. and Samha, M. (1985) 'The impact of
    international migration on the urban structure
    of Amman', Population, Espace et Sociétés,   ·
    3(1), in press.
Hashemite Kingdom of Jordan (1983) Statistical
    Yearbook 1982, Department of Statistics, Amman.
King, R.L., Mortimer, J. and Strachan, A. (1984)
    'Return migration and tertiary development',
    Anthropological Quarterly, 57(3), pp. 112-124.
Royal Scientific Society (1983) Workers Migration
    Abroad, RSS, Amman.
Saket, B. (1983) Economic Uses of Remittances - the
    Case of Jordan, RSS Economics Department,
    Amman.
Samha, M. (1984) 'Replacement migration to Jordan
    with special reference to Amman governorate,
    1980', Diraset, 11, pp. 123-154.
Seccombe, I. (1984) International Labour Migration
    and Skill Scarcity in the Hashemite Kingdom of
    Jordan, ILO International Migration for
    Employment Project Working Paper 14, Geneva.
Serageldin, I. (1983) Manpower and International
    Labour Migration in the Middle East and North
    Africa, Oxford University Press, Oxford.
Simon, G. (ed.) (1982) Les Travailleurs Emigrés et
    le Changement des Pays d'Origines, CIEM,
    Poitiers.
Simon, G. (ed.) (1984) Villes et Migrations
    Internationales de Travail dans le Tiers-Monde,
    Migrinter, Poitiers.
Swanson, J. (1979) Emigration and Economic
    Development, Westview, Boulder.

Chapter Nine

THE IMPACT OF RETURN MIGRATION IN RURAL NEWFOUNDLAND

George Gmelch and Barnett Richling

Since Newfoundland joined Canada in 1949, the greatest proportion of Newfoundlanders have migrated
internally to various destinations in mainland
Canada. Nevertheless, return migration to rural
Newfoundland bears much in common with cases in
which the migrants are moving from one cultural
system to another, such as Filipinos returning from
Hawaii or Turks from Germany. This is due chiefly
to Newfoundland being a distinct social and cultural
entity within the Canadian national context, the
result of its geographical isolation and long history
as a separate colony and dominion. Also, Newfoundland is economically underdeveloped in comparison to
other Canadian provinces. Therefore, while Newfoundland migrants are not crossing international boundaries, they are crossing important social and
economic boundaries.

The aim of this study is to examine some of the
social and economic consequences of return migration
in rural Newfoundland.[1] In assessing the return
migrants' impact three areas are examined: the introduction of new work skills; the investments
migrants make with their repatriated earnings; and
the role migrants play in introducing new ideas into
their home communities.

THE SETTING AND OUT-MIGRATION

Newfoundland, England's oldest North American colony,
did not confederate with Canada until 1949. The
population of Newfoundland (567,681 in 1981) is
mainly spread along the coastline; the interior of
the island, which is primarily forest and tundra, is
uninhabited except for a few towns adjacent to pulp
and paper mills and mines. Newfoundland's economy

185

is weak and displays most of the classic characteristics of underdevelopment: a low level of industrialisation, primary production of raw materials,
reliance on one or few products for export, and
foreign ownership and control.

Two distinct socio-economic sectors can be
identified in Newfoundland: one traditional, the
other modern. In broad terms they correspond to
rural and urban life. This dualism does not merely
reflect differences in settlement pattern and local
economic base but also involves pronounced differences in values and expectations. Rural life in
Newfoundland is characterised by widely dispersed,
low-density settlements (outports), interdependent
domestic economies with limited access to cash
resources, emphasis on subsistence-oriented production (e.g. logging, hunting, fishing, gardening),
high occupational variablity (i.e. working at several different jobs during the year), kin-based
social organisation, and low or intermediate levels
of technology. In contrast, urban Newfoundland is
characterised by centralisation, depersonalised
organisation tied to industrialism, and independent
domestic economies dependent on cash flow. Unlike
the rural and urban components of mainstream
Canadian society, which are integrated at virtually
all levels of organisation and value, the rural and
urban spheres in Newfoundland show less integration
and are structually more independent.

The existence of such differences between the
urban and rural sectors is largely due to the development policies pursued by the Newfoundland government from the beginning of the confederation period
until the mid-1970s. During this period a major
priority of the provincial government was to
centralise the region's widely scattered rural
population into 'growth centres' where jobs and
municipal services could be provided more efficient-
ly. During the period of direct assault on the
outports by federal and provincial resettlement
programmes (1951-1976), the rural sector's share of
Newfoundland's population declined from just over 73
per cent to 60 per cent. In short, the government's
policy of forced urbanisation and modernisation has
been carried out at the expense of small, rural
communities. Nonetheless, despite government policy
many Newfoundlanders have continued to voice strong,
positive sentiments about the outport way of life,
idealising its traditional lifestyle and rural values
as representative of true Newfoundland society and
culture. And the most recent provincial government

census shows that the shift of the province's population from rural to urban has stabilised
(Newfoundland and Labrador,1983).

Both out-migration and return migration in
Newfoundland are linked to this socio-economic
dichotomy between the province's rural and urban
sectors. Since confederation with Canada, levels
of out-migration from Newfoundland have been on
average twice as high as they were during the
preceding 25 years.[2] Between the mid-1950s, when
the resettlement programmes began, and the early
1970s, out-migration reduced population growth by
natural increase by an average of 36 per cent. But
Canadian census data since 1966 show a decreased
outflow and an increased inflow. Net out-migration
for Newfoundland changed from 20,000 in 1966-71 to a
low of 1500 in 1971-76, rising slightly to a loss of
4500 in 1976-81. While Newfoundland is still a net
exporter of people, it is significant that in the
past decade there has been an increased in-flow of
people settling in rural areas. A government study
of immigration to Newfoundland in 1980-81 found that
43 per cent of all arrivees settled in rural areas;
among native-born Newfoundlanders the rate of return
to rural areas was 51 per cent (Newfoundland and
Labrador,1982).

METHODS

Data were gathered through a multi-method approach
involving a questionnaire survey, in-depth interviews,
and some participant-observation in two Newfoundland
communities. A sample of 420 return migrants was
interviewed in the summer of 1979. A team of 12
interviewers administered a 98 item questionnaire
consisting of five parts: the circumstances of the
migrant before emigration, the emigration experience,
the reasons for return, the post-return adjustment,
and the impact of the migrant in his workplace and
community. The communities in which the survey was
conducted were located on the Bonavista, Avalon, and
Burin Peninsulas in eastern Newfoundland, Notre Dame
Bay in the north central part of the island, and the
Bay of Islands in western Newfoundland. In each
Newfoundland community the names and addresses of
return migrants were obtained from the post office,
shopkeepers, and/or local residents. An effort was
made to acquire as near a comprehensive listing as
possible and then to contact every person on the
list; that is, to interview the known universe of

migrants within each community. The sampling procedure may have resulted in married couples being
overrepresented and single migrants underrepresented
due to the greater likelihood of at least one spouse
being at home when the interviewer called.

In conjunction with the survey, 15 migrants were
selected for in-depth interviews. These interviews,
which were tape-recorded, focussed on the returnees'
migration history and readaptation to life in
Newfoundland. Finally, one of us gathered additional
data through participant-observation and informal
interviewing in two outports in the Bay of Islands
region over a seven-week period in 1981 and 1982
(see Richling, 1985).

CHARACTERISTICS OF THE SAMPLE

Of the returnees interviewed, 53 per cent were men
and 47 per cent women. The mean age at which the
sample had first migrated from Newfoundland was 22.5
years. At the time of emigration only one-fifth
planned to leave the province permanently; most of
the remainder either had no plans (53 per cent) or
planned to be away less than 3 years (18 per cent).
Hence, most of the migrants left Newfoundland on a
trial basis, letting their decision of whether or not
to return be guided by the opportunities they found
in the new setting.

The majority of the migrants -- 88 per cent --
went to other places within Canada, 10 per cent to
the USA, and 2 per cent to Europe, mostly to the UK.
Most of the respondents (71 per cent) travelled to
places where they already had kinsmen or friends
from home. Nearly half joined siblings, the remainder joined other relatives or friends. These relationships were instrumental in helping the migrants
get established in the new settings: 61 per cent of
the sample received direct aid in finding housing
and 45 per cent were helped in finding a job.

Two-thirds of the sample were unmarried at the
time of their emigration. At the time of their
return to Newfoundland, however, less than one third
were still single. All but 8 per cent of those who
married while away selected other Newfoundlanders as
their mates.

The majority of the migrants returned between
the ages of 25 and 34; only 10 per cent came back
after their 45th birthday. In general, from age 30
onward there was a steady decline in the numbers
returning. This pattern deviates only slightly in

the 65-69 year age bracket, representing persons who
returned for retirement. It is significant that all
but a handful of the migrants returned home during
the prime years of life. In other words, the bulk
of the homeward flow of returnees was unrelated to
retirement. The reasons for the migrants' decision
to return home have been discussed at length
elsewhere (cf. Gmelch, 1983; Richling, 1985).

A comparison of the place of residence of the
migrants before and after their return reveals that
for the majority return migration was essentially an
urban to rural movement. Over 64 per cent of the
sample left cities in North America and Britain with
populations of more than one million. The same
percentage of the sample then resettled in rural
outports in Newfoundland with populations under
1,000; only 6 per cent of the sample returned to
urban areas with populations greater than 5,000.

THE IMPACT OF RETURN MIGRATION

Introduction of Work Skills

In Newfoundland, as in other underdeveloped societies, a large proportion of emigrants are unskilled
and poorly educated when they leave home. Some pro-
ponents of emigration (see e.g. Rose, 1969) argue,
however, that during their stay abroad many emigrants
acquire industrial work skills and training, that,
for migrants who eventually return home, contribute
to the economic development and modernisation of
their underdeveloped homelands. But do Newfoundland
migrants return with more work skills and training
than they had before they left? And if so, what kind
of skills do they acquire? We attempted to measure
this by comparing the migrants' occupational status
before they left Newfoundland with their status after
they returned. We also asked the respondents
directly if they had learned a trade or skill while
away, and if so what. The picture which emerges
from responses to these questions is not as clear as
we hoped for, but it does offer us some clues as to
what the migrants' economic impact might be.

Table 9.1 compares the migrants' occupations
before emigration and after their return home. It
shows a sharp decline in the percentage of migrants
in skilled jobs, from 27 per cent prior to emigration to just 10 per cent after their return. And
the categories requiring skills or advanced education (i.e. executive/professional, administration/
business, skilled) all show small to moderate

189

Table 9.1: Occupations of Migrants Before Emigration and
After Their Return to Newfoundland (n = 420).

	Before Emigration %	After Returning Home %
Executive/professional	1	2
Administration/business	7	11
Service	13	14
Skilled	10	12
Semi-skilled	6	7
Fishing	8	4
Unskilled	27	10
Unemployed	28	28
Retired	0	12
	100	100

Source: Authors' survey.

increases. Conversely the proportion of migrants
in fishing declined from 8 to 4 per cent. In short,
there is some evidence for the migrants having
improved their occupational status. However, it
must be remembered that most migrants left Newfoundland in their late teens and early twenties, and that
some would have moved up to better jobs at home had
they never left Newfoundland.

Table 9.1 also shows that 28 per cent of the
returnees are unemployed after returning home, a
figure identical to the number unemployed before
emigration. Hence, having mainland work experience
does not appear to improve the migrants' prospects
of obtaining a job.

Next, we asked the migrants if they had learned
a trade or skill while living outside Newfoundland.
Thirty-nine per cent said yes, although it was clear
that many defined 'skill' or 'trade' rather loosely.
For example, many included in this category any type
of job training, from driving a taxi to nurse's aid,
in which they had learned something new. The percentage of the sample that actually acquired new
work skills, defined as knowledge of a specific art
or trade, was probably closer to 15 per cent. The
most common trades or skills in this category were
electrician, mechanic, machinist, welder, heavy
equipment operator, health care worker, nurse, and
office worker (e.g. typist, computer operator). Far
less common were those, mainly in urban areas, who

acquired business or professional expertise: among
them were an insurance broker, pilot, wildlife bio-
logist and physician.

But obtaining a skill abroad does not guarantee
that it will be used at home. Rural Newfoundland
simply lacks the industrial base to support a skilled
or even semi-skilled work force of any size. Rather,
employment opportunities are concentrated in the
primary industries, notably the fisheries and
fishery-related manufacturing, such as fish processing plants, and in the service sector. These areas
rely mainly on unskilled labour. But some skilled
returnees were able to resettle in a small outport
and work at jobs which utilised their skills by
commuting to urban regional centres. This type of
commuting was found to be a typical adaptation
among returnees in the Bay of Islands region, and
occurs commonly in other rural districts that are
within reach of urban centres.

Investment of Repatriated Earnings

After years of hard work and saving, many migrants
return home with considerable amounts of capital.
More than 40 per cent of the sample claimed to have
saved between $5,000 and $10,000, and a quarter of
the sample returned with more than $10,000. Repatri-
ated capital was derived not only from income saved
from work outside the province, but also from the
sale of assets accumulated while away which could
not easily be transported home, such as houses, cars,
appliances and large pieces of furniture.

In considering the potential impact of repatriated capital, the most significant question is
perhaps not how much money the returnees bring back
but what they do with it. Rhoades (1978) and
Swanson (1979) believe the key issue is whether the
migrants invest their repatriated earnings in enterprises, such as new businesses or cooperatives,
which will raise the productive capacity of the
region and generate further capital, or whether they
spend their earnings on housing and consumer goods
to raise their living standards.

Using a list of seven possible investments we
asked the migrants how they had invested their
savings. The results (see Table 9.2) show that the
main investment priority for over half the sample
was housing. Another 16 per cent spent the largest
share of their savings on furniture or appliances,
and 9 per cent on land for either a future house
site or as an investment. Over one-quarter (27 per

Table 9.2: Investment of Repatriated Earnings at Home
(n = 420).

Type of Investment	Migrants %[1]
House purchase	53
Living expenses while looking for work	27
Furniture and electric appliances	16
Land for a house or for investment	9
Business (to start or expand)	10
Fishing boat and gear	4
Automobile	8

Note: 1. Percentages total more than 100 due to migrants
making more than one major investment.

Source: Authors' survey.

cent), mostly those who were unable to find work
immediately, spent their savings on living expenses
to support their families. Ten per cent used their
savings to open a business. Most common were small
general stores or 'groceterias', fast food take-
away stands, and auto repair shops; the list also
included a few larger enterprises, such as a lounge
bar and a motel. A prominent incentive behind such
investments was the desire for the owner to be his
own boss. Several respondents indicated that small
businesses were ideally suited to meeting the needs
of their families, require few specialised skills to
establish and operate (with the exception of repair
businesses), and freed them from the uncertainties
of the rural Newfoundland labour market. Small
enterprises abound in the outports and tend to be
remarkably resilient despite the poor conditions
affecting the small business sector generally. This
can be attributed to the absence of property taxes
in most rural communities, the common practice of
running the business out of the proprietor's house
(e.g. in a front room or porch), employing family
members, and the small but regular local clienteles.
In contrast to this type of investment, few
returnees -- only 4 per cent -- used repatriated
savings to purchase fishing boats, gear, or fishing
licences. Despite the relative importance of the
fisheries in Newfoundland, several factors weigh
heavily against entry into this type of work. They

include the expense of licensing new inshore fishing
boats, the emphasis on employment in capital intensive off-shore fisheries (or in related fish processing), and the general and widespread instability in
the fishing industry. Moreover, those engaged in
local inshore fishing, especially on a full-time
basis, tend not to be migratory in the first place
-- only 8 per cent of survey respondents were employed in the fishery before emigration. Other
studies (e.g. Wadel, 1969) have indicated that full-
time fishermen comprise the core of permanent (non-
migratory) residents in many outports.

When investments in small business and fishing
are considered together, we find that approximately
one out of seven returnees invested savings in an
income-producing activity. In view of the fact that
such investments tend to provide subsistence for
the proprietors and their families and do not
generate surplus capital or create employment, the
economic benefit of this use of repatriated savings
is minimal for the larger community.

In other societies observers (e.g. Griffiths,
1979; King, 1978; Rhoades, 1978; Swanson, 1979) have
cited the returnees' expenditures on lavish homes
and furnishings, and their failure to invest in new
businesses, as evidence of economic conservatism and
of their minimal contribution to the development of
the home society. We should not expect so much,
however, since in the Newfoundland context housing
is a basic requirement that must be satisfied by all
migrants. The reason many migrants left Newfoundland in the first place was to find work that would
enable them to save enough money to purchase or build
a home of their own. Given the comparatively small
amounts of capital that the migrants returned with,
most simply would not have had enough money to both
buy a house and start a business. Unfortunately,
the survey does not tell us how many migrants were
eventually able to start up a business once they got
established.

Investment in housing does have some benefit
for the community and local economy. The presence
of many new or renovated houses gives an air of
prosperity to areas where there is a lot of emigrant
financed housing, and the new construction and reno-
vation increases local employment. On the other
hand, the jobs created are usually of a temporary
nature, with the continuation depending upon a
regular flow of returnees with capital to invest in
housing. And many returnees bypass local labour,
choosing instead to build their own houses. They

may even acquire the wood from nearby forests, using privately-owned machinery to prepare it for use. What extra labour or equipment is required is often obtained through reciprocal cooperation with kinsmen and neighbours. Hence, the construction of new housing may not in fact bolster the local economy in any significant way.

Introduction of New Ideas

Have the migrants introduced modern ideas acquired on the mainland into their home communities? And if so, have these new ideas stimulated changes at the local level, leading to greater efficiencies in production and investment, or encouraging new trends in consumerism? Or, conversely, has the migrants' role been a conservative one, simply encouraging the maintenance of traditional values and practices? This dimension was by far the most difficult of the three areas of the returnees' impact to measure. In the main, our data, which are here derived mostly from informal interviews, suggest that the return migrant's impact is minimal. This is partially due to the fact that present-day rural Newfoundlanders, unlike those in the pre-confederation period, have already been exposed to many mainland ideas and attitudes through national television and radio, the print media, tourism, and in many cases travel to the mainland itself. In short, it is difficult to disentangle the possible role of return migrants as culture change agents from other mainland influences. In many cases the return migrants' urban mainland experience only distinguished them from their non-migrant neighbours in terms of their degree of exposure to mainland culture -- the differences between them being of degree, not of kind.

The fact that Newfoundland return migrants are not accorded special status in the outports minimises the likelihood that others will adopt or emulate what new ideas and attitudes they do bring back. The rural Newfoundlander's numerous contacts with the outside and the increased frequency of return migration in the last decade have relegated the arrival home of return migrants to the status of non-events. While returnees in some societies are accorded a special status, such as the Italian americano or returnee from the USA (Gilkey, 1967), or the Spanish alemán or returnee from West Germany (Rhoades, 1978), no such status or appellation exists in Newfoundland.[4]

The returnees' minimal impact may also be due
to some migrants simply not having assimilated much
of urban or Canadian values during their residence
on the mainland. In Toronto and other large cities
many working-class or rural migrants live in ethnic
enclaves which act as a buffer between them and the
mainstream urban world. Even in the workplace some
migrants worked primarily with other Newfoundlanders.
Some evidence of the migrants not having assimilated
much of an urban ethos can be seen in the migrants'
negative evaluations of mainland life when discussing their motivations for returning home. Below is
a selection of remarks migrants made about urban
mainland life:

> I got a little sick of Toronto...You always had
> to be looking over your shoulder when you walked
> down the street, because you never knew!...It's
> just too big, and getting bigger and worse all
> the time.

> I couldn't stand Toronto! I don't like the big
> city and all that. I'd rather have a little
> space -- wide open, like here...

> 'The Harbour' is home! All the places I ever
> been, I wouldn't trade home for any of them.
> I don't mind going so much, but I'm coming home
> just as soon as I get my ten weeks in (unem-
> ployment insurance qualifying period).

Hence, while many migrants valued the city for its
amenities and activity, they preferred the outport
for its greater social comfort and familiarity.
These migrants felt a sense of relief at being home
in the small, close-knit, quiet outport of their
youth; they believed that rural Newfoundland offered
them an escape from the ills -- crime, drugs,
impersonality -- of city life. Migrants with this
frame of mind are less likely to promote mainland
ideas and attitudes.

CONCLUDING SUMMARY

This study has found only limited evidence in the
three areas investigated for return migrants having
a significant, beneficial impact in rural Newfoundland. The migrants' ability to apply work skills
acquired on the mainland and to invest in new
businesses or other productive enterprises is, to

some degree, hindered by structural economic factors
relating to rural underdevelopment. Simply, there
is often a mismatch between the migrants' new
industrial skills and the preindustrial economy to
which they return. Nevertheless, rural return migration in Newfoundland does contribute in an important
way to the stability of the once beleaguered rural
sector. By settling in small communities and en-
during high rates of unemployment, geographical
isolation, and the lack of urban-style amenities
return migrants express by their example a preference for the outport way of life -- its intimate
social relations, community cooperation, opportunities for home production, and affordable housing.
In this respect the impact of return migration in
outport Newfoundland is a beneficial one, offering
an unambiguous message that rural society and culture
are both vibrant and viable.

NOTES

    1. The authors wish to thank the Center for
Field Research and Earthwatch for a grant for the
1979 study, and the Social Science and Humanities
Research Council of Canada for a grant (No. 410-81-
0083) for the ethnographic follow-up study in 1981-
82 conducted by Barnett Richling. The latter also
acknowledges the contributions of field assistants
Linda Parsons and Vince Walsh in 1982.
    2. Before 1949, Boston and New York City were
the main destinations for migrants. Since confederation, the heaviest migrant traffic has been to Nova
Scotia, to the larger cities of Ontario, and more
recently to Alberta and British Columbia.
    3. The sharing of resources and labour is an
important and traditional adaptation in rural
Newfoundland, enabling residents to achieve highly-
valued goals, such as debt-free or inexpensive
housing.
    4. Newfoundlanders refer to out-migration
itself as 'going up' to the mainland, and occasionally to those who leave as 'up-alongs'. But they
have no term for returnees, though non-Newfoundland-
ers who settle in the province may be referred to as
'come-from-aways'.

REFERENCES

Gilkey, G.R. (1967) 'The United States and Italy:
    migration and repatriation', Journal of Develop-
    ing Areas, 2(1), pp. 23-35.

Gmelch, G. (1983) 'Who returns and why: return
    migration behaviour in two North Atlantic
    societies', Human Organization, 42(1), pp. 46-
    54.
Griffiths, S. (1979) 'Emigration and entrepreneur-
    ship in a Philippine peasant village', Papers
    in Anthropology, 20(1), pp. 127-144.
King, R.L. (1978) 'Return migration: review of
    some case studies from Southern Europe',
    Mediterranean Studies, 1(2), pp. 3-30.
Newfoundland and Labrador (1982) Survey of Migrants
    to Newfoundland and Labrador, 1980-81, New-
    foundland Statistic Agency, St. John's.
Newfoundland and Labrador (1983) Persistence and
    Change: The Social and Economic Development of
    Rural Newfoundland and Labrador, 1971 to 1981,
    Department of Rural Agricultural and Northern
    Development, St. John's.
Rhoades, R.E. (1978) 'Intra-European return migra-
    tion and rural development: lessons from the
    Spanish case', Human Organization, 37(2),
    pp. 136-147.
Richling, B. (1985) 'You'd never starve here:
    return migration to rural Newfoundland',
    Canadian Review of Sociology and Anthropology,
    2(2), in press.
Rose, A. (1969) Migrants in Europe, University of
    Minnesota Press, Minneapolis.
Swanson, J. (1979) 'The consequences of emigration
    for economic development: a review of the
    literature', Papers in Anthropology, 20(1),
    pp. 39-56.
Wadel, C. (1969) Marginal Adaptations and Moderniza-
    tion in Newfoundland: A Study of Strategies
    and Implications of Resettlement and Redevelop-
    ment of Outport Fishing Communities, Memorial
    University of Newfoundland, St. John's.

Chapter Ten

IMPLICATIONS OF RETURN MIGRATION FROM THE UNITED
KINGDOM FOR URBAN EMPLOYMENT IN KINGSTON, JAMAICA

Richard Nutter

Jamaican society, like many others in the Caribbean,
can be seen as a migration oriented or migration
dependent society. Emigration from Jamaica has occurred to a wide variety of destinations and has, at
some time or other, affected every sector of Jamaican society in the 150 years since Emancipation.
This chapter sets out to examine the manner in which
such a history of emigration can influence the behaviour of migrants upon return to their home
society. This examination will focus upon the idea
that return migrants can, given favourable conditions, significantly affect the course of regional
or national development (cf. Cases Mendez, 1976).
Early studies of the effects of emigration and return in the Caribbean were often optimistic about
the long-term gains of migration (Tidrick, 1966).
While this original optimism has been tempered recently (Stinner, de Albuquerque and Bryce-Laporte,
1982), it is still recognised that returnees can,
and do, act as agents of social, cultural or economic change but that the scale, impacts and benefits
of such change are debatable (Bovenkerk, 1982). The
Jamaican case shows that, while certain aspects of
return migration are of undoubted benefit, these
benefits are limited; this limitation stems in part
from the nature of the ideology which exists as an
integral element of the Caribbean migration tradition.

THE DEVELOPMENT OF A MIGRATION TRADITION

Slavery was abolished in Jamaica in 1834, but it was
not until 1840 and the end of the apprenticeship
system that the majority of the population became
officially free. In the years immediately following
1840 there were substantial labour movements out of

the island as many newly freed slaves attempted to seek economic or social independence, both of which were still largely unattainable within Jamaica itself. Statistics for this period are patchy but large movements can be discerned to a number of Caribbean and Central American destinations, principally Panama, Costa Rica and Cuba. Jamaicans emigrated to Panama during the 1850s to aid the construction of the Panama railroad. The two attempts to construct a canal across Panama, between 1883 and 1888 and between 1908 and 1914, drew further migrants; nearly 70,000 Jamaicans left for Panama between 1907 and 1914 alone (Lewis, 1980). There was a high level of emigration to Costa Rica during the late nineteenth century (Thomas-Hope, 1978), and the early decades of the twentieth century saw large-scale movements to both Cuba and the United States (Roberts, 1957). Jamaica was characterised by almost continuous emigration in the century between emancipation and the depression of the 1930s which closed most emigration outlets for Caribbean labour. Since World War Two there have been further movements, principally to Britain, Canada and the United States.

There is no doubt that these emigrations have had wide-ranging effects upon the social and economic structure of Jamaica, but this is not to suggest that the movements have been uni-directional. The failure of the first canal project, the completion of the second project in 1915, the closure of countries like Cuba and Costa Rica to alien immigrants and ultimately the Great Depression, all resulted in sizeable return flows to Jamaica (Taylor, 1976). In addition to these time-specific return flows there existed a constant level of circular migration since, as Lewis (1980, p. 28) comments of the migrants to Panama, 'it was the dream of every worker to save his money, work out his contract for labour and return to his homeland for a life of ease and comfort'.

What occurred during these years was not therefore a series of permanent emigrations but the development of a migration system containing strong elements of circularity and return. Substantial numbers of emigrants did remain overseas but at the outset the move was never intended to be permanent; instead emigration made available a potential channel of advancement and resource acquisition which operated outside the rigid constraints of Jamaican society (Thomas-Hope, 1980). The ultimate aim of every migrant was to return to the island and realise

199

the assets gained through emigration. Almost a century of continuous emigration and return has made this migration system an institutionalised part of Jamaican society and Jamaican life.

There are several damaging aspects to this institutionalisation, one of which has been the development of an externally oriented psychology and a tendency to denigrate all things Jamaican and enhance all things foreign. Early notice of this fact was given by Hadley (1949). More recently Stone (1980, p. 64) has criticised the importance placed upon migration since it breeds 'a sort of escapism, ambivalence and lack of commitment to the Jamaican political community that weakens the development of ties of loyalty and affinity to the nation'.

A positive aspect of this institutionalisation, however, lies in the importance placed upon return to the home society and the beliefs and hopes which surround the return. Returnees, and specific large-scale return flows, have had important influences on Jamaican society. The return of servicemen from Britain after World War Two is believed to have provided a direct stimulus to the migration which began in the 1950s. The huge influx of returnees during the 1930s depression was a contributing factor to the 1938 labour rebellion (Post, 1978). Many of the popular leaders of the 1930s, such as Garvey, Howell, Hibbert, Bustamante and Hart, had spent time abroad. Indeed most of Jamaica's leaders have either lived or studied abroad and the role played by these men is perhaps one of the reasons why there has developed within Jamaican society a strong association between foreign experience and domestic social or economic advancement. The belief that a person is somehow better for having been abroad is still widely held in Jamaica (Thomas-Hope, 1980).

The movement of Jamaicans to Britain, and, more particularly, the return movement cannot therefore be viewed in isolation but must instead be seen within the cultural and historical institutionalisation of migration within Jamaican society and consciousness.

RETURN MIGRATION SURVEY DATA

The data upon which this analysis of return migration is based were collected during a survey of manufacturing, retail and financial premises in the Kingston Metropolitan Area (KMA) between June 1983 and January 1984.[1] This survey utilised a 1 in 5

(20 per cent) sample of manufacturing and financial establishments supplemented by a smaller 1 in 7 (14.3 per cent) sample of retail premises within the KMA. These samples were drawn from a listing compiled from National Insurance returns and supplied to the researcher by the Ministry of Industry. The total sample comprised 576 premises in seven industrial categories: food and beverage; clothing, footwear and textile; wood and paper; metal and metal products; glass, chemical and miscellaneous manufacture; retail and wholesale; and finance and financial services. The original intention was to visit each of these 576 premises and interview any returnees from the United Kingdom employed by the particular company. However the field survey had to be prematurely halted in January 1984 when incidents of politically motivated violence occurred in Downtown Kingston. Thirty-two sample locations in Downtown and West Kingston were not considered safe to visit and were removed from the survey. The total of returnees interviewed is thus drawn from visits to 544 premises within the KMA.

A total of 93 returnees were contacted during the survey, all of whom completed the designed questionnaire. Fifty five (59.1 per cent) of those interviewed were males and 38 (40.9 per cent) females. Ages ranged from 18 to over 60 but a large proportion of the returnees (48.4 per cent) were in the 36-50 age bracket. Males were generally older than females.

The pattern of emigration for this group would seem to reflect the overall national pattern for emigration from Jamaica to the United Kingdom. The earliest year of departure was 1938, the most recent 1979. Five of those interviewed were born in the United Kingdom. The majority of the sample (47, or 50.5 per cent) left Jamaica between 1961 and 1966. The earliest year of return was 1950, the most recent 1983, although a large proportion of those interviewed (36.6 per cent) returned to Jamaica between 1971 and 1973. The number of years spent living in the United Kingdom ranged from a minimum of just over 1 year to a maximum of 27, the mean stay being 11.4 years.

ECONOMIC AND SPATIAL DISTRIBUTION OF RETURNEES

The location of returnees by industrial category is shown in Table 10.1. In total 77 premises (14.1 per cent of the sample) employeed returnees from the

Table 10.1: Employment of Returnees by Industrial Category

Category[1]	Sample Premises % total[2]	Premises with Returnees %	Returnees no.	%	Returnees per Estab.
Food and beverage	9.7	20.7	13	14.0	0.22
Textiles and clothing	12.0	11.1	9	9.7	0.12
Wood and paper	11.9	8.4	7	7.5	0.10
Chemicals and miscellaneous manufactures	11.2	6.0	5	5.4	0.07
Metal and metal products	17.4	21.2	29	31.2	0.28
Retail and wholesale	31.6	11.1	17	18.3	0.13
Financial	6.2	27.0	13	14.0	0.35
Total	100.0		93	100.0	

Notes: 1. Industrial categories based on Jamaican Ministry
            of Industry Industrial Classification.

         2. Where appropriate percentage figures have been
            adjusted using inverse sampling ratio multiplica-
            tion to compensate for the smaller sample in the
            Retail and wholesale sector. The same applies to
            Tables 10.2, 10.3 and 10.4

Source: Author's survey.

United Kingdom; 1 establishment employing 5 returnees, 1 employing 3, 10 employing 2 and 65 establishments employing a single return migrant. Table 10.1
shows that returnees were not evenly distributed
between the various industrial categories. For
example, only 6 per cent of Chemical and Miscellaneous Manufacturing premises employed returnees, compared to 27 per cent of financial concerns. This
tendency towards employment in particular sectors is
also shown by the fact that 59.1 per cent of those
returnees located were employed in three out of the
seven industrial categories, these three categories
containing only 33.3 per cent of the total sample
premises. An analysis of the average number of returnees per establishment (the final column in Table

Table 10.2: Employment of Returnees by Size of Premises

Workforce Size	Sample Premises % total	Premises Employing Returnees %	Returnees no.	%	Returnees per Estab.
10 - 24	54.0	6.0	17	18.3	0.06
25 - 49	25.5	18.1	28	30.1	0.20
50 - 74	11.1	23.9	22	23.7	0.36
75 - 99	4.7	28.6	9	9.7	0.35
over 100	4.7	43.6	17	18.3	0.65
Total	100.0		93	100.0	

Source: Author's survey.

Table 10.3: Employment of Returnees by Area of KMA

	Sample Premises % total	Premises with Returnees %	Returnees no.	%	Returnees per Estab.
Downtown	30.5	5.4	9	9.7	0.05
South West	9.4	21.4	15	16.1	0.29
Spanish Town Rd.	9.2	30.9	21	22.6	0.43
West	8.0	9.2	4	4.3	0.09
West Central	3.1	--	--	--	--
Central	14.0	22.4	20	21.5	0.25
East Central	0.6	--	--	--	--
North Central	13.9	17.1	18	19.3	0.24
North West	3.2	12.5	2	2.1	0.11
North	3.6	9.2	2	2.1	0.09
North East	3.2	7.2	1	1.1	0.06
East	0.3	50.0	1	1.1	0.50
Other	0.9		--	--	--
Total	100.0		93	100.0	

Source: Author's survey

10.1) also reveals this tendency towards concentration.
    Table 10.2 shows a similar analysis of returnee
location by size of premises based on workforce size.
A tendency towards employment in the larger

establishments clearly emerges. An analysis of returnee location by area of the KMA (Table 10.3)
reveals a similar tendency towards clustering.
Nearly 80 per cent of the returnees are employed in
four areas of the KMA (Spanish Town Road and South
West, Central and North Central St. Andrew) yet
these four areas contain only 46.5 per cent of
sample premises. By contrast Downtown Kingston,
with 30.5 per cent of sample premises, provides the
employment location of only 9.7 per cent of
returnees.

From these data it would seem that returnees
tend to be employed in one of three industrial categories, in one of four areas of the KMA and in
larger sized premises. The interrelationships be-·
tween these factors -- function, area and size --
provide only a partial explanation for this distribution, however. The spatial variation in returnee
location, for example, is to some extent a reflection of spatial variation in the location of the
various industrial categories. Similarly spatial
variation in plant size could be used to account for
the patterns of returnee location, since both South
West St. Andrew and Spanish Town Road have an over-
representation of larger size plants. However these
interrelationships are not constant since Central
St. Andrew, another area of returnee employment, is
dominated by smaller sized concerns. Moreover, no
relationship seems to exist between category and
plant size which could aid explanation of the spatial
and economic distribution of returnees.

A fuller explanation of returnee distribution
must therefore be sought elsewhere, and here an examination of the post-war evolution of the spatial
and economic structure of the KMA becomes particularly relevant. Radical change has taken place in
Kingston since the late 1940s, the central aspect of
which has been the decline of the traditional business and commercial centre of Downtown Kingston.
The age and structure of Downtown, which led to
severe problems of congestion and overcrowding, as
well as the rapid expansion of the KMA, have removed
most of the commercial and business attractions of
the old colonial centre (National Planning Agency,
1978). The relocation of the city's port facilities
to Newport West during the early 1960s sounded the
death knell for Downtown but the area had essentially
been in serious decline since the 1930s (Clarke,
1974; George and Warren, 1984).

The movement of activities from Downtown, as
well as the alternative locations chosen by

industries new to the KMA, have benefited two areas
of the city. The first of these areas is centred on
Three Mile in West Kingston, where a major industrial
estate established by the Industrial Development
Commission in 1952 stretches south east along
Marcus Garvey Drive as well as north west along
Spanish Town Road towards Six Mile. This area has
become the centre for large scale manufacturing,
retailing and import/export companies, many of them
attracted by the development legislation enacted by
Jamaica during the 1960s. The second area to benefit is situated around Half Way Tree and Crossroads
in St. Andrew. The rapid growth of New Kingston as
a major financial and commercial centre, the development of a series of modern shopping plazas on
Constant Spring Road above Half Way Tree, and the
presence of several prestige establishments, government offices, embassies and international hotels,
have all served to stimulate an area with a traditionally mixed manufacturing and commercial base
(National Planning Agency, 1978).

These two areas now form the modern cores of
the KMA despite the recent regeneration of the
waterfront (George and Warren, 1984). In central
Kingston are located many of the commercial and
financial institutions vital to Jamaica's current
development policy. Around Three Mile, Six Mile and
Marcus Garvey Drive are found a selection of the
plants at the forefront of Jamaica's emphasis on
manufacturing development for both domestic and export consumption. It is to industries within these
areas, often larger and more modern than industries
located elsewhere, that emigrants would seem to be
returning.

Before considering the significance of this
fact in more detail it is worth examining other aspects of the return flow, in particular the types of
occupations held by, and the individual motivations
of, the returnees interviewed.

OCCUPATION AND INDIVIDUAL MOTIVATION

Table 10.4 shows returnee occupation broken down by
industrial category. The most striking feature of
this table is the extremely high proportion of those
in professional and managerial positions. Fifty one
returnees are in this category and in total 78 (83.9
per cent) are employed in white collar occupations.
This occupational distribution is perhaps to be expected given the educational background of those

Table 10.4: Returnee Occupation by Industrial Category

Occupation[1]	Industrial Category[2]							Total	
	Food & Beverage	Text. & Clothing	Wood & Paper	Chemical & Misc.	Metal	Retail	Finance	no.	%
Professional & managerial	6	1	4	4	18	11	7	51	54.8
Clerical	2	5	1	1	7	5	6	27	29.0
Processing	5	--	--	--	1	--	--	6	6.4
Machine trade	--	1	1	--	--	--	--	2	2.1
Benchwork	--	1	--	--	--	--	--	1	1.1
Structural	--	--	--	--	3	--	--	3	3.2
Miscellaneous	--	1	1	--	--	1	--	3	3.2
Total	13	9	7	5	29	17	13	93	100.0

Notes: 1. Based on US Department of Labor Dictionary of Occupational Titles.
2. Based on Jamaican Ministry of Industry Industrial Classification.

Source: Author's survey.

interviewed. Forty people had been trained to degree, HNC or HND level and a further 26 had obtained
at least one 'A' level. However,the interesting
fact here is that for a large proportion of this
group this education was obtained in the United
Kingdom. Of the 78 people employed in professional,
manageral and clerical occupations, 43 had been
classified as students or juveniles at the date of
departure and a further 4 were born in the United
Kingdom. A major proportion of those in top occupational categories can thus be classified as second
generation migrants, either travelling with family
to the United Kingdom or coming to join family already settled in the country.

Two points are worthy of comment here. Firstly,
data available on the experiences of West Indians in
the United Kingdom suggest that second generation
blacks are suffering disproportionately in terms of
educational and employment opportunities (see e.g.
Home Affairs Committee, 1981). The flow of returnees detected by my survey may therefore represent
some form of creaming off process, whereby the most
skilled or the most highly motivated return home.
However, without some form of comparable survey in
the United Kingdom the truth and significance of
this assertion are difficult to assess. Secondly,
data available on the national occupational structure of Jamaica show that in 1982 77,330 people or
8.3 per cent of the total workforce were employed in
professional and managerial positions (National
Planning Agency, 1983). The difference between this
proportion and that of the returnee sample, where
54.8 per cent are employed in this category, cannot
be accounted for by any discrepancies in the classification systems used. It would seem therefore that
those returning to Jamaica for urban or industrial
employment are a skilled minority of not only the
West Indian community in the United Kingdom but also
of those in employment in Jamaica.

There are undoubted benefits in this type of
return since Jamaica has traditionally been, and
still is, drastically short of skilled manpower. At
the same time it is obvious that this return flow is
not large enough to offset losses through emigration,
for between 1978 and 1981 746 professional, administrative, technical and managerial staff were lost to
Canada alone (National Planning Agency, 1983).

Even if this numerical imbalance is disregarded,
other reservations must be held about any benefits
accruing from this return flow. Firstly, of the 93
people interviewed 23 (24.7 per cent) had definite

jobs arranged before their return to Jamaica. These
included jobs arranged through friends, inter-
company transfers, direct recruitment and jobs obtained through personal approaches to companies in
the island. Of the remaining returnees, 38 found
employment through personal contacts, that is family
or friends, after their return. A further two returnees set themselves up in business, one with a
friend from the United Kingdom. All this means that
only 30 returnees (32.2 per cent) had to seek work
through official or non-personal channels such as
adverts or the media. The majority of returnees
thus either had jobs pre-arranged or acquired employment through institutional, family or friendship
ties. The significance of these figures, which reflect the widespread social networks underpinning
the operation of the migration system in Jamaica, is
further discussed in the Conclusion.

A second reservation as to the true benefits of
this return migration stream centres upon the personal motivations of returnees. The question of
migrant motivation is a difficult one to address;
indeed given the strong return orientation in
Caribbean migration to even begin to ask about
reasons for return may be a false process. However,
it seems that two very general reasons can be discerned from this survey, one or both of which were
mentioned by all those interviewed. Firstly, it was
frequently stated that a 'better life' could be
lived in Jamaica and secondly, that Jamaica was
'home'. The concept of a better life seems to include obvious advantages, such as the climate,
friends and family, as well as more abstract benefits such as the prestige and social status associated with return and the type of occupations in
which skilled or educated returnees can expect to be
employed. Despite relatively lower wages in Jamaica
nearly all the returnees claimed to be enjoying a
better standard of life than that which they had
been able to obtain in the United Kingdom. Further
it would seem that for the majority of returnees
their particular occupation may not, in itself, be
important; satisfaction for many seems to come from
the lifestyle often associated with their occupation
and from the social and economic benefits attached
not only to their occupation but also to their
position in society as a returnee.

CONCLUSIONS

To assess the likely impacts and benefits of return migration from the United Kingdom it is necessary to attempt a synthesis of these hitherto disparate threads -- types of industry and occupation to which migrants return and the role of these in national development, methods of job acquisition, personal motivation and the existence of an institutionalised migration tradition.

Firstly, from this survey it would seem that emigrants who return for urban employment in Kingston enter industrial sectors at the forefront of Jamaica's modern economic development strategy. Serious doubts have been expressed as to the long-term gains from this strategy and it has been argued that this style of development can be seen to be increasing the social and economic inequalities which currently exist in Jamaica (Girvan, 1983). The occupations held by many returnees within these sectors are of central importance to this development strategy. The number of white collar workers in Jamaica has grown rapidly in recent years (National Planning Agency, 1983) and the presence and relative wealth of this expanding social elite are clearly visible in metropolitan centres like Kingston. Clearly return of this type cannot be detrimental to the island since it does help to offset, albeit to a limited extent, the loss of skilled manpower through emigration. However the imbalance between the number of those emigrating and those returning is just one limitation on the potential benefits of return.

The individual orientation of most returnees along with the strong emphasis placed upon the importance of personal success were two of the overriding features detected by this survey. These features are in part the result of a century during which the idea of escape from the constraints of Jamaican society through emigration and eventual successful return became deeply embedded in the social consciousness of the population. The importance of these features stems from the manner in which they condition the views which returnees hold about themselves, their occupations and their position in society. For many returnees the particular type of industry or occupation to which they return is not in itself of major importance. Instead it is the fact that the modern urban sector makes available a prestigious and enviable lifestyle, befitting their status as returnees, which seems for many to be the major attraction. The links which undoubtably exist in Caribbean societies between a migration tradition, return and development need a great deal more study but in this case a clear conflict would seem to arise between national development and individual priorities of migrants. The migration tradition places great emphasis on personal success and achievement. Employment in the modern urban sectors gives returnees an obvious channel through which such success can be realised, yet at the same time the wider social benefits of the development strategy upon which the growth of these sectors is dependent are debatable.

Secondly, it would seem that the traditional prestige attached to foreign experience, and in particular to a foreign education, may give skilled returnees such as those detected by this survey an edge over their domestic counterparts in the field of job competition. In Jamaica patronage relationships and social contacts underpin successful occupation acquisition. These factors may lead to a circular, self-reinforcing process of reasoning. Returnees obtain prestigious employment partly because of their foreign experience and often through personal contacts; prestigious employment then reinforces the social belief that time abroad somehow makes a person 'better' and deepens the external psychological orientation of Jamaican society. Furthermore while such systems of patronage and social support are not necessarily bad -- in small societies heavily dependent upon emigration and return they are often a necessary part of survival -- in Jamaica they may have serious consequences. The opportunity to emigrate is becoming increasingly the preserve of either the middle classes or of skilled personnel and a system of social support such as that which exists in Jamaica merely magnifies the privileges already held by a relatively privileged social class.

In conclusion it must be said that migration, in particular flows of skilled return migrants, can benefit Jamaican society. At best, though, these benefits are limited by the small scale of the return flows over both time and space and by the individual motivations of the returnees. At worst the operation of the migration system can be seen to be not only reinforcing a particular system of economic development, cultural values and patronage ties but also strengthening an emphasis on personal success and advancement, and both are leading to increased social and economic inequalities within the island.

NOTE

   1.   This work was undertaken during the tenure
(1981-84) of a Social Science Research Council
Linked Studentship in UK-Caribbean Migration Studies,
supervised by Dr. Elizabeth Thomas-Hope in the
Geography Department, Liverpool University.

REFERENCES

Bovenkerk, F. (1982) 'Why returnees do not turn out
     to be "agents of change": notes on the litera-
     ture', in W.F. Stinner, K. de Albuquerque & R.S.
     Bryce-Laporte (eds.) Return Migration and
     Remittances: Developing a Caribbean Perspec-
     tive, Smithsonian Institution, Occasional Paper
     3, Washington, DC, pp. 183-216.
Cases Mendez, J.I. (1976) 'The relation between
     migration policy and economic development and
     the promotion of new employment possibilities
     for returnees', International Migration, 14,
     pp. 134-162.
Clarke, C.G. (1974) Kingston, Jamaica: Urban Growth
     and Social Change, 1692-1962, University of
     California Press, Berkeley.
George, V. and Warren, C. (1984) 'The Kingston
     waterfront: evaluation of a redevelopment
     scheme', Caribbean Geography, 1, pp. 203-207.
Girvan, N. (1972) Foreign Capital and Economic
     Underdevelopment in Jamaica, ISER, Kingston.
Hadley, C.V.D. (1949) 'Personality patterns, social
     class and aggression in the British West
     Indies', Human Relations, 2, pp. 143-148.
Home Affairs Committee (1981) Racial Disadvantage:
     Fifth Report, HMSO, London.
Lewis, L.S. (1980) The West Indian in Panama: Black
     Labour in Panama, 1850-1914, University Press
     of America, Washington, DC.
National Planning Agency (1978) Urban Growth and
     Management Study: Final Report, Government
     Printer, Kingston.
National Planning Agency (1983) Economic and Social
     Survey: Jamaica 1982, Government Printer,
     Kingston.
Post, K. (1978) Arise ye Starvelings: The Jamaican
     Labour Rebellion of 1938 and its Aftermath,
     Martinus Nijhoff, The Hague.
Roberts, G.W. (1957) The Population of Jamaica,
     Cambridge University Press, London.

Stinner, W.F., de Albuquerque, K. and Bryce-Laporte, R.S. (1982) Return Migration and Remittances: Developing a Caribbean Perspective, Smithsonian Institution, Occasional Paper 3, Washington, DC.

Stone, C. (1980) Democracy and Clientelism in Jamaica, Transaction Inc., New Jersey.

Taylor, E. (1976) 'The social adjustment of returned migrants to Jamaica', in F. Henry (ed.) Ethnicity in the Americas, Mouton, The Hague, pp. 213-229.

Thomas-Hope, E.M. (1978) 'The establishment of a migration tradition: British West Indian movements to the Hispanic Caribbean in the century after emancipation', in C.G. Clarke (ed.) Caribbean Social Relations, University of Liverpool, Centre for Latin American Studies, Monograph Series 8, pp. 66-81.

Thomas-Hope, E.M. (1980) 'Hopes and reality in the West Indian migration to Britain', Oral History, 8, pp. 35-42.

Tidrick, G. (1966) 'Some aspects of Jamaican emigration to the United Kingdom, 1953-62', Social and Economic Studies, 15, pp. 22-39.

Chapter Eleven

RETURN MIGRATION TO ALGERIA: THE IMPACT OF STATE
INTERVENTION

Richard Lawless

ALGERIA AND THE FRENCH LABOUR MARKET

Algeria was the first Maghreb country to become in-
corporated in the French labour market. The French
military conquest of Algeria in 1830 was quickly
followed by massive settler colonisation and the
expropriation of the most fertile lands which passed
under the control of European farmers. The majority
of Algerians were condemned to eke out a meagre and
miserable livelihood in the more inhospitable mountains and steppelands. As the colonial period pro-
gressed and the Algerian population increased,
pressure of population on a limited and fragile
resource base provoked new patterns of migration.
Dispossessed and impoverished in their own country,
Algerians began to seek employment across the
Mediterranean in Europe, the vast majority in France.
     At first the movement grew slowly but during
the First World War Algerian labour was recruited
directly by the French government, especially the
Ministry of War, to work in munitions factories,
army service workshops, transport and the mines.
During 1914-1918 North Africa supplied France with
175,000 soldiers and 150,000 workers, of whom the
great majority were Algerians. Immediately after
the First World War most Algerian workers were
repatriated. However, the boom of the 1920s soon
resulted in a new and considerable influx of
Algerians to France, despite restrictive pressure
from the European settlers who were opposed to the
departure to France of their supply of cheap labour.
The economic slump of the 1930s caused many to return home again and the Algerian labour force
employed in France fell to a third of its former
size. Emigration was suspended during the Second
World War but after the liberation of France one of

the main preoccupations of the French government
was the supply of labour needed for economic re-
covery and reconstruction. Free circulation was
gradually re-established and once again the Algerian
migratory movement swelled. By 1950 there were
about a quarter of a million Algerians working in
France. Migrant workers were cheap labour for the
European capitalist economy because they were imported as 'ready-made' wage workers whose upbringing
had been paid for by the countries of origin. Wages
for unskilled labour were kept low and this in turn
held down unit labour costs at the time when economic growth and full employment in France would
otherwise have caused them to soar. By 1962, the
eve of Algerian Independence, the Algerian population in France had reached 350,484, equivalent to
nearly a fifth of the adult male population of
Algeria.
     During the first decade of Algerian independ-
ence the Algerian population in France more than
doubled. By 1973 the 850,000 strong Algerian community had become the largest foreign group in
France accounting for almost a quarter of the total
foreign population in the country. The Evian
Accords (1961), which set out in detail the nature
of relations between France and the independent
Algerian Republic, provided for the continued access
of Algerians to the French labour market. But the
freedom of circulation guaranteed by those accords
soon came under attack from French officials who
felt that a renewed influx of Algerians seeking work
in France would strain the absorptive capacity of
the French economy. In Algeria the continuing reliance on the export of labour as a solution to the
country's unemployment problems was denounced by
left wing forces within the Front de Libération
Nationale (FLN). Their leading spokesman, Mohamed
Harbi, declared that 'the only valid solution is the
stabilisation of employment at home and the immediate halt to emigration'. But the Algerian government of Ben Bella regarded the interruption of emigration as unrealistic given the legacy of acute
economic and social underdevelopment inherited from
colonialism. Nevertheless, Ben Bella desired to
bring emigration more firmly under government control, and in November 1962 the Office National
Algérien de Main d'Oeuvre (ONAMO) was set up. One
of its tasks was to apply selective criteria to
prospective emigrants and check the outflow.
     In 1964 Algeria and France signed the Nekkache-
Grandval Accord on emigration. Almost at once the
214

new agreement was criticised in Algeria because it
gave the French the right to determine unilaterally
how many Algerians were to be admitted to the French
labour market. The annual contingent of Algerians
to be admitted was fixed by France at about 12,000
per year which the Algerians considered insufficient.

After the military coup in 1965 which overthrew
Ben Bella and installed Boumedienne and the Oujda
group in power, major changes took place in the
Algerian government's attitude towards emigration.
Boumedienne's government embarked upon a development
policy which involved the nationalisation of foreign
economic interests, the control of all key sectors
of the economy by state-owned monopolies and the
development of the economy by concentrating investment on the creation of a relatively small, highly
efficient modern sector, based upon hydrocarbons
and other heavy industry. The choice of modernisation on the basis of a high technology, heavy
industrialisation programme created relatively few
jobs in its early stages and hardly touched the
agricultural sector where some two-thirds of the
population gained their livelihood. The ability to
export surplus labour remained a vital safety valve
for the relief of social pressures due to unemployment and underemployment. The Nekkache-Grandval
Accord was, therefore, a considerable obstacle to the
new regime's industrialisation strategy. Algerian
economic planners wanted a substantial and reliable
exodus of labour from rural areas so that resources
could be devoted to the industrialisation programme
and not sidetracked into what they regarded as less-
productive rural investment. Their objective in the
next round of negotiations with France was, therefore, the establishment of a fixed multi-annual
contingent. In the Accord which was eventually
signed in October 1968 a contingent of 35,000 workers
was authorised to enter France each year for the
next three years, after which a new contingent would
be negotiated. ONAMO selected the candidates for
emigration so that the choice of age, education and
skill of the emigrants was made by Algeria in accordance with its own perceived development needs
rather than by France in accordance with its
requirements.

In particular further efforts were made to
diversify the regions from which emigrants were
drawn so as to ensure a more even distribution of
revenues and other 'benefits' of migration for
employment. The vast majority of Algerian emigrants
came from rural areas. However, after 1962 there

was an increase in the number of emigrants from
urban areas, although many in reality were recently
arrived peasants who had been forced off their land
during the War of Independence -- the city had become merely a stage in the migratory chain linking
the Algerian countryside with the industrial centres
of France. But in addition the development plans
adopted by the Boumedienne government required a
considerable amount of skilled labour which was in
short supply in Algeria. This led the Algerian
authorities to consider the necessity of reintegrat-
ing qualified Algerians working in France into the
Algerian economic system. However, they believed
that it was more difficult to attract a worker from
one part of Algeria to another than it was to
attract him back from abroad. Migrants returning
from France almost always wished to go back to their
home area rather than to other parts of the country.
Therefore, a policy that diversified the sources of
emigration would make it much easier to bring about
the subsequent return of skilled workers into those
areas where they were needed (Adler, 1977).

The method introduced to promote this diversification was the adoption of new criteria for the
distribuiton of the annual contingent according to
the wilaya (department) of the migrants. This
system gave a weighting coefficient of three for the
wilaya's population, two for the number of residents
already absent and one for the actual number of
demands to emigrate. The areas which traditionally
have had the highest rates of emigration are not
those with the most population. Consequently the
coefficient of three for population disfavoured
these regions as did the weight of only one for the
criterion of demand. This policy of regional diversification of emigration was accompanied by a series
of special measures initiated by the government to
create employment in areas which had traditionally
experienced high rates of underemployment -- notably
the wilayas of Tizi Ouzou, parts of the Aurès and
Setif. Kabylia was selected for the first of these
special programmes which started in 1968 and included the opening of special credits for the
construction of factories, schools and infrastruc-
tures.

Because of the growing demand in Algeria for
skilled manpower the authorities sought to restrict
the departure of qualified workers. By the early
1970s the proportion of skilled workers had fallen
to just over 2 per cent of all departures. Indeed
the level of skill on entry was very much lower for

Algerians than for almost every other nationality
with significant immigration to France. But to take
advantage of training facilities in France workers
had to be literate. As most Algerian unskilled
workers were also illiterate the increase in the proportion of such labourers among departures implied
that their chances of acquiring skills abroad would
probably be reduced (Adler, 1977).

Other criteria for selecting candidates were
designed to favour those most in need in order to
ensure that the benefits of emigration were distributed as widely as possible. Although in theory no
one who could be found a job in Algeria was allowed
to emigrate, in practice Algerians who might have
found work at home were given permission to leave.
In an attempt to tighten up procedures, in January
1972 the Minister of Labour issued a circular requiring ONAMO to accept applications only from unemployed married workers with at least one child and
unmarried unemployed workers over 24 years of age.
Applications from other persons were to be refused.

On the whole the 1968 Accord was a much more
advantageous agreement for Algeria than the 1964
Protocol. The 35,000 holders of an ONAMO card and a
medical certificate from the French medical authorities were allowed to enter France to look for work
for a period of up to nine months. When they found
a job they were issued with a residence certificate.
Few problems arose over these arrangements. In 1971
a new contingent of 25,000 per year was negotiated
for the following two years at the end of which dis-
cussions were to take place to revise existing
arrangements.

THE TERMINATION OF EMIGRATION AND THE THREAT OF
EXPULSION FROM FRANCE

In the early 1970s both the Algerian and French governments, though for very different reasons, sought
to terminate all new labour migration from Algeria
to France. France, like its neighbours West Germany,
Belgium and the Netherlands, was becoming concerned
over the high level of immigration which had been
occurring and the tendency for some sectors of the
economy to become overdependent on foreign labour
reserves. It was becoming clear that France could
not escape the social costs of the reproduction of
the labour force. As migrant workers grew in number
and stayed longer, they demanded the right to bring
their families and called for better housing and

social conditions. These demands were backed by the growth of political organisations and strike movements. As the economic recession began to bite, France banned completely the entry of workers from outside the EEC in 1974 and a few years later, in the face of rising national unemployment, sought to persuade the established immigrant community to return home. In 1977 for example the French government introduced an 'aid to return' programme offering a repatriation allowance of 10,000FF (about £1,000) to all foreign workers who had worked in France for at least five years. By the end of the 1970s a deepening of the European recession resulted in mounting hostility to migrant workers who were accused of taking jobs that would otherwise have been made available to French job seekers. The French government made every effort to convince public opinion that the size of the foreign community was a cause of the high level of unemployment among French nationals, even though there was little evidence that a reduction in the number of foreign workers would release an equivalent number of jobs for the French. In March 1981, during the French presidential campaign, M. Giscard d'Estaing declared 'We have a million and a half unemployed and we have a million and a half foreign workers, without counting those who enter freely from the countries of the Common Market. The number of immigrant workers must be reduced by several hundred thousand in the next few years' (Lawless, Findlay and Findlay, 1982). As early as 1979 Lionel Stoleru, the French Secretary of State at the Ministry of Labour with responsibility for migrant workers, made it clear that he intended to adjust the size of the foreign community to the employment situation by restricting the renewal of residence permits; an annual reduction of between 3 and 5 per cent was required, representing an annual departure of some 120,000 to 200,000 persons.

However, in September 1973, almost a year before France's decision to suspend immigration and only a few months before new negotiations on Algerian migration to France, the Algerian government terminated unilaterally all new emigration to France declaring that this represented the first step in a new programme to reintegrate the migrant community into the Algerian economy and society. The decision followed a series of racist incidents in the south of France directed against Algerians. Some observers were convinced that Algeria would break off diplomatic relations with France if these incidents were not rapidly brought under control. Adler (1977), however, points out that racism against Algerian workers was a long-established problem. He suggests that the decision to terminate emigration to France was political and that international considerations probably led to this dramatic gesture. According to Adler, Algeria's apparent dependence on France in labour matters was a source of embarrassment to the government's self-image as a leader of the non-aligned world -- a perception heightened by the fact that the summit conference of non-aligned nations was due to take place in Algiers in September 1973.

By contrast, the Amicale des Algériens en Europe, the FLN's antenna in Europe, no doubt articulating the official Algerian government's position, stated that the decision to suspend emigration was made possible by the creation of new employment opportunities through planned industrialisation and the land reform introduced in late 1971. A shift in the government's emphasis in labour policy is illustrated by the Second Four Year Development Plan (1974-77) in which the creation of new employment became the 'major priority aim of development'. Indeed, by 1973 some local improvements in employment opportunities had certainly occurred, but at the national level the labour situation had hardly improved by comparison with 1968. Employment had barely kept pace with the natural growth in the labour force, leaving untouched the backlog of existing unemployed people. Some idea of the intensity of pressure on the labour market can be seen from the fact that in January 1972 there were over 200,000 candidates for emigration in the different Bureaux de Main d'Oeuvre in a year when the contingent was fixed at 25,000. The decision to terminate all new emigration to France therefore does appear to have been basically a political one.

Whatever the original intention, it soon became clear that the suspension was not to be temporary. The National Charter, which defines the fundamental principles for the organisation of Algerian society, reaffirmed the country's commitment to the return and progressive reintegration of the migrant community as one of the major objectives of the Socialist Revolution. It states:

> Because of the development of the country workers no longer need to emigrate to find a job. Moreover by the different actions which it has undertaken to transform the society and to build socialism, the Revolution has created

for each Algerian the obligation of making his
contribution to that common task of national
reconstruction...The necessary efforts will be
accomplished to facilitate the reinsertion of
our migrant workers into the national community.

THE THREE 'AGES' OF ALGERIAN EMIGRATION AND THE
CHANGING PATTERN OF RETURN MIGRATION

Abdelmalek Sayad (1977) in a seminal article entitled 'Les trois "âges" de l'émigration Algérienne
en France' argues that the different phases of
emigration to France relate to the internal processes of transformation affecting the rural communities
which have produced the migrants. The first age of
emigration, from its origins to the Second World War,
was a response to the destructive impact of French
colonisation on the traditional peasant economy and
society. Emigration provided the Algerian peasant
with additional resources to support his family.
The migrant left for France as the representative of
the extended family or community for a limited
period of time and with a limited set of objectives
-- to pay off debts, to buy a piece of land or farm
animals, to rebuild the family house or to pay for
a brother's marriage. Such representatives were
carefully chosen by the community, giving rise to a
certain division of labour between those peasants
who worked within the village economy and those who
were employed outside it. The 'sponsored' migrants
should not be too young or unmarried and had to
enjoy the confidence and trust of their group. They
had to be able to adapt to the new conditions of
work in France while remaining true to their peasant
values. Even in exile the migrant was called upon
to live and think like a peasant and in an alien
environment he took refuge among other migrants from
the same region in an attempt to reconstruct in
France the community he had left behind. The rhythm
of their departures and return was determined by the
demands of the agricultural calendar rather than by
the requirements of the industries in which the
migrant found employment. Departures normally took
place after ploughing had been completed at the end
of the autumn or the beginning of winter. Return
coincided with harvest time and the period of intense social activity (in particular the marriage
season) which followed. The migrant's mission to
France was to be completed in the shortest time
possible and any prolonging of the stay abroad

incurred the reprobation of family and community.
On his return the migrant was submitted to a ritu-
alised 'reintegration' into the community. After a
number of years had passed a new mission might be
undertaken, but as before this would be determined
and carefully controlled by the extended family and
village community.

An acceleration of the process of 'depeasantisation' ushered in the second age of emigration.
The impoverishment and disintegration of peasant
society could not be reversed by temporary migration
to France. Contact with the colonial society, the
penetration and generalisation of monetary ex-
changes, and the impact of emigration itself in up-
rooting the peasant from his land, even if only for
a limited period of time, reinforced the process of
depeasantisation. New conditions in the countryside,
in particular a growing dissatisfaction with agricultural work and traditional ways of life, gave
rise to a new form of emigration and a new type of
emigrant. Anxious to seek a new life beyond the
traditional peasant community, the new migrant
aspired to a full-time job outside the Algerian
agricultural sector and to an economic and social in-
dividualism that had been denied to his predecessor.
Whereas emigration during the first age was firmly
under the control of traditional society and aimed
to reinforce and strengthen that society, the second
age was characterised by a sharp break with the
village community and its traditional values. It
was no longer a mission conferred by the group on
one of its members but the act of an individual who
sought to free himself from the constraints of the
community. In particular it was the young men of
the village who wished to abandon traditional agricultural pursuits and the old lifestyle for a
permanent job in the modern sector. Emigrants of
the 'second age' were on average much younger when
they first arrived in France than their predecessors
and were also unmarried. Furthermore emigration was
no longer restricted to certain families but spread
throughout rural society.

Whereas migrants during the first age saved
money for a specific purpose and returned home as
soon as this task had been completed, under the
second .phase the period spent in France increased
and in many cases was continuously extended so that
the migrant spent his entire active life away from
home. Returns to Algeria were merely for short
vacations, the dates of which were determined by
French employers not by the Algerian farming

calendar. The peasant migrant was thus transformed
into the immigrant worker who adopted a different,
more urban lifestyle compared to peasants who remained in the village. Returning for the vacation,
the migrant became increasingly a stranger over
which his community exerted less and less control.
For a growing number of migrants permanent return to
Algeria was only on retirement at the end of their
working life. This evolution was confirmed in 1968
when the French census revealed that some 30 per
cent of the Algerian population in France had been
resident for at least 13 years, including 13 per
cent for at least 18 years. A later estimate provided by the Amicale des Algériens en France revealed that more than 32 per cent of Algerians resident in France had lived there continuously for at
least 16 years. Remittances were sent back to
Algeria on a regular basis, often monthly, and were
increasingly used to ensure the daily needs, in
terms of food and clothing, of the migrants' families. High rates of unemployment in Algeria and the
conviction that Algeria was a 'pays du chômage'
discouraged migrants from searching for jobs at home
before emigrating to France or from looking for work
when they returned home to Algeria on vacation.
      The third age, beginning in the 1960s, is
marked by an increase in family reunion in France
as migrants are joined by their wives and children.
Family migration increased significantly during the
War of Algerian Independence when many rural families were uprooted from their homes by the French
army. The termination of all new emigration in 1973
brought a new acceleration in the process of family
regrouping. By 1982, the date of the most recent
French census, the demographic structure of the
Algerian community in France had been transformed.
It was no longer a community of which the vast
majority were adult male workers; now only about
half of the community are active workers. Whereas
in 1963 out of a total Algerian population in France
of 458,210 there were 328,710 men over 16 years of
age, 29,500 women over 16 years and 100,000 children
of less than 16 years, by 1982 the 795,920 strong
Algerian community was composed of 360,960 men over
15 years of age, 180,040 women over 15 years and
254,920 children under 15 years of age. With the
closure of the French labour market in 1974, it was
no longer possible for workers to return to Algeria
for one or two years and then to re-emigrate. Consequently, the number of years that the migrant
spent in France continued to increase. By 1980 some

42 per cent of Algerians holding residence certifi-
cates had lived in France for more than 18 years,
30 per cent between 10 and 18 years and 28 per cent
less than 10 years. As a result the Algerian community in France has become increasingly autonomous,
possessing its own internal organisations and structures, its own support mechanisms to provide assistance during unemployment or illness, its own
marriages, births, investments, properties and
businesses. The community has its own shops, hotels,
restaurants and travel agents, and its own lawyers
and doctors. It is no longer necessary for a young
Algerian to return to Algeria in order to marry. In
1973 for example 36 per cent of marriages of Algerian
men and 70.5 per cent of Algerian women were to
other members of the Algerian community in France.
An estimated 20,000 children are born into the
Algerian community in France each year and, having
been educated in France, eventually enter the French
labour market. The community has also become more
diversified in its social composition, with its own
internal stratification and hierarchy.

Return migration during the third age of emigration has become more complex. Chaker (1982)
identifies three groups of migrants with different
attitudes towards return migration to Algeria:
migrants who have left their families in Algeria;
those who have been joined by their families in
France; and the migrants' children born or brought
up in France, the so-called 'second generation'. He
argues that very often it is only those migrants
whose families have remained in Algeria who have
prepared a definite plan for their return, either on
completion of a specific project, such as the construction of a house, sufficient capital to invest
in a small shop or taxi, or because of retirement,
ill health or unemployment. Le Masne (1982), who
interviewed 80 Algerian workers in the Rhône-Alpes
region, found that whereas the majority (60) wished
to return, few had any clear plans as to how and
when this would be achieved. This uncertainty and
insecurity, he suggests, arises from the contradic-
tions inherent in their situation as migrant workers.
In the economic sphere of those who wished to return
to work in industry, few had acquired the qualifications in France that would enable them to secure
jobs in Algeria's modern industrial sector. Cul-
turally the migrants found themselves poorly integrated into French society. Yet, attracted by the
Western consumer mentality they had become increasingly alienated from the cultural values and aims

223

of their country of origin.

Safir and Khalladi (1982) point to contradic-
tions in the attitudes of migrants to return.
Almost all of those interviewed in the survey they
refer to had not formulated a plan for their return
and yet expressed their strong attachment to Algeria
and to its cultural values. Even those who expressed their desire to return had established no
time-scale for the project, making it difficult to
estimate the scale of future return migration.
Migrants under 30 years did not have a clear perception of the future; for most of them the date of
return was in the distant future. For the group
aged over 45 years, many of whom were unable to work
because of poor health, return was conditioned by
problems of social security and retirement. For the
age group 30-45 years the responses were diverse and
uncertain. Whether they were accompanied by their
families or not, they felt strangers both in France
and in Algeria, highlighting the problem of adaptation. They demanded the maximum number of guarantees -- in terms of employment, housing and the
children's education -- before considering return.
Among this group it was those workers without qualifications, often the first victims of unemployment,
who perceived return as a firm possibility. For
single workers and those who had left their families
in Algeria, the sacrifices involved in separation
had to be compensated by significant material success before return could be envisaged. Those workers who had been joined by their families experienced an agonising cultural crisis. In particular,
their children, the second generation, felt strangers when they visited Algeria, an experience reinforced by the barriers of language and culture.

Khellil (1979) in his study of migrants from
the Kabyle douar (district) of At Fliq focusses on
the problems of return migration resulting from the
increase in the period of time that migrants spend
in France. He found that every family in the 15
villages of the douar had at least one of its
members working in France. The vast majority of
migrants from At Fliq were employed as labourers in
garages or the automobile industry in the Paris
region. In spite of legislation to promote the professional training of Algerian workers, few had acquired any qualifications in France and only 3 per
cent were skilled workers. In 1976 only one migrant
was enrolled in a training programme.

Until the 1950s Khellil's typical Kabyle migrant
returned to his lands in the village at the age of

224

around 45 years and became a farmer again. His
place in France would be taken by a brother or
cousin in a system of 'rotation'. After 1950 the
migrants' sojourn in France lengthened and by the
1970s 50 per cent of migrants from At Fliq had lived
in France for more than 20 years, 35 per cent for
more than 30 years. At home, few opportunities for
employment were available in the village, and without qualifications the migrant found difficulty
securing a permanent job in the urban economy.
Salaries in Algeria were much lower than in France
and yet the urban cost of living was often higher,
while the housing crisis in Algerian cities merely
aggravated the problem of return. Return to the
village was inconceivable until a worker had sufficient savings to buy a car or build a house. But
the rising expectations and aspirations of families
at home had become increasingly difficult to satisfy. Many migrants indicated that they could no
longer return even on vacation because of the high
cost of the goods now demanded by their relatives.
The migrants themselves had acquired a European
pattern of consumption and had become 'prisoners' of
these European models. Those migrants who had been
joined by their families in France used their
earnings to ensure their immediate needs and only
then considered saving to return to Algeria. Those
whose families remained in Algeria had often married
late, at the age of 30 or 40 years, and with children to support had been forced to delay their return.
Those migrants who had returned had invariably built
a new house in the village in the European style.
As a result the physical fabric of the villages has
been transformed by emigration. However, many of
the new houses remained empty for most of the year
and were only occupied during the summer holidays or
during religious festivals. Their owners had returned from France to live and work in Algiers 250
km away, but they had invested their savings in the
construction of a modern house in the village and
all indicated that they would return there on retirement or when the children were grown up. Only
recently had these former migrants begun to build
modern houses in Algiers.

For some migrants, however, there will be no
return. A survey carried out by Simon (1979) revealed that although the majority of Algerians
interviewed, some 65 per cent, planned to return
home eventually, 13.7 per cent indicated that they
wished to settle permanently in France. Relatively
few Algerians apply for French citizenship but the

numbers have increased significantly during the last
decade.
     Statistics on return migration to Algeria from
French and Algerian sources are inadequate but all
the estimates available confirm that the scale of
this movement is relatively limited. Cordeiro
(1982) for example estimates that around 75,000
Algerians returned between 1975 and 1978 -- an
average of 18,750 a year. This figure is close to
that proposed by Chaker (1982) who estimated that
about 15-20,000 Algerians return permanently each
year.

THE ALGERIAN GOVERNMENT'S REINSERTION PROGRAMME

The idea of the progressive return and reintegration
of the migrant community into the Algerian economy
dates back to the first years of independence. One of
the tasks assigned to ONAMO at the time of its creation in 1962 was 'to study, promote and organise the
progressive return of Algerian workers living
abroad'. In May 1966 a national seminar on emigration organised under the aegis of the FLN while
recognising the urgent need to secure new outlets
abroad for those Algerian workers unable to find jobs
at home also underlined the necessity of preparing
for the return and progressive reintegration of
migrants who wished to return permanently to Algeria.
In 1971 a <u>Rapport sur l'Emigration</u> published by the
Algerian Economic and Social Council argued that
reinsertion -- the return and reintegration of the
emigrant community -- should be a major principle of
future policy. Although it was recognised that the
return of all the Algerians then in France would
have to wait a considerable period of time, the
return of certain categories of skilled workers
urgently needed to satisfy the demands of Algeria's
new public sector industries was to be an immediate
priority. During the years 1971-73 various measures
were taken to promote reinsertion. The major state
companies were encouraged to recruit from among the
emigrant community, and in June 1973 the Ministry
of Finance announced a series of measures designed
to alleviate customs restrictions on goods imported
by migrant workers as an inducement to them to
return. In 1972-73 ONAMO recorded the number of
Algerian workers who requested jobs back home as
614, 73 of whom were unskilled. The Ministry of
Labour annexe at the Algerian Embassy in Paris,
however, claims to have helped the repatriation of

between 1,000 and 2,000 Algerians in 1973-74 -- a more substantial figure. In 1972 the President of the Amicale des Algériens en Europe, Abdelkrim Gheraieb, went on public record deploring that the policy of reinsertion had not been better defined; he criticised the state companies for not trying hard enough to recruit from among Algerians in France.

Reinsertion received a new impetus in the summer of 1977 when half a million Algerians returned from France to spend their vacation in Algeria. ONAMO, now responsible for coordinating the policy of reinsertion, used this opportunity to publicise the programme among the migrant community. A 'service de réinsertion' was established by ONAMO in each Algerian wilaya, and four offices were opened in France (at Paris, Marseilles, Lille and Lyon) to receive requests for repatriation and centralise offers of employment in Algeria from the various state companies. A migrant worker interested in returning home permanently can either contact one of the four offices in France (réinsertion à distance) or register with the service in his wilaya of origin (réinsertion spontanée). The latter course is preferred by the authorities because it is much easier to administer.

Other measures were taken to facilitate reinsertion. Under the terms of a finance law introduced in 1977 a migrant returning permanently to Algeria who has worked abroad for at least three years can import a car and his family's personal belongings free of customs dues. Workers and members of the liberal professions (e.g. doctors and dentists) can also bring back their professional equipment free of tax. In addition local government offices were instructed by the Interior Ministry to make every effort to resolve quickly any administrative difficulties encountered by returning migrants. Local authorities were also instructed to allocate a quota in all their new housing projects to returning migrants.

The figures available on return migration through the official reinsertion programme indicate that, despite the new structures established by ONAMO, the response has been limited. Statistics published by ONAMO's Department of Reinsertion reveal that from 1976 to 1979 a total of 40,000 jobs in state enterprises were made available to Algerian workers in France. According to level of skill 72 per cent of these 'offers of employment' were for level 2 (skilled jobs), 12 per cent for level 1

(jobs requiring no professional qualification and
general labourers) and only 7 per cent for level 3
(foremen, middle level management). The majority of
jobs were in Building and Public Works (20.5 per
cent) and Mechanical and Metal Construction (20 per
cent), with others in Electricity (10 per cent),
Chemicals (9.5 per cent), Metallurgy (2.5 per cent)
and Transport and Communication (8 per cent).
During the same period 1976-79, 20,000 demands from
migrant workers for jobs in Algeria were received
by ONAMO under the réinsertion spontanée scheme and
20,000 under réinsertion à distance. Out of a total
of 40,000 demands for jobs, 18,000 or 45 per cent
resulted in a permanent placement. Little more than
10 per cent of demands for jobs registered in France
under the réinsertion à distance scheme were satisfied. This proved to be the most costly of the two
reinsertion schemes introduced by ONAMO, with lead
times of between six months and one year before a
placement could be successfully completed. Greater
success was achieved by réinsertion spontanée. This
scheme involved mainly those workers well motivated
toward a permanent return to Algeria; the vast
majority were workers who had left their families at
home and were therefore not dependent on accommodation being made available so long as the job was
located in their wilaya of origin. As to the level
of skill of workers returning to Algeria, ONAMO
states that the vast majority of return migrants
belong to level 2.
    Khandriche (1982) has analysed in detail the
statistics provided by ONAMO for 1977. In that year
11,718 offers of employment were made by state
enterprises, 6,544 through the ONAMO offices in
France and 5,174 through the regional offices in
Algeria. The majority of the jobs on offer through
ONAMO's offices in France (69.5 per cent) were for
skilled workers in the industrial sector (level 2);
and only 23.3 per cent were for unskilled workers.
Four main branches of activity, chemicals, petro-
chemicals and construction materials, mechanical and
metal construction, electricity and building and
public works, all of which were experiencing rapid
growth, accounted for 72 per cent of the offers.
Offers made through the regional offices of ONAMO in
Algeria, aimed at recruiting migrants when they
returned for the summer vacation, were overwhelmingly for skilled workers (81.5 per cent) in the
industrial sector. One branch, building and public
works, accounted for 41.6 per cent of the jobs
available, reflecting the employment created by the

regional development programmes.

Khandriche found that only 4,856 demands for jobs were made through the ONAMO offices in France in 1977 compared with the 6,544 offers available. Two-thirds of the applicants were originally from Kabylia and eastern Constantinois, 9 per cent were from the Algiers region, 16 per cent from Western Algeria, and 7 per cent from the south, figures which reflect the major source areas of Algerian emigration. Eighty-four per cent of demands were from either single workers or those who were not accompanied by their families; 78 per cent were under 40 years of age. Over half of the applicants were unskilled labourers. Some 4,996 applications were made to the regional offices of ONAMO in Algeria compared with the 5,217 jobs being offered. Three-quarters of demands were from skilled workers (level 2). The major group of applicants (28 per cent) were employed in building and public works; 41.6 per cent of the jobs on offer were in this branch. The regional offices in Algeria proved more successful in terms of matching offers with demands than the ONAMO offices established in France. The service de réinsertion at the wilaya level was, not unnaturally, better informed about the local needs and possibilities of employment; the migrant was thus able to obtain first-hand information about the jobs on offer during his return on vacation.

Of the 9,762 demands received by ONAMO in 1977 only 2,063 (21 per cent) resulted in a definite placement: a mere 8.3 per cent (403) of demands received through the ONAMO offices in France and 34.1 per cent (1,676) of demands received through the regional offices of ONAMO in Algeria. Khandriche identifies a number of reasons for the very low proportion of placements made through the ONAMO offices in France. He highlights the fact that whereas the recruiting agents from the state companies insisted on applicants possessing a diploma relevant to their professional status, most migrant workers had gained their skills through on the job experience and did not have the necessary paper qualifications. Even those with the relevant skill level were often adapted to the specific needs of their employers in France and did not always meet the requirements of the newly established Algerian state enterprises employing the most up-to-date technology. The delegation sent to France by the state companies rarely contained the chef du personnel with the result that dossiers had to be referred to Algeria for consultation leading to long delays before a final decision was made.

The success rate for placement was higher for applications made through the regional offices in Algeria but varied according to the branch of activity recruiting labour and the skill level of the migrant. In Mechanical and Metal Construction 42 per cent of demands for employment were met and in Building and Public Works the figure was very similar (43 per cent). On the other hand, only 13 per cent of demands in Metal Production and Transformation were satisfied; in this sector the location of the production units resulted in serious housing problems. Sixty-two per cent of job offers for unskilled workers (level 1) were satisfied and 43 per cent of demands from workers in this category. In contrast at level 3, 55 per cent of demands were satisfied but only 19.4 per cent of offers because of the small number of applicants (108) with this qualification. Delays in processing applications appeared to be an even more critical factor than for the ONAMO offices in France in explaining the limited success rate. As the majority of applications were made during the summer months, those candidates who had not received a reply by the end of the vacation simply returned to France. Khandriche noted that 49 per cent of successful placements had been made within a month of application and 80 per cent in less than three months. Administrative delays were the major reason identified by migrants for the failure of their application. Housing, as might be expected, appeared to be a much less serious problem than in the case of reinsertion via the ONAMO offices in France.

No data are published on the spatial distribution of migrants reinserted into the Algerian economy through official schemes. However, in a study of the reinsertion of migrant workers into enterprises in eastern Algeria, Royoux (1983) found that the wilaya of Annaba, which is not a major region of emigration, had nevertheless received an important part of those workers reinserted into state industrial enterprises. This can be explained by the location of major new public sector industries in Annaba-El Hadjah (iron and steel, phosphate fertilisers, wagon construction, building and public works) providing some 30,000 jobs. Seventy per cent of migrants reinserted into the industrial economy of the wilaya of Annaba were skilled workers, 27 per cent unskilled labours. Over three-quarters had found employment in the iron and steel complex and associated construction projects. While problems

230

had arisen concerning conditions of work, especially salaries, the shortage of housing close to the place of work was a major difficulty and had resulted in some applicants for reinsertion refusing offers of jobs. High rates of absenteeism characterised those return migrants who lived 15-20 km from Annaba or came from the neighbouring wilaya of Guelma. Recruitment of migrant workers reached its peak during the late 1970s, the period of rapid industrial expansion and job creation, and has declined sharply since 1980.

It is clear that only a small proportion of return migration is accounted for by the official reinsertion programme. In a survey of 114 return migrants working in state enterprises in 1977 Khandriche (1982) found that only 27 had been placed by ONAMO, 15 through their offices in France and 12 through the regional offices in Algeria. The vast majority had obtained their jobs by applying directly to the enterprise concerned. Almost all the workers interviewed (90.3 per cent) were under 45 years of age; 35 per cent had departed for France between 1954 and 1962 and 58.7 per cent after 1962. Khandriche suggests that motivation to return might be inversely proportional to the length of time spent abroad. Just over half (52 per cent) had been unemployed before emigrating to France, 21 per cent had worked in agriculture and 22 per cent in industry (Table 11.1). Most of the industrial workers had departed after 1962, a movement associated with the collapse of the fragile colonial manufacturing sector after independence. Many of the workers classified as industrial were no doubt from the small-scale units that characterised colonial industry and from informal craft industries. In 1962 86 per cent of industrial enterprises employed less than 100 workers and 53 per cent less than 20 workers. Eighty-five per cent of the sample indicated that they had emigrated in order to find work. More than 90 per cent were married but 81.6 per cent had left their families in Algeria when emigrating to France. In France they had lived with other Algerians and two-thirds indicated that they had returned to Algeria at least once every two years and had maintained close links with their families. More than a third of the workers interviewed were illiterate and 72 per cent had not reached the level of CEP, generally regarded as the minimum qualification for promotion. Almost half were unskilled labourers for whom there was little prospect of promotion within the French labour market given their low level of

Table 11.1: Occupations before Emigration of a Sample of Algerian Return Migrants

| | Date of Emigration | | | | | | | |
| | Before 1954 | | 1954-1962 | | After 1962 | | Total | |
Occupations	Number	%	Number	%	Number	%	Number	%
Industrial			4	3.51	22	19.30	26	22.80
Agriculture	2	1.75	12	10.52	10	8.77	24	21.05
Unemployed	4	3.51	16	14.04	27	23.68	47	41.24
Other			8	7.02	8	7.02	17	14.90
Total	6	5.26	40	35.08	67	58.77	114	99.99

Source: Khandriche (1982), p. 191.

education. Consequently Khandriche argues that their
return to Algeria was motivated by lack of prospects
for promotion in France and separation from their
families in Algeria. Moreover the fact that unskilled labourers represented 46 per cent of return
migrants in the survey but only 21 per cent of placements through the ONAMO reinsertion programme in 1977
suggests that emigrants with few qualifications had
a better chance of finding employment in Algeria by
applying direct to the enterprises rather than
through the official channels. Delegations sent by
the state companies to France have given priority to
the recruitment of highly qualified workers who were
in very short supply in Algeria rather than pick up
unskilled labourers who could be recruited more
economically within Algeria. On the other hand, a
migrant worker lacking paper qualifications who applied directly to a state enterprise in Algeria had
the advantage of on average some 10 years' experience
in manufacturing industry in France and was accus-
tomed to the rhythm and conditions of industrial
work. Interviews with the directors of personnel
confirmed that the return migrants had adjusted well
to their new jobs in terms of levels of productivity
and maintenance of industrial machinery. Most of
the return migrants interviewed by Khandriche had
also experienced delays of from one to three months
before securing their jobs, but it was clear that
the bureaucratic procedures of the state enterprises
could be accelerated for highly qualified workers.
    Highly qualified workers also received priority
in the allocation of housing for which there remains
an acute shortage in the major cities of Algeria.
Key state industries such as the SNS complex at El
Hadjah (steel), the SONACOME plant at Constantine
(mechanical construction), have found accommodation
for those return migrants who were highly qualified
workers and foremen. These workers are essential to
the successful operation of the new production units
established by the state companies and satisfactory
housing was clearly perceived as a key element in the
maintenance of a stable workforce. Many of the migrants provided with accommodation have been joined
by their families in France; provision of housing by
the company appears to be an important factor in
their willingness to return. In contrast the vast
majority of the workers interviewed in the survey,
some 82.1 per cent, had not been provided with housing by their new employers; 35 per cent had returned
to the family home in their village of origin, while
some 34 per cent were living in hotels, with friends

or relatives (sometimes with 6-7 persons to a room) and others in spontaneous settlements. In response to this difficult situation the state companies have found it necessary to establish a network of company buses to transport workers and other personnel from their home villages to the factory each day. The SONACOME complex at Rouiba near Algiers, for example, transports personnel up to a radius of 150 km from the plant extending deep into Greater Kabylia, an important source of its workforce. Even so some workers interviewed had to travel a further 20-25 km in order to catch the company bus, and it was not unusual for workers to spend 5 hours a day travelling to and from work. Khandriche estimates that over half of the workforce in his sample were affected by the double problem of housing and travel to work.

On the whole the salaries obtained by the return migrants were about half those which they had enjoyed in France -- the reduction being less pronounced for the highly qualified workers. Nevertheless this was not regarded as a problem for most of the workers and to a certain extent the drop in salary was compensated for by the security of employment offered by the state companies and the fact that the migrants had been reunited with their families and relatives. There also appeared to have been few serious problems of socio-cultural adaptation for the majority of migrants interviewed, and it was only those migrants who had been joined by their families in France who had experienced difficulties in adapting to a new socio-cultural milieu. Their children's education was identified as the most acute difficulty.

THE PRIVATE SECTOR: RETURN MIGRATION AND THE
CREATION OF SMALL BUSINESSES

In spite of the dominant role accorded to the public sector in industrial development, by the late 1970s the private sector controlled 40 per cent of industrial value added in Algeria, provided 23 per cent of all industrial employment, and contributed 33 per cent of production of capital and intermediate goods and 66 per cent of production of goods for final consumption. Algeria's private sector industries have also attempted to recruit highly skilled workers in France. Some have succeeded by offering higher salaries than those available in the public sector, but private industrialists complain that recruitment has been difficult because migrant workers demand housing and guarantees concerning their children's

education. Other industrialists have been cautious
about employing return migrants because of the
latter's experience of union organisation and activity in France and their criticism of working conditions and salaries in Algeria.

The Algerian Government has also taken measures
to encourage migrants to invest in the private industrial sector. Although the role of this sector has
always been carefully defined by the Government, in
1966 a new code was introduced to encourage investment by Algerian nationals in private industry.
Patriotic appeals were made to the Algerian community in France, especially to the tradesmen, to invest their capital in industrial enterprises in
Algeria. Some notable successes were achieved such
as the creation of SOMITEX, a textile manufacturing
company established with capital from a number of
Algerian tradesmen in France through the initiative
of the Amicale Générale des Commercants Algériens en
France (Peneff, 1981).

One of the most striking characteristics of the
private industrial sector in Algeria is its heavy
spatial concentration in and around the capital
Algiers. In 1970 the wilaya of Algiers contained 56
per cent of all private manufacturing enterprises,
64 per cent of all industrial workers in the private
sector and some 77 per cent of the private sector's
industrial value added. In contrast the wilaya of
Oran provided only 13 per cent of the industrial
value added in the private sector and the rest of
the country a mere 10 per cent. Little information
is available about the role of return migrants in
the establishment of these enterprises but one
recently published survey by Peneff (1981) reveals
that return migrants have made only a limited contribution to the expansion of the private industrial
sector. Commercial capital from within Algeria,
provided by wholesalers, importers and retailers,
has played the most dynamic role in the rapid expansion of private industry.

Peneff (1981) interviewed some 217 Algerian
industrialists in the private sector with enterprises in the wilaya of Algiers. All the enterprises had been established during 1962-1971. The
enterprises were small with half employing under 50
workers and a third between 8 and 15 workers. Only
33 of the industrialists interviewed had previously
worked in France. Table 11.2 provides a brief biographical synopsis of this group. The table shows
that only two had been born in Algiers and only four
had migrated to the capital before emigrating to

Table 11.2: Return Migrants who set up Small Businesses in
the Wilaya of Algiers

Place of Birth	Age	Previous Occupation	Industrial Branch	No. of Workers
Biskra	40	Office worker in France	Textile	25
Sidi Aïch	36	Tradesman in France; account-ant in the Algerian adminis-tration	Textile	20
Mekla	33	Tradesman in France	Chemicals	-
Alger	37	Manager of a hair-dressing salon in France and then in Algiers	Chemicals	10
Dra El Mizan	35	Insurance inspector in France	Textile	50
Boghni	32	Hotelier in France; civil servant in Algeria	Leather	15
Taher	42	Tradesman in France and then in Algiers	Clothing	20
L'Aarba N Irathen	45	Tradesman in France then in Blida, Algeria	Clothing	10
Ain El Hammam	51	Tradesman in France	Metal	10
Taka	36	Tradesman/manu-facturer in France; importer in Algeria	Clothing	60
Guelaa	39	Waiter in France; tradesman in Algeria	Weaving	60
El-Kseur	45	Tradesman/hotelier in France	Chemicals	60
Ain El Hammam	53	Wholesaler in France	Weaving	30

Table 11.2 (cont'd)

Place of Birth	Age	Previous Occupation	Industrial Branch	No. of Workers
Ain El Hammam	44	Labourer and hotelier in France	Textile	20
L'Aarba N Irathen	44	Taxi driver in Paris; farmer in Kabylia	Metal	8
El-Asnam	43	Labourer in Algiers; boiler-smith in France; foreman in Algiers	Metal	10
El Milia	40	Labourer in France	Metal	15
Bougaa	40	Labourer and then mechanic in France	Textile	30
Guémar	40	Foundry worker in France; tradesman in France then Tunis	Textile	50
Akfadou	36	Shepherd, labourer in France; FLN member and President APC	Paper	10
Sour El Ghozlan	33	Fitter in France; worker in a state company in Algiers	Metal	20
Boudouaou	33	Labourer in France; then tailor in France and Algiers	Clothing	10
Dra-El-Mizan	58	Labourer in France; hotelier in Paris	Food processing	15
Laghouat	39	Labourer in France	Metal	20
Algiers	33	Print worker in France; labourer in Algiers	Paper	15
Algiers	31	Fitter in Algiers and then in France	Wood	30

Table 11.2 (cont'd)

Place of Birth	Age	Previous Occupation	Industrial Branch	No. of Workers
Beni Douala	39	Clothing worker in France; tradesman in Algeria	Clothing	25
Ain El Hammam	48	Labourer in France; small business in France	Food processing	20
Algiers	36	Bakery worker in Algiers; pastry cook in France	Food processing	10
Bou-Mazza	35	Landing stage attendant	Chemicals	10
L'Aarba N Irathen	33	Unskilled labourer and then skilled worker in France; foreman in Algiers	Paper	9
Tunis	33	Electrical mechanic in France	Metal	8
Tlemcen	32	Clothing worker in France; head of workshop in Algiers	Clothing	15

Source: Peneff (1981).

France; nine had been office workers but by far the most important group (20) had been manual workers. Twelve out of these 20 were from Kabylia and their social origins reveal three distinct groups -- 9 were the sons of peasant farmers, 5 the sons of craftsmen or traders and 6 the sons of manual workers. Emigration had allowed these men to improve their qualifications and to accumulate enough capital to buy a shop or a small business. The majority of the 'emigrant entrepreneurs' had already obtained a solid primary education in Algeria and had at least achieved the CEP. In France 12 had improved their qualifications by taking evening courses, attending a technical school or by work experience. For the others (8) emigration had not only enabled them to obtain a qualification but to invest their savings in a cafe or hotel or to establish a small business (taxi, transport) in France or in Algeria. Five out of the eight had emigrated to France before 1950. This represents an earlier phase of emigration than the movement to secure better qualifications. Already installed in France, they were able to offer certain services (cafe, hotel, restaurant) to the wave of new migrants that arrived after 1950. Their savings were achieved by economising on housing and food and for many by marrying late so that without family commitments they could save and then invest the major part of their salary. The enterprises of the 'emigrant entrepreneurs' were among the smallest in Peneff's survey, with 16 out of 20 employing no more than 20 workers. They were often located in garages or apartments in low income residential quarters.

The reinsertion of migrants into the private sector through the creation of small businesses has met with strong criticism in certain quarters, particularly from those opposed to the expansion of the role played by the private sector in Algerian development. These criticisms were strongly voiced in 1980 when Algeria and France signed a new accord on emigration. Under the terms of this accord the two countries agreed to introduce a number of measures to encourage voluntary return and to facilitate the reinsertion of Algerian workers and their families into the Algerian economy and society. Algerian workers in France were offered three possibilities: a repatriation allowance; the opportunity of undertaking a training programme before taking up a job in Algeria; or, for craftsmen and traders, the provision of loans enabling them to set up a small business in Algeria. The French Government agreed to pay the cost of feasibility studies and engineering work for these enterprises and to provide loans for up to 85 per cent of the cost at preferential rates guaranteed by the Algerian Treasury for the purchase in France of machinery to equip them. This measure should be seen against the background of preparations for the Five Year Plan (1980-1984) which underlined the enhanced role of the private sector and small-scale enterprise in Algerian development.

Opposition to the accord has focussed on the creation of small industrial enterprises in Algeria by return migrants. They are seen as providing a privileged market for French equipment and machinery in Algeria, as creating unfair competition for the state-owned enterprises of the same scale being

set up at commune level, and as facilitating the
penetration of the Algerian economy by French
capitalist ideology (Garson, 1982). For some com-
mentators the only legitimate deployment of those
migrants who have completed training programmes
under the terms of the new accord is for them to
spend a minimum period working in the state sector
of the Algerian economy. As one critic put it: 'It
is unthinkable that the Algerian Socialist Revolution should provide funds, guarantees and aid to
these "capitalist apprentices" whose principal
object is the exploitation of man and the destruction of Socialism' (quoted in Lawless and Findlay,
1982).

CONCLUSION

Closure of the French labour market in 1974 consoli-
dated the third age of emigration from Algeria to
France characterised by family reunion. Return was
delayed and in many cases, perhaps for the majority,
it became a retirement movement at the end of the
migrant's working life. For those who have chosen
reinsertion into the productive sector of the
Algerian economy, only a small proportion have returned through state-sponsored initiatives, i.e.
the recruitment of skilled workers and technicians
for the public sector enterprises or incentives to
establish small businesses in the private sector.
Others have secured employment by applying directly
to the state enterprises. The available evidence
points to the concentration of these travailleurs
émigrés réinsérés in the major industrial growth
poles, Algiers, Oran-Arzeuw and the eastern triangle
of Skikda-Annaba-Constantine. These three major
industrial development poles have absorbed the
lion's share of investment since 1970 and have experienced the most rapid growth in employment opportunities. Although the Second Four Year Plan
(1974-1977) called for a greater geographical dis-
persal of industrial investment and proposed the
setting up of small and medium-sized industries
in the mountains and steppelands of the interior,
notably along the east-west axis Tiaret-Barika-
Batna and Tebessa, a zone of strong outmigration, by
1979 over half the projects still remained at the
design or study stage. Thus the pattern of state
investment has exerted a powerful influence on the
pattern of migrant reinsertion. For those migrants
returning to establish small industrial enterprises

in Algeria, the <u>wilaya</u> of Algiers, where the private
sector is heavily concentrated, has proved to be the
most attractive region for investment, so that this
movement has made little impact on regional development. Indeed it could be argued that the presence
of return migrants in productive employment represents a good barometer of the economic vitality of a
region. There is little evidence that return migration has contributed to the development of those
areas outside the major industrial development poles.
Traditional regions of emigration serve as retirement homes for those migrants returning at the end
of their working lives or in some cases dormitories
for those workers returning to jobs in industry who
cannot find housing close to their new place of
work.

REFERENCES

Adler, S. (1977) <u>International Migration and
    Development,</u> Saxon House, Farnborough.
Chaker, R. (1982) 'Les perspectives des flux migra-
    toires France-Algérie', in <u>L'Emigration Magh-
    rébine en Europe: Exploitation ou Coopération?</u>
    Centre de Recherches en Economie Appliquée,
    pp. 445-460.
Cordeiro, A. (1982) 'Emigration algérienne en France:
    crise économique et nouveau modèle migratoire',
    in <u>L'Emigration Maghrébine en Europe: Exploit-
    ation ou Coopération?</u>, Centre de Recherches en
    Economie Appliquée, pp. 70-85.
Garson, J.P. (1982) 'La réinsertion productive des
    émigrés algériens: retour et création d'entre-
    prises', in <u>L'Emigration Maghrébine en Europe:
    Exploitation ou Coopération?</u>, Centre de
    Recherches en Economie Appliquée, pp. 518-564.
Khandriche, M. (1982) <u>Développement et Réinsertion:
    l'Exemple de l'Emigration Algérienne,</u> Office
    des Publications Universitaires, Algiers.
Khellil, M. (1979) <u>L'Exile Kabyle,</u> Editions L'Harma-
    ttan, Paris.
Lawless, R.I., Findlay, A.M. and Findlay, A. (1982)
    <u>Return Migration to the Maghreb: People and
    Policies,</u> Arab Research Centre, Arab Papers 10,
    London.
Lawless, R.I. and Findlay, A.M. (1982) 'Algerian
    emigration to France and the France-Algerian
    Accords of 1980', <u>Orient</u>, 23, pp. 454-467.
Le Masne, H. (1982) <u>Le Retour des Emigrés Algériens,</u>
    Office des Publications Universitaires, El
    Djazair.

Peneff, J. (1981) _Industriels Algériens_, Editions
     du CNRS, Paris.
Royoux, D. (1983) 'La réinsertion des travailleurs
     dans les entreprises de l'Est Algérien', in
     Les Travailleurs Emigrés et le Changement
     Urbain des Pays d'Origine, Maghreb-Proche
     Orient-Pays Tropicaux, Centre Interuniversi-
     taire d'Etudes Mediterranéennes, Fascicule 4,
     Poitiers, pp. 104-117.
Safir, T. and Khalladi, M. (1982) 'Stratégies in-
     dividuelles de retour', in _L'Emigration Magh-_
     rébine en Europe: Exploitation ou Coopéra-
     tion?, Centre de Recherches en Economie
     Appliquée, pp. 429-444.
Sayad, A. (1977) 'Les trois "âges" de l'émigration
     algérienne' _Actes de la Recherche en Sciences_
     Sociales, 15, pp. 59-79.
Simon, G. (1979) 'Faiblesse et difficultés des
     retours définitifs en Tunisie', _Hommes et_
     Migrations, 975, pp. 19-25.

Chapter Twelve

BRIDGING THE GULF: THE ECONOMIC SIGNIFICANCE OF
SOUTH ASIAN MIGRATION TO AND FROM THE MIDDLE EAST

Vaughan Robinson

This chapter is concerned with recent labour migration from Bangladesh, India and Pakistan to the six
Arab states which together make up the Gulf Cooperation Council (Bahrain, Kuwait, Oman, Qatar, Saudi
Arabia and the United Arab Emirates). More particularly, it focusses on the economic significance of
this movement for the sending societies, and the
relative balance of advantages and disadvantages
which accrues to those societies through emigration,
expatriate remittances, and return migration.
     There are several reasons for selecting this
particular case-study. Firstly, the scale of the
movement. The International Labour Office (1984)
estimates that there are now some 292,200 Pakistani,
and 244,000 Indian workers in the Gulf, in addition
to an unspecified number of Bangladeshis. The combined total of these groups in the Gulf is comparable to the number of South Asian workers in the UK.
Secondly, despite the scale of the movement the
literature on the position of South Asians in the
Gulf is still poorly developed when compared to the
work on Indians and Pakistanis in the UK, America,
the Caribbean or East Africa. And thirdly, there is
the economic significance of the movement for both
sending and receiving countries. This is evidenced
by the fact that remittances finance some 86 per cent
of Pakistan's trade deficit, and by the statistic
that expatriates form over 80 per cent of the labour
force in the United Arab Emirates. However, even
though there are good reasons for investigating this
case-study, it is important to note at the outset
that it is not immune from the usual difficulties
concerning the availability or reliability of data
on migration and remittances.

DUBAI CHALO! THE MOVEMENT TO THE GULF

Clearly, it is impossible to discuss the issues of
expatriate remittances and return migration without
first providing details of the scale, timing and
selectivity of outward migration. Motives also need
to be considered since these are instrumental in
determining the permanence of settlement, the likelihood of return and the extent to which links will
be retained with the sending society through time.

     The catalyst in the process of labour migration
to the Gulf was the discovery and exploitation of
oil reserves. Extraction began as early as 1947 in
Kuwait although other states such as Oman exported
their first oil as late as 1967. The rapid expansion in demand for oil in the developed world generated by economic growth, and the later rise in the
crude oil prices engineered by OPEC in 1973 have
ensured that the Gulf states have enjoyed sizeable
and sustained revenue beyond their immediate economic needs. This revenue has been used to erect
welfare systems which have few parallels in the
world, and also to diversify the economic base of
the states away from primary extraction and over-
dependence on oil. Both of these strategies have,
however, generated demand for unskilled and skilled
labour which cannot be met from the indigenous populations. The same can also be said of the oil industry itself. The indigenous populations are not
only few in number -- for example the entire population of Qatar is only 300,000 -- but record low
activity rates and low levels of skill. More than
half the adults in the Gulf states are illiterate.
Furthermore, the shortage of labour and skills is
exacerbated by the relative size and growth of public
sector employment: 54 per cent of the local labour
force in Qatar, for instance, is employed by the
government. Lastly, the relatively high income
levels enjoyed by the local labour force do not encourage employment in semiskilled or unskilled manual occupations. Per capita income in the United
Arab Emirates (UAE), for example, exceeds £30,000 per
year (Ahmed, 1984).

     Labour migration from outside the Gulf was the
natural response to the shortage of manpower and
skills. Migrants came from four major source regions: Western Europe and North America via multinational employers; poorer Arab states; South Asia;
and East Asia. Whilst workers from the Western
industrialised nations tended to fill key skilled
posts, it was to their Arab neighbours that the Gulf

states first turned for employees for the construction and service sectors. Geographical proximity, and cultural and linguistic similarity meant that workers were drawn from Egypt, Jordan, Syria, and North and South Yemen. However the period of major industrial diversification and welfare expansion which then followed coincided with a shift of source area from neighbouring Arab states to the Indian subcontinent. Weiner (1982) explains this shift in relation to tensions within the Arab world between Sunni and Shiite Muslims, between capitalists and communists, and between those who were pro-West and pro-East in their political allegiances. Rather than introduce what was seen to be an undesirable degree of heterogeneity into the resident Arab population, the Gulf states turned instead to India, Pakistan and Bangladesh for their labour needs. Weiner (1982, p. 12) explains that Asian migrants do not bear the baggage of political ideologies and make few demands; 'they do not interact with the local Arab population, do not make claims on the state for benefits, do not expect to live in the country permanently, and can be expelled at will... and they are willing to engage in jobs that Arabs often will not accept'. Consequently, whereas only 3,534 Pakistani workers had emigrated to the Middle East during 1971, this figure rose to 16,328 during 1974, 41,690 during 1976, 129,533 during 1978, and 153,081 during 1981 (Shah, 1983).

However, Weiner's argument does not indicate why the Gulf states turned specifically to the countries of South Asia for labour rather than to other non-Arab sources. The explanation for this is largely historical, although contemporary economic factors have also been of importance. The Gulf has had a long-established economic and political link with the Indian subcontinent. Dubai, for example, has traditionally been an entrepôt for trade between the Middle East and India, and Hindu merchants dominated both the gold and textile trades. Oman, as a second example, was nominally independent in the nineteeth century but was in practice policed and administered by British officials from India, whilst the trade and banking of the country were in the hands of Khojas, Ismailis and Kutchis. Given these precedents, levels of remuneration for similar occupations which could be as much as eight times higher in the Gulf and the endemic rural unemployment and underemployment which had stimulated successive waves of overseas emigration from the subcontinent, it is not difficult to see why the labour link developed.

More recently, though, the relative importance of this link has declined in the face of competition from other labour surplus countries in Asia. The nature of the link has also changed with increasing emphasis being placed on the skill levels of South Asian migrants rather than sheer numbers. Ling (1984) has documented why these changes should have occurred, and argues that East Asians are replacing South Asians in the labour market because the latter had become so numerous as to encourage the growth of nationalistic sentiments within South Asian communities in the Gulf. In addition, South Asians are thought to be more militant because of strikes about poor wages and working conditions. And finally, with the cutback in capital spending by Gulf administrations has come a change in recruitment patterns so that workers enter the region for a specified time period to work on a designated project. This 'project-tied recruitment' was first offered by South Korean and Taiwanese companies who imported their own nationals in preference to South Asians. The corollary of this increased recruitment of low-skill workers from East Asia is likely to be seen in the skills of those South Asians who are successful in gaining employment in the Gulf (Tsakok, 1982).

Although labour migration to the Gulf has seen these three major phases, involving Arab, South Asian and East Asian workers, the differing times at which the countries of the Gulf Cooperation Council have found and exploited their oil reserves have meant that each state has a different ethnic mix within its expatriate labour force. Saudi Arabia has the lowest percentage of its migrant labour of South Asian origin (8.4 per cent), followed by Kuwait (22.4 per cent), Qatar (47.3 per cent), Bahrain (60.3 per cent), UAE (64.3 per cent) and Oman (89.5 per cent). In contrast, Saudi Arabia is the main destination for East Asians and also has the highest proportion of its workforce made up of non-national Arabs (see Table 12.1). This table also reveals the overwhelming dominance of the United Arab Emirates as a destination for South Asian workers since the Emirates contain some 45.6 per cent of all Pakistanis, Indians and Bangladeshis in the Gulf. The next most important destinations are Oman (14.9 per cent) and Kuwait (14.6 per cent), followed by Saudi Arabia (11.3 per cent), Bahrain (7 per cent) and Qatar (6.6 per cent).

Whilst the volume of migration hints at the potential economic significance for the sending

Table 12.1: The Relative and Absolute Number of South Asian Workers in the Gulf, 1980 ('000 and column per cents)

	Saudi Arabia No.	%	Kuwait No.	%	UAE No.	%	Oman No.	%	Bahrain No.	%	Qatar No.	%
Non-national Arabs	570.7	73.8	244.1	64.4	89.7	21.8	5.5	5.7	8.9	13.1	19.4	24.1
Indians	29.7	3.8	45	11.9	109.5	26.6	35.6	36.8	12.3	18.2	11.9	14.8
Pakistanis	29.7	3.8	34	9.0	137	33.3	44.5	46.0	26.2	38.7	20.8	25.9
Bangladeshis	6.1	0.8	5.7	1.5	18	4.4	6.5	6.7	2.3	3.4	5.3	6.6
Other Asian	87.4	11.3	4.3	1.1	2.7	0.6	–	–	7.7	11.4	–	–
Total	773.4		379		411		96.8		67.7		80.3	

Note: Because of data difficulties these figures must be regarded as estimates only. Total figures also include 'others'.

Source: Bangladeshi data from Ali et al (1981); all other data from International Labour Office.

societies, the degree of governmental intervention
in the planning, promotion and organisation of the
migration provides further indications. The Bangladeshi case illustrates this well. Bangladeshi
labour migration to the Middle East began in earnest
around 1972 when the country was visited by a number
of unofficial delegations seeking to recruit unskilled workers. This informal arrangement persist-
ed for a further four years until the government
became concerned about the mistreatment of Bangladeshis abroad and also, one suspects, about the
relatively small scale of emigration and therefore
remittances. As a consequence, in 1976, the Bangladeshi administration became directly involved when
it established the Bureau of Manpower, Employment
and Training (BMET). BMET processes requests for
labour from all foreign employers and attempts to
match these to individuals who have registered with
the bureau as overseas job-seekers. BMET charges no
fee and is currently responsible for around 35 per
cent of all Bangladeshi emigration to the Middle
East (Ali et al, 1981). There is a not dissimilar,
but more complex, administration in Pakistan with
the Overseas Pakistanis Foundation, the Overseas
Employment Corporation and training centres all contributing to the expansion and economic success of
labour migration (Addleton, 1984).

The last feature which contributes to the likely development potential of emigration is the degree
of selectivity within the migration stream. Selective migration can have both negative and positive
consequences exemplified by the loss of scarce
skills and the syphoning-off of excess agricultural
labour. In the case of South Asians in the Gulf,
generalisation is difficult since a broad spectrum
of classes and occupations have been involved in the
migration. At one extreme there are the merchants
of Dubai, at the other the construction workers in
Kuwait. Weiner (1982) suggests that the majority of
Indians fall into five groups: construction workers
(including both management, professionals and labourers); private sector workers such as hotel staff,
bank clerks and factory workers; public sector workers such as nurses and civil engineers; servants;
and merchants. Clearly, each of these groups will
have been drawn from different backgrounds and enjoy
different conditions of service. The Christian
nurses from Goa and the professionals are both settled and likely to remain in the Gulf for some time
to come. In contrast, the Keralite construction
workers are far more transitory and are also a more

marginal element within the receiving societies.

Various micro-scale studies allow a more detailed analysis of the selectivity of Indian emigration. Prakash (1978), for example, notes how emigrants from Kerala are largely unemployed prior to
emigration, how they have few skills and a low level
of education, and how they had already been involved
in rural-urban migration within India before departure for the Gulf. Mathew and Gopinathan Nair's
(1978) study of two villages in Kerala confirms many
of these points. Migrants were male, young, unmarried, poorly educated, and from households headed by
casual labourers. Given that Kerala has furnished
many of the unskilled construction workers in the
Gulf, these characteristics are perhaps not unexpected.

Data on Pakistani emigration reveal selectivity
of a similar nature. Shah (1983) describes how
emigrants are largely males in the 25-40 year-old
age group, how 70 per cent are married but how only
4 per cent are accompanied by their families. Two-
thirds are originally from rural areas but many had
already moved to urban centres prior to emigration.
Gilani, Khan and Iqbal (1981) provide a detailed
breakdown of the occupational structure of Pakistani
labour migrants and this reveals that 83 per cent
could be categorised as production workers prior to
migration to the Middle East, 6 per cent as sales/
businessmen, 4 per cent as professional workers, 2
per cent as service workers and less than 2 per cent
as clerical staff. Within the category of 'production workers' there was an equal division between
skilled and unskilled employees with key occupations
being agricultural workers, labourers, drivers,
masons, electricians, carpenters and tailors. The
most numerous professional groups were engineers,
accountants and teachers whilst the largest groups
of service workers were cooks and watchmen.

Finally, Ali et al's (1981) survey of a sample
of 3,572 Bangladeshi emigrants indicates that migration from that country to the Gulf is also of a very
similar type. They also provide data on three further areas of selectivity which are of importance.
Firstly, two-thirds of respondents were going to the
Gulf on contracts with a duration of only one year.
Secondly, more than half the sample came from only
three districts within Bangladesh, namely Chittagong,
Dacca and Sylhet. And thirdly, whilst the majority
(89 per cent) of emigrants were taking up employment
in the private sector, it was those with more skills
who were destined for the less volatile public

sector.

Clearly then, these various sources indicate
that whilst there are professional people and white
collar workers within the migration stream to the
Gulf, it is the manual workers who form the majority
of Indians, Pakistanis and Bangladeshis in the Gulf.
Moreover, the characteristics of these individuals
are exactly as expected given their role as replacement labour in expanding economies. There is a
close parallel, for example, between the character
of the movement to the Gulf and the period of mass
migration of South Asians to the UK (Robinson, 1981).

There are also parallels in the way that the
native populations of the UK and the Gulf states
view the presence of South Asian labour. Evidence
is increasingly suggesting that racism and discrimi-
nation are not uncommon in the Gulf. The Financial
Times (30 November 1983) has commented on the existence of discriminatory practices in both employment
and housing within the UAE and also upon the parti-
ality of the judiciary and police force. On a day-
to-day level 'nationals always go to the head of the
queue, always manage to get on aircraft that seemed
to be fully booked. They live in separate identifi-
able areas, and always are deferentially treated'.
Other reports of the treatment of Pakistani labourers suggest that these attitudes are not confined to
the UAE. Indeed whilst objective observers might
point to the similarity of underlying attitudes
towards South Asians in the Gulf and in the UK,
further analysis indicates that the legal relationship between state and migrant worker is fundamental-
ly different. Whilst there is no doubt that successive restrictions on immigration and redefinitions
of citizenship have weakened the position of Asians
in Britain, they are still entitled to permanent
residence, participation in the political process,
and access to all welfare rights. The same cannot be
said for South Asians in the Gulf, who enjoy a very
precarious position indeed. It is also impossible
for them to gain citizenship, there are stringent
criteria to be met before dependants are admitted,
residence is related directly to the possession of a
work permit, there are limitations on ownership of
businesses by foreigners, expatriates are allowed to
play no part in the political process, and there is
no right of access to welfare benefits. In short,
South Asians in the Gulf occupy a structural niche
more akin to that occupied by guestworkers in West
Germany than Asian settlers in the UK. This trans-
ience, and marginality, which is recognised by the

sending and receiving governments as well as by the
participants in the migration, has obvious and direct implications for how significant an element
that migration is likely to be for the economic
development of the source regions.

CONSEQUENCES OF THE MIGRATION

The consequences of labour migration for the sending
societies are both economic and social as well as
positive and negative.

Economic Consequences

The most immediate consequence of emigration relates
to the cost of that act itself. Potential emigrants
have to raise the necessary finance to pay for visas
and travel. Mathew and Gopinathan Nair (1978), for
example, discovered that the cost of a 'No Objection
Certificate' to enter the Gulf can be as high as
£2,000, or five times the average monthly household
income in sending villages. Furthermore, the other
direct costs of emigration -- up to another £2,000
-- also have to be considered. Case studies in
Pakistan and Kerala indicate that around half the
emigrants finance their move by raising loans, predominantly from friends and relatives and sometimes
through banks and moneylenders. Interest rates on
short-term loans from moneylenders reach 120 per
cent per annum in certain cases (Gilani et al, 1981;
Mathew and Gopinathan Nair, 1978). The other major
sources of capital for emigration are personal savings and the sale or mortgaging of belongings or
land. Migration can thus have a debilitating short-
term impact on household finances and it is likely
that this reinforces the moral obligation on emigrants to remit a high proportion of their incomes
whilst overseas.
        The early stages of labour migration also impose
financial burdens on the state. Each of the governments with which this chapter is concerned is openly
seeking to promote emigration to the Gulf. One of
the key policy mechanisms which they employ to
achieve this is the training of their nationals to
provide them with the skills which are currently in
demand in the Gulf. The Pakistani government's
crash programme for training skilled and semiskilled
workers for overseas employment, instituted in 1975-
6, aimed to produce 50,000 trained workers per annum
(Shah, 1983, p. 412); whilst it never achieved this

ambitious goal, the creation of facilities and institutions required the injection of resources, manpower, and time. The parallel programme begun by the Overseas Pakistanis Foundation in 1980, for instance, spawned 44 new training institutions in less than two years.

Whilst there are thus short-term costs involved in labour migration both for the state and for the individual, there are also obvious short-run benefits. The most obvious of these is that large-scale emigration can act to relieve pressure on unemployment and underemployment. Weiner (1982) argues this case in relation to Indian emigration, and in particular to the emigration of educated individuals. He notes how, of the 1.2 million people unemployed in Kerala in December 1979, approximately half were educated, 54,000 were graduates and 8,500 were postgraduates. He, and others, point out that under such circumstances, the migration of educated people must be regarded nct as a 'brain drain' but as a 'brain overflow'. It provides qualified but inexperienced individuals with the opportunity to practise and develop their skills.

There are also long-term economic consequences of labour migration but here the literature tends to stress disadvantages at the expense of benefits. There is the continuing cost of maintaining manpower training for emigration and if anything this increases with time. Gilani et al (1981) note that the cost of technical training at a formal institution in Pakistan varies between £200 and £600 per head per year. The costs for skilled and white collar occupations are even higher: up to £4,000 for a clerk, £5,800 for a teacher, £8,600 for a technician, and £22,200 for an engineer. The state bears between 38 and 49 per cent of these costs directly.

Labour migration on the scale occurring between the Indian subcontinent and the Gulf can produce manpower shortages within specific occupations. Addleton (1984) and Gilani et al (1981) explain these as follows. About 1.8 million Pakistanis work in the Middle East and they form 7.5 per cent of the total recorded labour force of the sending society. However the predominantly unskilled nature of emigration means that not all of these emigrants are net losses to the Pakistani labour force since many can be replaced by the unemployed and underemployed who have not emigrated. This transition can be smooth and inexpensive and need not entail a loss of productivity. Gilani et al apply this logic to not only unskilled labourers but also clerical workers, service workers, salesmen and businessmen. They argue that the skills possessed by these groups are relatively easily learnt. The same cannot be said of professional or skilled workers where the acquisition of skills is a lengthier and more complex procedure. In these cases, replacements can be trained but the substitution of these for emigrants often involves a lowering of productivity. Furthermore, training capacity is presently insufficient to match the scale of emigration, and shortages have developed as a consequence. The Pakistan Ministry of Labour forecasts that emigration will create significant shortages of well drillers, tool makers, welders and heavy equipment operators in addition to skilled construction workers (Addleton, 1984). Gilani et al (1981) note that bus drivers and engineers are already in short supply in Pakistan, whilst Ali et al (1981) note shortages of doctors, technicians, engineers, agricultural professionals and fibre technologists in Bangladesh. Mathew and Gopinathan Nair (1978) show how shortages can develop even of unskilled labour at a local level and how this can stimulate rural-urban migration to fill the manpower vacuum created by emigration.

Local or sectoral labour shortages have a number of corollaries. Not only the quantity but also the quality of output suffers. Gilani et al (1981) indicate that as skilled workers depart, their jobs are taken up by hurriedly trained unskilled workers, leading to a decline in output and productivity. Decreased international competitiveness results, or alternatively costs have to be passed on to indigenous consumers. The same is also true of increased labour costs which result from higher wage rates, themselves the product of skilled labour shortages. In this case, though, labour migration seems to have differentially affected the three Asian societies under discussion. Ali et al (1981) note that wage inflation has not been a problem in Bangladesh since the majority of the 'modern sector' is publicly owned and controlled, and therefore wage rates are determined by central government. Gilani et al (1981) point to different circumstances in Pakistan. Here wage rates have increased sharply and it is generally acknowledged that this is as a direct consequence of international migration. The evidence for India is more anecdotal, but if Mathew and Gopinathan Nair's (1978) conclusions about Kerala have any generality then it appears that emigration has prompted modest

increases in wage rates. Clearly, though, this may
be the result of purely local circumstances.

Social Consequences

The social consequences of labour migration are less
easy to quantify and to isolate as direct products
of emigration. Moreover, probably because of the
economic benefits derived by the governments of
sending nations, they are less frequently investigated and aired in public. Nevertheless, sufficient
evidence exists to suggest tentatively that a number of consequences have resulted directly from
emigration.

Firstly, the absence of men from home has had
two consequences. It places women in a situation
where the reputation of the family can be tarnished;
and it also reduces the potential for reproduction,
and thereby population growth rates. Ahmed (1981)
provides an example of the former problem and argues
that this strikes at a cardinal feature of the social
code of the Pukhtans. Mathew and Gopinathan Nair
(1978) quantify the second consequence. They discovered that as a result of male emigration the sex
ratios in the Keralite villages of Perumathura and
Puthukurichi were respectively 136.6 and 173.5 females per 100 males. This feature was also reflected in the number of births: only about 7 per
cent of the two villages' populations were less
than 5 years old.

Secondly, emigration, and the economic advantages which families enjoy as a result of it, is
producing an emergent nouveau riche which is chal-
lenging the traditional structure and hierarchy of
local political life. Ahmed (1981) describes an
example of this trend in relation to elections. He
provides an account of how a member of the nouveau
riche won an election on the strength of bribery,
his ostentatious life-style and his lavish entertainment. Each of these was made possible by wealth
accumulated in the Gulf and this was sufficient to
achieve the defeat of the other candidate, a Cabinet
Minister and Malik (tribal elder).

Thirdly, there are the psychological costs of
the migration borne by the participants themselves.
Dr. Mubas Mubashar Malik has recently produced a
research report on this topic which received considerable publicity in the Pakistani press (Ahmed,
1984; Wallis, 1985). He argued that up to a quarter
of the Pakistani population is suffering from psychological problems as a direct result of emigration.

The Dubai Syndrome, as he termed it, can be divided
into three stages, 'pre-Dubai', 'Dubai', and 'post-
Dubai'. The last of these will be discussed in a
subsequent section of this chapter, but the first
two stages are of relevence here. In the pre-Dubai
phase, individuals suffer intense jealousy of those
families who are in receipt of remittances and goods
from the Gulf. They experience a deep sense of
deprivation leading to anxiety and acute depression.
However, once the family head emigrates the problems
change but do not disappear. The head feels isolated and lonely and compensates by working overtime
and minimising his expenditure in order to send more
money home. As a result, he may even become under-
nourished. At home, in Pakistan, the migrant's
family also experiences a sense of loneliness and is
deprived of its father figure. In this way labour
migration extracts psychological costs from both
migrant and non-migrant families, and from both the
labour migrant and his dependants. One should add
that these psychological costs are in addition to
the physical costs which may be borne by the migrant
himself -- recent reports in The Sunday Times (6
January 1985) describe, for example, how some
Pakistani construction workers in Saudi Arabia are
living in a camp without electricity, water and air
conditioning despite temperatures which reach 49°C.
Many are having to sell their blood in order to
survive because of the collapse of the construction
company to which they were sub-contracted. Whilst
this may be an exception it involves some 2,000
foreign workers.

THE ECONOMIC SIGNIFICANCE OF A BELIEF IN RETURN
MIGRATION

Remittances: Volume and Value
Evidence presented so far makes it clear that migrants to the Gulf regard their stay there as a
finite opportunity to improve the economic and social
status of their household. The predominance of
fixed-term employment contracts and the absence of
dependants in the Gulf make it plain that most migrants are planning and working towards their
eventual return to the subcontinent. A direct consequence of this is the transfer of money and goods
back to the source regions in the form of
remittances.
    Remittances represent an under-researched

255

aspect of return migration. Perhaps this is because they are the product of a belief in return,
rather than return itself. Nevertheless they pos-
sess the potential to have a radical and permanent
impact on levels of regional economic development.
Whether this potential is realised is a separate
issue. However, before discussing this, it is
important to note that remittances have a significance beyond the purely economic. They represent a
continuing and quantifiable statement about the
strength of links which exist between a migrant and
his homeland, and they are frequently interpreted
both by academics and recipients as a commitment to
the traditions and culture of the sending society.
     Statistics on the volume of remittances to
India, Pakistan and Bangladesh, and the extent to
which the national economies of these countries
rely upon them, are both surprising and revealing.
In all three cases, though, data are intermittent,
contradictory and plagued by inconsistent definitions. Having said this, there does seem to be
general agreement about the volume of remittances
into Pakistan and Bangladesh. Data supplied by the
Embassy of Pakistan Investment Centre in London
reveal the dramatic growth in expatriate remittances:
from £90 million in 1971/2 to £2,405 million in
1982/3. What is more difficult to prove, however,
is the way in which the source of these monies has
progressively shifted from the UK in the early 1970s
to the Middle East in the 1980s. Swamy (1981) cal-
culates that in the early 1980s remittances contributed 8 per cent of Pakistan's GNP, 40 per cent of
its total foreign exchange earnings and nearly 80
per cent of its merchandise export earnings. Tsakok
(1982) also notes that remittances have been running at a level roughly twice that of receipts from
international aid. Thus, whilst Pakistan has not
yet become a 'remittance economy' like North Yemen
(Swanson, 1979) or Montserrat (Philpott, 1977), it
is already heavily dependent on expatriate money to
maintain its balance of payments.
     Ali et al's (1981) data allow a similar analy-
sis for Bangladesh. Total overseas remittances
have risen from £67 million in 1977 to about £160
million in 1979. In the first of these years
Britain was still the dominant source with over 70
per cent of the total, but by 1979 this had declined
to less than 40 per cent. As the UK contribution
fell, Middle East sources became more important with
Saudi Arabia alone being responsible for 20 per cent
of the total in 1979. In the same year, the six

Gulf States accounted for 35 per cent of Bangladeshi
receipts. Swamy (1981) has again calculated the
overall importance of remittances to the Bangladeshi
national economy and has found that expatriate money
constitutes 21 per cent of merchandise export earnings.
     India represents a more problematic case,
since it is the policy of that country's government
not to publish data on private remittances. Helweg
(1983) is consequently forced to present data which
relate not only to personal remittances but also to
export receipts from shipping, insurance, tourism
and dividends. The total amount of earnings from
all these sources has risen from about £1.8 billion
in 1977 to £4.3 billion by 1981/2. The opposite of
these inflated figures are those provided by Reserve
Bank of India statistics. This source records only
private cash remittances and more particularly only
inward remittances which exceed 10,000 Rs. Amounts
less than this need not be notified to the Reserve
Bank by currency dealers. As a result, the Bank's
data must be regarded as a gross understatement of
the total value of remittances. Nevertheless, they
indicate a doubling of expatriate money from around
£75 million in 1975/6 to £150 million in 1978/9.
Swamy (1981) suggests that remittances have increased from 10 per cent of merchandise export earnings in 1967 to 15 per cent by 1977. As with Pakistani data, it is extremely difficult to credit remittances to particular source countries. Weiner
(1982) estimates that perhaps half of India's overseas remittances come from the Middle East. One of
the reasons it is impossible to be more accurate
about this, or indeed about the overall volume of
remittances, is the wide variety of channels through
which expatriate money can enter a country. Cash
can be sent through official banking channels,
through 'hundi' or money-changers, and by making a
personal visit. Goods can be sent in place of cash.
Insurance policies or government bonds can be bought
and sold. It would be almost impossible to record
all of these transactions accurately.
     Given the shortcomings of official data it is
not surprising that many researchers have turned to
social surveys of specimen villages in order to
collect data on the more sensitive or detailed aspects of remittance flows. Studies of this nature
are invaluable for assessing the impact of remittances on regional economic development, but like
all local studies they have to be seen as part of a
larger canvas. Gilani <u>et al</u>'s (1981) national study

is an exception to this generalisation since they
interviewed a sample of 1153 households in Pakistan
during 1980. The results of this research are of
considerable significance. They discovered that 84
per cent of the sample had received remittances at
some time during the migrant's absence and that 76
per cent had received remittances during the last 12
months. The average value of remittance per household during 1979 had been £2,922 in transmitted
cash, £1,068 in cash brought during visits home, and
a further £410 in consumer durables. Gilani et al
also found that the levels of remittance varied according to the occupation of the migrant: a professional person remitted an average of £7,478 whilst
an unskilled worker sent £3,298. Interestingly,
these contrasting amounts did not represent very
different proportions of earned income; if anything,
manual workers sent home a higher percentage of
their earnings than white-collar workers. A further
unexpected finding was that the volume of remittances did not decrease as the length of time that
the emigrant spent abroad increased. In fact, the
reverse was the case. Ali et al's (1981) national
study in Bangladesh for the World Bank produced com-
patible results. Their survey revealed that incomes
rose by a factor of ten on emigration, and that the
average unskilled worker saved £2,033 per year from
his salary of £3,986. Only 31 per cent of savings
were remitted through official channels, the remainder finding its way into Bangladesh in the form of
gold, watches, gifts or under-invoiced goods.

Again, national surveys of this type are not yet
available for India, and it is therefore necessary
to rely upon local studies such as those of Mathew
and Gopinathan Nair (1978), Oberai and Singh (1980)
and Prakash (1978). Oberai and Singh, in their
study of Ludhiana in the Indian Punjab, found that
those most likely to remit were married, from a low
caste, small landowners and earning a low income
prior to emigration. They also noted that the propensity to remit increased with time. Their sample
of 504 households received an average of £691 per
annum in remittances although, naturally, different
sub-groups of the population tended to receive different amounts. The average for their Ludhiana
sample proved to be less than that for other Indian
studies. Prakash (1978) found that households in
the village of Chavakkad in Kerala received an average of £1,070 per year with a range of £420 to
£2,500 per annum. Mathew and Gopinathan Nair's
(1978) figures, also for Kerala State, are very

similar, with an average of £1,101 per year and a minimum of £170 and a maximum of over £3,300. Interestingly, half of the sample in this study declared that they had no income other than remittances. Clearly, then, whilst national economies are not yet dependent solely on remittances, this need not be the case at a local level. Moreover the extent of this dependence is likely to be understated by average figures such as those provided above, since these consist only of declared cash remittances, not personal transfers of cash on visits, or the purchase of durable goods by emigrants.

The five studies cited above are in broad agreement on three points which are relevant to a discussion of regional economic problems. Firstly, remittances represent a significant flow of capital and goods whether considered in relation to the national, regional, or household economy. Extrapolation of Mathew and Gopinathan Nair's data, for example, indicates that the two villages studied received approximately £353,000 and £296,000 in cash remittances each year. Secondly, these remittances seem not to be subject to time-decay through natural forces, and appear to be remarkably resilient in the short term to economic recession in the societies where labour is employed. Thirdly, although there are variations in the size of remittances which different socio-economic groups receive, remittances do seem to be spread broadly throughout society in the receiving areas. These points suggest that a belief in return migration -- and the remittances which go with this -- could make a significant and permanent contribution to regional economic change. Remittances are a net gain to society's resources; they ease the balance of payments crisis and therefore allow the importation of equipment and raw materials for development; they provide government revenue which can be invested in infrastructure; they have the potential to improve income distribution; they reduce the dependence of individual households on the natural environment; and they allow individuals to instigate improvements in nutrition, housing, education, and agricultural practices. However, only empirical analysis of how remittances are actually used can reveal whether cumulative economic growth and social change really are occurring as a result of expatriate remittances.

Bridging the Gulf

<u>Remittances: Use</u>
An evaluation of the benefits which accrue from remittances must again rely upon specific studies of
sample populations, but it is worth noting that
several authors have posited generalised chronolo-
gies of the use to which remittances are put.
Helweg (1983) suggests that there are three main
phases: the family maintenance stage; the conspicuous consumption stage; and the business investment
stage. If Helweg is correct in his assumptions,
economic benefits are derived at the very start of
the remittance flow since emigrants ensure their
families' economic future by investing in land and
improved agricultural practices. The second stage
will continue to offer local economic benefits since
money is spent on improved housing and the provision
of conspicuous public works. The last stage main-
tains the economic momentum since remittances are
invested in small local enterprises which will
generate multiplier effects. Curson (1981) seems
not to disagree with such a chronology.
     The available evidence on the use to which
remittances are put makes generalisation across the
subcontinent difficult. Ali <u>et al</u> (1981), discussing Bangladesh, comment that households in receipt
of remittances have no greater propensity to spend
on consumption and do not shift their spending from
essential to luxury goods, but instead save more
and invest more in land, housing and housing improvements. Little money is invested in agriculture or
industry. This suggests that Bangladeshis, perhaps
because they were the last of the three groups to
become involved in the migration, are still using
remittances to improve their local social status
through the acquisition of land and superior accommodation. Gilani <u>et al</u>'s (1981) data suggest a
slightly different picture in Pakistan. Their calculations revealed that 62 per cent of remittances
were used for current consumption (food, fuel,
clothing, transport, marriage costs, and the purchase of consumer durables) with the majority of
this (92 per cent) being used for recurrent consumption. Twenty-two per cent of remittances were
channelled into 'consumption-type investment' such
as the purchase/construction/improvement of residential accommodation, the acquisition of commercial
real estate and the extension of landholdings. And
only 12 per cent were invested either in savings or
industrial and agricultural concerns.
     It would be easy to conclude on the basis of
these data that remittances are not being channelled
260

into the productive investment which might bring
about cumulative economic development. Indeed Shah
(1983) does just this. However, closer inspection
of the data suggests less pessimistic conclusions.
Increased demand for food creates the incentive for
agricultural change and modernisation. Increased
demand for new and improved properties stimulates the
construction industry and its suppliers, both of
which are labour-intensive. A significant proportion of households used their remittances to modern-
ise their agricultural methods, to establish workshops, or to inject capital into an existing
business. Each of these uses of remittances will
produce multiplier effects with consequent gains in
employment and productivity.

Similar conclusions could be derived from the
Indian studies. Oberai and Singh (1980) found 86
per cent of households using remittances for current
consumption, 25 per cent using them for luxury goods
and housing, 6 per cent using them for 'productive
investment' (defined as agricultural land and machinery, fertilisers, pesticides and seeds), 4 per
cent using them for debt repayment and only 1 per
cent using them to educate their children. The
authors however commented on the fallacy of interpreting these percentages at face value and noted,
for instance, how remittances might be used for
daily recurrent expenses thereby allowing the investment of other income. Thirty-seven per cent of
their sample found that, as a result of remittances,
they were now able to spend more on at least one
category of productive farm investment (i.e. land,
land improvement, implements, and improved methods
of cultivation). The percentage breakdown of
Mathew and Gopinathan Nair's (1978) sample was very
similar indeed to that of Oberai and Singh: 82-84
per cent of expenditure was on 'unproductive' items
(which again included real estate and housing), 2-7
per cent on 'productive' items and 11-13 per cent on
arranging marriages for children. Prakash's (1978)
data were more problematic from the point of view of
classification. Fully 90 per cent of savings were
invested in land, real estate, and marital costs.
Twenty-seven per cent of households had purchased
land with remittances (usually one-tenth of an acre)
34 per cent had built brand new houses with an approximate average value of £4,850 and 34 per cent
had improved their current properties at an average
cost of £1,800.

In short, empirical data on the economic value
of remittances to regional economies are amenable to

alternative interpretations. It is possible to
argue that the majority of remittances are used
simply to raise the living standard of the household, increase its perceived status and purchase
imported luxury goods such as tape players, radios,
cars and white goods. Alternatively, one can point
to the household's investment in agriculture, industry and housing and argue that once multiplier
effects are included, and once notice is taken of
how emigrant investment releases indigenous capital
which can then be reinvested, the local significance
of remittances is considerably greater than bare
percentages indicate. The difference between these
two schools of thought is far from being semantic
although, in the end, adherence to one or the other
may be a matter of faith.

The impact that remittances have had upon local
wage rates and commodity prices is equally unproven.
Prakash (1978) argues that remittances and the way
in which they have been spent have been responsible
for sharp increases in the cost of building land in
Chavakkad village. Building materials have also
risen in cost by 60 per cent in four years and the
wages of masons and carpenters have doubled.
Prakash, however, does not enumerate the relative
contributions to these increases of domestic inflation and remittance-generated inflation. The same
flaw permeates Mathew and Gopinathan Nair's (1978)
statements that land prices have risen by around 100
per cent over the last five years and that wage
rates have increased in the construction industry.
Other authors, such as Addleton (1984) and Shah (1983)
claim, but do not prove, such inflation.

The implications of expatriate income for the
social structure of sending regions are also an
under-researched area where conclusions are still
tentative. Ahmed (1981), as has already been noted,
argues that remittances give families the economic
power to challenge the local political hierarchy.
He also implies that they have been responsible for
secularising the Pukhtan culture and undermining
many traditional codes of behaviour. Gilani et al
(1981) comment that expatriate income creates a
standard of living and expectations which could
never be sustained without it and which is therefore
ultimately destructive. For those who are not in
receipt of remittances, they generate feelings of
relative deprivation and frustration. They have
also been responsible for creating a cash economy
which has threatened the mutual interdependence
upon which village life is based. The concrete

manifestation of these trends towards fission is
seen in the impact of remittances on income distri-
butions. Oberai and Singh (1980) provide a detailed
case study of this. They show that 36 per cent of
all remittances are received by the wealthiest 10
per cent of households, whereas the poorest 50 per
cent of families receive only 19 per cent of the
total. This is despite the fact that the wealthy
are less dependent upon remittances. In short, remittances serve to raise living standards for most
households but they do so least for the poorest, and
therefore income disparities widen rather than weak-
en. Gilani et al (1981) agree that this is also the
case in Pakistan.

An unintended, but nevertheless highly significant, side-effect of remittance sending is the
development and extension of the banking system into
the rural areas of the subcontinent. Addleton (1984)
sees this as an important development and notes how
the number of rural bank branches in Pakistan has
increased from 2,432 in 1972 to 6,966 in 1981.
Mathew and Gopinathan Nair (1978) look at the growth
of bank usage within one village: they describe how
within two years of the branch opening in Perumathura
there were 750 deposit accounts and 120 non-resident
external accounts. In the first twelve months of
operation the bank received deposits of £560,000.
These deposits, in turn, would become available to
borrowers and would therefore provide a source of
capital for agricultural development and business
investment.

The balance of disadvantages and advantages
generated by remittances is thus difficult to dis-
cern. Remittances do provide a net addition to
societies' resources but this is unequally distributed between regions and between social groups.
They allow a higher level of investment in agriculture and industry than would otherwise be the case
but a relatively large proportion of remittances is
spent on 'unproductive uses'. They stimulate a
change to a cash economy with attendant access to
banks and credit, but this undermines the basis of
mutual cooperation upon which village life is built.
And lastly, whilst they increase household income,
they also seem to produce inflation of labour and
commodity costs. It is interesting, given these
paradoxes, that the governments of India, Pakistan
and Bangladesh seem so committed to stimulating
labour migration and remittances almost at any cost.

THE SIGNIFICANCE OF RETURN MIGRATION

Whilst remittances are often taken as a sign of intentions towards return migration it is important
to consider whether these intentions ever come to
fruition and, if so, whether return is of an innovative or conservative kind, and whether it is a product of failure, family pressures or simply retirement (Cerase, 1967; 1974). The various typologies
into which it is possible to group different permu-
tations of the cause and timing of return migration
have been thoroughly discussed by Gmelch (1980) and
King (1978).

As other chapters in this book have shown,
quantifying the volume of return migration is not an
easy task. An issue which has particular importance
for South Asian migration back from the Gulf is the
distinction between 'permanent return migration'
(the movement of emigrants back to their homelands
to resettle) and a temporary return to the homeland
in anticipation of further emigration. Given the
fact that most migrants leave the Indian subcontinent for employment in the Gulf on fixed-term contracts, it would not be unreasonable to assume that
the majority of returns are temporary sojourns
prior to re-emigration. The social and economic
importance of these two types of return will clearly
be very different.

Two major studies exist which allow an analysis
of return migration and its likely economic impact.
These are Iqbal and Khan's (1981) work in Pakistan
and Ali et al's (1981) report on circumstances in
Bangladesh. Sadly there is no comparable study of
return migration which uses national data for India.
One is forced, therefore, to extrapolate from
Pakistani and Bangladeshi experience.

Iqbal and Khan's (1981) work formed part of the
Pakistan Institute of Development Economics' International Migration Project and relies for the most
part on a sample survey of 277 returnees. Data from
the sample survey indicate that 9 per cent of returnees left the Middle East because they had a-
chieved the target which they had set prior to
emigration, 31 per cent returned for domestic reasons,
and the remainder were forced to leave because of
the expiry of contracts (40 per cent), visa problems
(5 per cent) or deportation. The prominent element
of compulsion in these figures indicates the unique
characteristics of labour migration, especially when
it is for short-term employment in societies where
immigration is tightly restricted. It also reveals

the vulnerability of South Asian labour to changes
in economic circumstances and therefore the tenuous
nature of their long-term contribution to the economic development of the source regions.

Having identified the volume of return, and
some of the reasons for this, Iqbal and Khan then
consider the likely economic impact of the movement.
They acknowledge that large-scale return would require an adjustment in the economy to accommodate
the loss of earnings from remittances. However,
since the Pakistani government has tended not to
build remittances into its forward planning, this is
thought to be less of a problem than the need to
find employment for returning workers. The large
majority of returnees sampled were of working age
and still wished to work, and whilst there was no
great difficulty in absorbing skilled or professional workers into the labour force the same could not
be said of unskilled and clerical employees, for
whom there is little demand. Iqbal and Khan (1981)
quantified the scale of this problem by asking
respondents what type of job they were seeking in
Pakistan (this included those who had already found
a job and those who were still seeking work) and
then calculating the number of jobs which would be
required each year to fill this need, assuming that
return migration continued at the rate of 21,000
per annum. Their results can be found in Table 12.2.
The authors conclude that the scale of the problem
is less than might have been expected: intending
businessmen would generate their own employment; the
agricultural sector is sufficiently elastic to accommodate returnees; and market demand would absorb
professionals and skilled workers. In short, the
problem had shrunk to 13.4 per cent of returnees who
wished to work as unskilled or clerical workers.
However, a second conclusion can also be drawn from
Table 12.2. This is either that return migration
has been very selective or, alternatively, that
working in the Middle East has raised the expectations of emigrants to the point where they are de-
manding jobs for which they were not qualified prior
to emigration. Comparison of the occupational
breakdowns of emigrants (Gilani et al, 1981) and
returnees (Iqbal and Khan, 1981) reveals, for
example, that whilst 88.3 per cent of emigrants were
manual workers the same can be said of only 57.6 per
cent of returnees. The percentage of professional
workers rises from 4.3 to 7.6 and the percentage of
clerical workers increases from 1.5 to 5.3 Which-
ever line of reasoning explains this apparent

Table 12.2: Employment Preferences of a Sample of Pakistani
Returnees (n = 277)

Occupation	% of Returnees Seeking Employment	Total number of jobs needed per annum to meet current levels of return migration
Unskilled	8.1	1,700
Skilled	37.1	7,790
Clerical	5.3	1,110
Business	29.5	6,195
Agriculture	12.4	2,605
Professions	7.6	1,600
Total	100.0	21,000

Source: Iqbal and Khan (1981)

Table 12.3: Return Migration and Loss of Income (£)

Occupation	1 Average domestic income p.a.	2 Annual cash remittances	3 Consumption from remittances	Column 1 as % of column 3
Unskilled	653	2,088	1,671	39.1
Skilled	1,111	2,542	1,779	62.5
Service	903	3,053	1,833	49.3
Clerical	875	2,778	1,667	52.5
Professional	2,014	5,279	2,640	76.3

Source: Iqbal and Khan (1981)

discrepancy more accurately, it is clear that emigration and return migration jointly benefit the
Pakistani labour force. Either employment in the
Middle East gives workers extra skills, or alternatively the skilled have a greater tendency to
return.
     Whilst Iqbal and Khan's early prognosis had
been that the problem of finding returnees work was
not numerically a difficult one, their later analysis showed this to be a simplistic conclusion. Data
from their social survey revealed that 38 per cent
of those seeking skilled and semi-skilled jobs had,

in fact, been unemployed for twelve months or more
on their return to Pakistan. A further 29 per cent
had been looking for work for between six and twelve
months. Yet it was these workers who ought to have
been finding immediate employment because of their
skills. Iqbal and Khan were forced to conclude that,
in these cases, unemployment resulted from an unwillingness to work for the lower levels of remuneration offered in the domestic economy.

This issue of relative income levels was also
at the heart of the second part of Iqbal and Khan's
analysis. Here they were studying the financial
impact of return upon household incomes. Table 12.3
summarises their findings, and reveals the dramatic
impact which return migration has upon household
consumption. Column 1 of the table indicates average
levels of income for different occupational groups
in Pakistan whilst column 3 contains the known consumption levels of those households in receipt of
remittances. Comparison of the two reveals that
return migration necessitates a reduction in consumption of between 61 and 24 per cent depending
upon occupational group. Even allowing for the use
of savings as a short-term method of maintaining
consumption, it is clear that return migration im-
poses severe financial restrictions upon the returnee's family and may well induce feelings of
frustration and relative deprivation. It is perhaps
this factor that produces the 'Post-Dubai' phase
noted by Malik. During this period, immediately
following return, the migrant finds he is valued
solely for his earning power and both he and his
family find it difficult to resume a normal relationship.

Ali et al's (1981) study is more concerned with
the characteristics of returnees than their economic
or social plight in Bangladesh. Their findings,
which must be treated with some caution, rely upon a
sample of 189 returnees which included permanent and
temporary returnees and which was admitted not to be
scientifically selected. Regardless, their results
are indicative. They show that returnees tend to be
older than emigrants (61 per cent aged less than 35
years old against 83 per cent), that they are better
educated (74 per cent of returnees had professional
diplomas or degrees whilst 82 per cent of emigrants
were educated to less than secondary standard) and
that the majority had been in the Middle East for
between 12 and 24 months. Comparison of the occupational breakdown of emigrants and returnees again
points to the selectivity of return migration:

whereas 80 per cent of emigrants were manual workers
only 25 per cent of returnees were; and whilst only
8 per cent of emigrants were professional or technical workers the figure for returnees was 75 per cent.
Ali et al also enquired about the type of employment
which returnees would be seeking. Of those who expressed an opinion, 43 per cent expected to return
to their old profession, 39 per cent wished to set
up private bus services, 7 per cent would become
farmers, 3 per cent intended to purchase a shop, and
2 per cent mentioned each of the following: setting
up a manufacturing plant; establishing an import/
export business; undertaking consultancy work in the
contracting industry; and gaining further qualifications. In total, then, some 48 per cent intended to
go into business in one form or another as a direct
consequence of the experience they gained in the
Middle East and the capital they were able to accumulate there.

Consideration of the points raised by Iqbal and
Khan, and Ali et al allows a number of conclusions
to be drawn. Firstly, because of the age structure
of the emigrants, return migration is not for retirement purposes. This is emphasised by the fact
that most intend to work on their return. Secondly,
returning Pakistanis and Bangladeshis are not returning because of their failure to adapt to life in
the Gulf. The majority never intended to adapt,
simply to work out their contracts and return as
wealthier men. Thirdly, whilst many migrants seem
to have benefited from their time in the Gulf they
do not return as innovators bent on changing the
social and economic structure. Rather they are conservative returnees who wish to alter their own
positions within structures rather than the structures themselves. With the exception of the Indian
middle classes in the Gulf, other labour migrants
simply see a period in the Gulf as a short-term
means of stabilising or improving their families'
economic position. The norms and standards of the
sending society are never rejected, simply held in
abeyance for a short period for economic gain. The
return of Gulf migrants is unlikely, therefore, to
have a major impact upon the rate and direction of
economic development and social change. To be sure,
certain new skills will be brought back and many
returnees will establish themselves in business, but
these changes will only accentuate existing trends
rather than create new trajectories.

THE FUTURE ROLE OF SOUTH ASIAN LABOUR MIGRATION TO THE GULF

Whilst labour migration from the Indian subcontinent
to the Gulf undoubtedly provides significant short-
term benefits it would be unwise to regard these as
anything other than short term. Emigration provides
temporary relief for the unemployed, remittances
allow existing economic and regional structures to
persist when they are threatened with change, and
return migration may create a petite bourgeoisie of
modest proportions. If, however, these changes are
set against the enormity of the problem of economic
underdevelopment, then it is clear that emigration
and return migration are palliatives not panaceas.
They sustain the existing system rather than create
new and innovative solutions. Furthermore, there is
every reason to believe that the current levels of
labour circulation between the Gulf and the subcontinent may well represent the peak of this movement
and that, henceforth, the medium term will see a
decline in numbers and remittances. Several factors
support this prognosis. Many of the Gulf states are
undergoing relatively slow economic growth because
of the glut in world oil markets and are therefore
curtailing the capital spending which would attract
South Asian construction workers. Furthermore,
those capital projects which are being put out to
tender are increasingly going to East Asian companies on a package basis. At the opposite end of the
occupational structure, skilled and professional
South Asians will come under increasing competition
from indigenous labour especially in Bahrain and the
United Arab Emirates. And the Asian business community is already fearful of the impact of 'Arabisa-
tion' policies in countries such as Oman. In future
Asian traders will have to have active and controlling Arab partners rather than the sleeping partners
who have allowed them to evade ownership laws to
date. In total, then, the South Asian presence may
well be restricted to limited numbers of professional, technical and business people who can comply
with local legislation or who have skills not
readily available within the indigenous Arab population. Their characteristics would consequently
come to resemble those of the expatriate European
and North American populations in the Gulf. If this
scenario is an accurate extension of present trends,
then South Asian governments would do well to regard
the benefits of Gulf labour migration as economic
windfalls of a transitory nature which, in the short

269

term, need to be channelled and exploited to the
full. Even whilst this is being undertaken, though,
they should be mindful of the volatile nature of
economic and political circumstances in the Gulf and
also of the historical precedents of East Africa.

REFERENCES

Addleton, J. (1984) 'The impact of international
    migration on economic development in Pakistan',
    Asian Survey, 24, pp. 574-596.
Ahmed, A.S. (1981) 'The Arab connection: emergent
    models of social structure among Pakistani
    tribesmen', Asian Affairs, 12, pp. 167-172.
Ahmed, A.S. (1984) 'Dubai Chalo. Problems in the
    ethnic encounter between Middle Eastern and
    South Asian Muslim societies', Asian Affairs,
    15, pp. 262-276.
Ali, S.A., Habibullah, A.K., Hossain, A.R.M.A.,
    Islam, R., Mahmud, W., Osmani, S.R., Rahman,
    Q.M. and Siddiqui, A.M.A.H. (1981) Labour
    Migration from Bangladesh to the Middle East,
    World Bank, Washington DC.
Cerase, F.P. (1967) 'A study of Italian migrants
    returning from the United States', Internation-
    al Migration Review, 3, pp. 67-74.
Cerase, F.P. (1974) 'Expectations and reality: a
    case study of return migration from the United
    States to Italy', International Migration
    Review, 8, pp. 245-262.
Curson, P. (1981) 'Remittances and migration: the
    commerce of movement', Population Geography, 3,
    pp. 77-95.
Gilani, I., Khan, M.F. and Iqbal, M. (1981) Labour
    Migration from Pakistan to the Middle East and
    its Impact on the Domestic Economy, Parts I and
    II, Pakistan Institute of Development Economics,
    Islamabad.
Gmelch, G. (1980) 'Return migration', Annual Review
    of Anthropology, 9, pp. 135-159.
Helweg, A.W. (1983) 'Emigrant remittances: their
    nature and impact on a Punjabi village', New
    Community, 10, pp. 435-443.
International Labour Office (1984) World Labour
    Report, ILO, Geneva.
Iqbal, M. and Khan, M.F. (1981) Economic Implica-
    tions of the Return Flow of Immigrants from the
    Middle East, Pakistan Institute of Development
    Economics, Islamabad.

King, R.L. (1978) 'Return migration: a neglected aspect of population geography', Area, 10, pp. 175-182.

Ling, L.H. (1984) 'East Asian migration to the Middle East: causes, consequences and considerations', International Migration Review, 18, pp. 19-36.

Mathew, E.T. and Gopinathan Nair, P.R. (1978) 'Socio-economic characteristics of emigrants and emigrant households', Economic and Political Weekly, 13, pp. 1140-1144.

Oberai, A.S. and Singh, H.K.M. (1980) 'Migration, remittances and rural development. Findings of a case-study in the Indian Punjab', International Labour Review, 119, pp. 229-241.

Philpott, S.B. (1977) 'The Montserratians: migration dependency and the maintenance of island ties in England', in J.L. Watson (ed.) Between Two Cultures, Blackwell, Oxford, pp. 90-120.

Prakash, B.A. (1978) 'Impact of foreign remittances: a case study of Chavakkad village in Kerala', Economic and Political Weekly, 13, pp. 1107-1111.

Robinson, V. (1981) 'The development of South Asian settlement in Britain and the Myth of Return', in C. Peach, V. Robinson and S.J. Smith (eds.) Ethnic Segregation in Cities, Croom Helm, London, pp. 149-169.

Shah, N.M. (1983) 'Pakistani workers in the Middle East: volume, trends and consequences', International Migration Review, 17, pp. 410-424.

Swamy, G. (1981) International Migrant Workers' Remittances: Issues and Prospects, World Bank, Washington DC.

Swanson, J.C. (1979) 'Some consequences of emigration for rural economic development in the Yemen Arab Republic', Middle East Journal, 33, pp. 34-43.

Tsakok, I. (1982) 'The export of manpower from Pakistan to the Middle East 1975-1985', World Development, 10, pp. 319-325.

Wallis, E. (1985) 'Migrants in the Gulf', Geofile, 48, pp. 1-4.

Weiner, M. (1982) 'International migration and development: Indians in the Persian Gulf, Population and Development Review, 8, pp. 1-36.

INDEX

Mezzogiorno 38-68; see also
    Italy
Middle East 45, 104, 171,
    243-71; see also Gulf
    States, oil, South Asia
migration cycle 34, 141, 199
migration data 1, 41;
    Algerian 213-15; Greek
    129-31; Irish 153-4;
    Italian 41-2; Jamaican
    198-200; Jordanian 172-5;
    Newfoundland 187;
    Portuguese 102-5, 108-9;
    South Asian 244-50
Monserrat 16, 26, 256
Moroccan migrants 6
motives for return 13-14,
    39, 42-6, 147-8, 195,
    208, 224, 231, 233, 264
Mozambique 103-4, 117
myth of return 12-13; see
    also motives for return

Netherlands 6, 217
Newfoundland 185-97
New York 156, 161, 196
Nigeria 9, 17
North America 48, 56, 103,
    154, 157, 189, 243-44;
    see also United States
    of America
Norway 9
nostalgia 13, 15, 46

oil 7, 38, 172-8 passim, 244,
    269; see also Gulf States
Oman 243-47, 269

Pakistan 101, 243-71 passim;
    Pakistani migrants 7, 16,
    25, 243-55, 264-8;
    remittances to 256-63
Palestinians 7, 171-82 passim
Paris 224, 226-7
Philippines 8; Filipino
    migrants 8, 16, 21, 185
pieds noirs 6
pilgrimage migration 5-6
political events and migra-
    tion 5, 38-9, 104, 172,
    213-19, 222, 239, 248;

see also refugees,
    repatriation
Portugal 100-28; Portuguese
    migrants 5-6, 16, 26,
    102-5, 108-9, 112-18;
    returnee investment
    118-26
professionals 7, 19, 72, 174,
    183, 189, 205-7, 227, 229,
    248-50, 253, 258, 265-9;
    see also brain drain,
    employment of returnees
Puerto Rican migrants 2-3,
    5, 21
Puglia 41-4, 63
Punjab 26, 258

Qatar 243-7 passim

racism 219, 250
Ravenstein's laws of
    migration 1
recession 3, 38, 104, 106,
    144, 218
re-emigration 4-5, 7, 10, 42,
    65, 104, 148, 150, 161,
    222
refugees 104, 172, 175-6, 181
regressados 101, 105, 108,
    111-22, 126-6; see also
    Portugal
reintegration 63-4, 143,
    147-50, 152, 156-69, 216,
    219, 221, 226-7; see also
    resettlement of returnees,
    social structure
remittances 13, 15, 18, 23-4,
    27, 39-40, 55-60, 62,
    96-7, 100-3, 110, 118-19,
    124, 147, 171-3, 178-9,
    181-3, 222, 243-4, 251,
    255-63; see also house
    construction by returnees,
    investment, land purchase
    by returnees, savings
repatriation 3, 5, 6-7, 18,
    38, 213, 218, 226-7, 239
replacement migration 173
resettlement of returnees 7,
    63-4, 70, 75-7, 114, 186;
    see also aspirations of